SHELTER IS NOT ENOUGH

Transforming multi-storey housing

Graham Towers

The POLICY
PRESS

First published in Great Britain in March 2000 by

The Policy Press
University of Bristol
34 Tyndall's Park Road
Bristol BS8 1PY
UK

Tel +44 (0)117 954 6800
Fax +44 (0)117 973 7308
e-mail tpp@bristol.ac.uk
http://www.bristol.ac.uk/Publications/TPP

British Library Cataloguing in Publication Data
A catalogue record for this book is available from the British Library

ISBN 1 86134 156 3

Graham Towers is an Architect and Town Planner.

Cover design by Qube Design Associates, Bristol.

Front cover: Before and after photographs of improvements to Priory Court Estate, Waltham Forest. The scheme is described on pp 167-8.

Printed and bound in Great Britain by Hobbs the Printers Ltd, Southampton.

SHELTER IS NOT ENOUGH

Also available from The Policy Press

The state of UK housing
by Philip Leather
Paperback 1 86134 228 4 £16.95 tbc Spring 2000 forthcoming
Published in association with the Joseph Rowntree Foundation

Two steps forward: Housing policy into the new millennium
Edited by Dave Cowan and Alex Marsh
Paperback 1 86134 229 2 £18.99 tbc October 2000 forthcoming
Hardback 1 86134 252 7 £45.00

Social housing in rural areas
by Mark Bevan and Julie Rugg
Paperback 1 86134 251 0 £12.95 tbc August 2000 forthcoming

Housing renewal in Europe
Edited by Hans Skifter Andersen and Philip Leather
Paperback 1 86134 135 0 £18.99 January 1999
Hardback 1 86134 157 1 £45.00

A good investment? The impact of urban renewal on an inner-city housing market
by Rick Groves and Pat Niner
Paperback 1 86134 105 9 £11.95 June 1998
Published in association with the Joseph Rowntree Foundation

Make do and mend? Explaining homeowners' approaches to repair and maintenance
by Philip Leather, Mandy Littlewood and Moira Munro
Paperback 1 86134 096 6 £11.95 May 1998
Published in association with the Joseph Rowntree Foundation

Uncommon currencies: LETS and their impact on property repair and maintenance for low-income homeowners
by John Pearce and Chris Wadhams
Paperback 1 86134 078 8 £11.95 February 1998
Published in association with the Joseph Rowntree Foundation

Contents

List of figures and tables

Figures

Tables

Acknowledgements

All illustrations are by the author except for the following:

Dedication

For Chlöe

Preface

At the end of the 1960s I spent two years working as an assistant architect on a large high-density housing development in inner London. The designers were socially committed and set high aspirations for environmental quality. We believed that we were creating local authority housing to the highest standards. The complexity of the scheme made the work demanding and interesting. But it eventually became evident to me that we were working in a blinkered fashion, unaware of broader issues. No thought was ever given to the possibility of not demolishing everything – of preserving and rehabilitating some of the better quality Victorian buildings. The brief had been set at the beginning and it was never questioned. During the design work the partner-in-charge had some contact with the Borough Architect and the Chair of the Housing Committee, but in the entire time I worked on the project I never once met a representative of the client. Worse still, no member of the design team ever had the slightest contact with the tenants – either those who were to lose their homes or those who would occupy the new housing.

To try to redress these shortcomings, both in the process and in my own experience, I took a job as a community worker in a part of North Kensington which had already experienced considerable slum clearance and where much more was in prospect. I was to remain involved in community politics in the area for several years. During this time I learned the value of involving users in the design and development process – user participation can produce different solutions which work better. I also became aware of the shortcomings of multi-storey flats – the hardship caused when lifts or services fail in high blocks; the health problems suffered by families with young children; the disturbance and noise nuisance caused by inadequate design; the degradation caused by fouling and abuse of lifts, stairs and other common areas; the dangers caused by dumped rubbish; and the insecurity caused by assaults and burglaries. For several years I experienced these problems at first hand as a tenant in multi-storey housing.

From 1981, for a period of 12 years, I worked in Islington Council Architects Department, mostly on the modernisation of housing estates. We found that, through close collaboration with tenants and housing officers, we could develop solutions for remodelling the inter-war estates which seemed to work well. Later, we successfully applied similar solutions to the smaller and lower-scale post-war blocks of flats. The larger blocks and the more complex inter-connected estates presented more difficult problems. In more than one case, large amounts of money were spent on improvement schemes which failed almost as soon as they were commissioned – security systems which quickly broke down and became inoperable; new entrance enclosures and amenities which were destroyed by vandalism. It became evident that other authorities were experiencing similar problems. This observation, together with my own experience in Islington, led me to question whether successful solutions could be worked out to solve the problems of large multi-storey estates. It was to seek an answer to this question that I embarked on this study.

The work was originally carried out for a research degree. In adapting my PhD thesis for publication extensive revisions have been carried out. These include two major changes. First, much of the detail of the original case study research has been removed. The findings are summarised in the text. Material on the methodology and summaries of the research results are included in the Appendix. This may prove useful for those especially interested in research methods. Second, the context of the study has shifted. The thesis included a lot of material on 19th-century developments in Britain. Most of this has been omitted in order to concentrate on more recent developments. At the same time, a new final chapter addresses broader issues – the parallel problems which have emerged in estates in Europe and the value of multi-storey housing in making cities more compact and sustainable on the Continental model.

It serves to emphasise the link with Europe that the title is a tribute to Elizabeth Denby's classic housing text. 'Shelter is not enough' is a direct quotation from *Europe rehoused*, published in 1938. The young researcher wrote about inter-war developments in Europe with an enthusiasm which must have done much to kindle the idealistic view of multi-storey housing. Her convictions on the quality of urban life, largely unrealised in the past, still have relevance and are now being rediscovered.

Many people have provided support for the project:

Special thanks are due to Tony Monk, Professor of Architecture at the University of Luton – he first suggested I carry out the work and has provided advice and encouragement throughout; and to Dr Richard Turkington, Director of Housing Research at the University of Central England in Birmingham – he has brought to bear his own expertise in the subject and has commented helpfully on the drafts at every stage. Recognition is also due to staff at Luton University who helped with the progress of the PhD – Dr Roger Harvey, Colin Osborn, Dr Kenal Ahmet, Dr Valerie Shrimplin and Lynn Abassi.

I would like to express my appreciation for the support given by three former colleagues from Islington – John Bussy, Pauline Nee and Cecelia Tredget. They not only supplied valuable material for the case studies but have also read the drafts and provided comments and advice. Finally, my thanks for the time given by those who agreed to be interviewed for the case study research – Kevin Byrne, Ros Tyrell, Alan Kirkpatrick, Olivia O'Connor, Alain Head,

Yvonne Hines, Cathy Donald, David Ford, Jackie McGeavour, Eddie Lenny, Nick McArthur, Steve Barnes, Raouf Ben-Salem, Chris Picton, Phillida Culpin, Gary Looker, Peggy Ovary, Rose Topless and Gerry Alexander.

Graham Towers

Foreword

Multi-storey housing remains the enigma of the British housing system. Tenement or apartment, penthouse or tower block – the history and place of multi-storey housing continue to defy easy explanation. There has been no more controversial addition to the 20th-century urban scene than the public sector tower block. Initially praised for its efficiency and innovation, the received view is that such a structure is an aberration. The spectacle of 'dropping a block' counts for nothing against the loss of modern homes, and such a negative view continues to dominate our thinking on multi-storey housing.

Such stigma has also influenced the extent of scholarly activity in the area. Dunleavy's 1981 study of the construction of multi-storey housing stands as a beacon in the literature available; but over a dozen years separates it from Glendinning and Muthesius' 1994 analysis of the 'tower block' phenomenon. Such accounts have focused attention on 'why?' and 'how?', but the experience of multi-storey living has been little studied, and largely subsumed within the broader question of the future of 'council estates'. Such a limited literature does not reflect the extent of practical activity. After a late start, a range of refurbishment schemes have achieved changes in the fortunes of tenements and tower blocks. The impact and potential of such activity has been neither collated nor communicated, even its extent has gone unrecorded.

This book represents the first significant attempt to explore the place of multi-storey housing in the British dwelling stock, from its varied origins and chequered history, to its future as a valued urban resource. While the perspective adopted is informed by sociological and public policy analysis, this book makes a distinctive contribution by developing and applying a practical and positive model for the regeneration of a range of multi-storey housing. The relevance of such an endeavour in both a British and European context is fully recognised, and this book provides a powerful counterbalance to the received and mainly negative view of the multi-storey legacy. As Britain seeks to rethink patterns of urban development and the future of our older industrial cities, Graham Towers' analysis provides a timely reminder of the continued, and growing relevance of multi-storey living.

Dr Richard Turkington
Director of Research, School of Housing,
University of Central England, Birmingham

ONE

Introduction

In the mid-1990s a leading newspaper published a survey of prosperity and poverty in 9,000 British 'postal sectors' – small neighbourhoods of up to 2,000 people (*The Observer*, 1996). The wealthiest district – narrowly ahead of Purley in the Surrey 'stockbroker belt' and Dulwich, an exclusive area in South London – was the Barbican. On the edge of the City of London, the Barbican is one of the densest developments of multi-storey housing in Britain. Originally designed to house a mixed community in which all social groups were represented, the Barbican has gradually become dominated by well-off professionals. At the other end of the scale, the poorest district in Britain was the east end of Sunderland – a dockside area of four-storey inter-war tenement blocks. Very run-down and neglected, these flats now provide homes only for the poorest and most needy tenants. Block by block they are being demolished.

This stark contrast neatly encapsulates the conundrum of multi-storey housing. While flats, even in the highest of blocks, provide successful housing for some of the wealthiest in society, those built for low-income tenants have, almost universally, become the focus of serious problems. Most of the multi-storey social housing in Britain was built in a 20-year period from 1955 until the mid-1970s. In an accelerating programme, which reached its zenith in the 1960s, 19th-century housing in the inner urban areas was demolished and replaced by estates of multi-storey flats. Initially these new dwellings, with high standards of space and servicing, were welcomed as a great improvement over the physically decaying, overcrowded and often unhealthy housing that fell to the bulldozers. However, very soon after they were built, these flats began to deteriorate. Many of the estates became stigmatised and 'hard-to-let'.

The environment of these new buildings, so different from the old terraced streets, quickly proved unsuitable for those who had been rehoused. It was not just the isolation felt by families with young children and by elderly people. The uncontrolled common parts – the lifts and staircases, the underground garages – quickly became abused and vandalised. The public spaces of the estates became despoiled, setting off a spiral of decline. Many inner-city estates are, today, beset by a multitude of problems. Socially they are characterised by high unemployment and low economic activity; by concentrations of single parents and large numbers of children; and by low levels of educational attainment. This complex of social deprivation helps to generate high levels of crime, ranging from vandalism and graffiti through to burglary, violent assaults and drug dealing. Physically, low standards of maintenance and repair, sometimes exacerbated by poor design or construction, have produced environmental degradation.

So serious is this interlocking nexus of seemingly intractable problems that many have concluded that the only solution is to demolish the estates and start again. All over Britain run-down multi-storey housing is being torn down. A good deal has already gone. But this draconian approach raises serious concerns. Will it really work? Does it provide value for money? Is there really no alternative? Why can't these generally substantial buildings be successfully adapted or re-used? The central question is whether such problematic multi-storey estates can be transformed; whether they can be modernised to provide good housing; or whether, indeed, the only solution is to consign them to oblivion.

The geographical focus

Housing is the world's most common building type and encompasses many different forms. The flat is, almost exclusively, an urban form. Blocks of flats can be found in almost all the world's cities. They provide homes for all sectors of society and all levels of income. Whatever the status of the occupants, much multi-storey housing is provided by the private sector. There is profit to be had from the poorest tenants provided standards are low enough and occupancy at a maximum. However, in most industrialised countries, extremes of housing deprivation are mitigated by intervention from the state. Through direct provision or indirect subsidy, most countries provide a degree of social housing. It may be minimal; it may be very extensive. In many industrial cities it takes the form of multi-storey estates. The history of the development of these estates and the policy framework varies widely from one country to another. As a result the location, form and standards of multi-storey social housing vary considerably. Many estates in other countries have technical and social problems. Although there are common factors, these problems are quite diverse in their nature.

The problems of multi-storey housing in the United States attracted a lot of attention in the early 1970s (Newman, 1972). The Pruitt Igoe Estate in St Louis became a potent symbol of the failure of multi-storey housing when several of the blocks were blown up in 1972 (Hackney, 1990, p 82). But it became apparent that social housing in the US was a very small part of total provision, catering only for the very poorest households who might be expected to have special problems. The total social housing in New York City, for example, was equivalent to that in just two of the 32 London boroughs – Tower Hamlets and Southwark (Coleman, 1990, pp 13, 23). The very limited scale of social housing in North America means that any lessons drawn from its study may not be widely applicable.

Like the USA, Europe has a strongly established urban culture of living in flats. But there has been a much stronger and extensive commitment to building social housing. A good deal of this has taken the form of multi-storey estates and many of these now have problems. In Western Europe there are many estates where serious difficulties have arisen from their planning, their physical form and their social mix. Since the fall of communism, the problems of multi-storey housing in Eastern European countries have attracted considerable attention. There, multi-storey blocks were a common form of housing for everyone and there are, as yet, few of the social problems found in the West. Standards are poor, however, and there are serious technical problems. There are strong contrasts between the housing pattern in Britain and Europe and significant differences in tenure and ownership and in location – in the main multi-storey estates are on the periphery of European cities, rather than in the inner areas as in Britain (Power, 1997, pp 12-14).

The differences are marked but there are also many similarities in the extent of social housing and the nature of the multi-storey legacy. The European experience forms the framework for this study. It had a strong impact on the design of multi-storey housing in Britain and has since experienced many similar problems. The main focus, however, is on developments in Britain. Concentrating on the British experience means that the history of the development and regeneration of multi-storey housing can be examined in a context which has many features in common. For most British cities the historical and cultural background is the same. The legislative and funding framework is standardised This means that multi-storey estates have been built in similar locations, in similar forms, with a similar social purpose. As a result, they have experienced similar problems. Worthwhile conclusions can therefore be drawn from a comparison of the various approaches to dealing with these problems. This in turn leads to recommendations which can improve the regeneration process in the future.

Within the context of the British experience the scope of investigation has been constrained for practical and historical reasons. No attempt has been made to include Northern Ireland. The sectarian divide there not only challenges the status of the province but overlays the housing issue through segregating residential areas. For historical reasons Wales also merits limited attention. Welsh industry was rooted around coal mines. Workers lived in industrial villages rather than cities. As a result, few flats of any sort were built in Wales. There are some multi-storey estates in the bigger cities but their problems are limited when compared with those in Britain's major industrial centres. There are also historical differences between England and Scotland. A tradition of living in flats was established early in major Scottish cities and this pattern continued throughout the 19th century and beyond. In England, multi-storey living developed in the older cities but not in the new. As industrial towns burgeoned during the 19th century they mostly consisted of individual houses. During the 20th century these differences between England and Scotland became blurred. In particular the massive post-war redevelopment drive had a similar impact on all large cities.

This study concentrates on multi-storey housing in the major British cities. Most estates of flats were built as a result of slum clearance and most of this was in the large industrial cities. There is a particular focus on London. This is partly because it is the locus of the author's work and experience which provides the source of much of the background material; partly it is because a very high proportion of Britain's multi-storey estates were built in London. In 1997 London was estimated to have 879 of the 1,400 most deprived estates in England (Wintour, 1997). It therefore merits special consideration. Within London, a seminal role is given to experience in Islington. In that borough during the 1980s, innovative programmes were carried out to modernise housing estates. While these were highly successful on many older estates, some of the newer estates proved resistant to regeneration. This experience helped to stimulate awareness of the critical questions surrounding the most difficult multi-storey estates.

Implications of housing form

In the relatively limited literature available on housing estates the term 'high rise' is often used indiscriminately to describe multi-storey housing. Several publications have drawn a distinction between 'high rise' and other forms described as 'medium-' or 'low-rise' flats. 'High rise' is most commonly defined as 'five storeys and above' (Cooney, 1974; Dunleavy, 1981) or sometimes 'six storeys and above' (Glendinning and Muthesius, 1994). The implication is that high-rise housing has special problems not experienced by low-rise housing. The distinction may have had some relevance in the 1950s and 1960s, when it could be applied to most developments, but it has no relevance to pre-war housing. Many inter-war tenements were less than five storeys high including those in Sunderland's east end or in Glasgow's notorious Gorbals. Such housing was among the most seriously deficient, both physically and socially. Nor has the distinction much relevance to housing built in the late 1960s and early 1970s. Many estates were developments of four, five and six storeys. In this study the definition of multi-storey housing is taken as any purpose-built block or estate comprising flats and/or maisonettes. This could include two-storey blocks although, in practice, it means three storeys and above.

Multi-storey housing takes various forms. Throughout the text there are references to five basic types. In approximate historical order, these are:

- *Tenement blocks:* these originated in the 19th century, although most were built in the inter-war period and in the 1940s. They vary from three to five storeys high. All were walk-up blocks without lifts. Some had staircase access only, but most were reached via staircases which served external access balconies at each level.

- *Tower blocks:* mostly built during the 1950s and early 1960s. The key distinctions are that the height of these blocks exceeds their width, and they have a single entrance point. Access is via a single lift and stair shaft which leads to landings or short corridors on each level. Blocks are normally at least 10 or 11 storeys high and can rise to over 30 floors. Tower blocks which are square in plan are sometimes called 'point blocks'.

- *Slab blocks:* these were built from the late 1940s onwards. In slab blocks the width exceeds the height and there are two or more entrance points. Access is via two or more lift/stair shafts. These may be separate, each serving two flats per landing. More commonly the shafts are connected by corridors or access balconies. Slab blocks can be as low as three storeys and are not normally higher than eight or nine floors. There are various hybrid types of block which are 'L', 'Y' or 'T' shaped in plan, but in most respects are the same as slab blocks.

- *Linked slabs:* essentially two or more slab blocks joined together. There are some examples from the 1950s but most date from the late 1960s. Commonly a lift/stair shaft would be linked by bridges to two or more blocks. Enclosed corridors, or sometimes open galleries, run through the blocks at several levels to link with other access shafts. A number of blocks might be linked together by a continuous access system which can be entered at several points.

- *Deck access estates:* these date from the 1960s and 1970s and are based on the 'streets in the sky' concept. As with linked slabs, many blocks may be linked together but the status of the access ways is enhanced. Usually there are only one or two access decks, each giving access to flats above and below. These are more than corridors – wider, open air and intended to have the atmosphere of a pedestrian street. The access system is completely open and can be entered at many points. Generally such estates are five or six storeys, but can be higher.

These five types cover most of the stock of multi-storey social housing in Britain. There is a degree of overlap, however, and some housing cannot be categorised precisely. There are differences of architectural style. The tenement blocks are often austere and traditional in appearance although many have quite decorative façades. Most of the blocks built in the early post–war period were influenced, to a greater or lesser degree, by the Modern Movement. They are characterised by flat roofs and façades, strip metal windows and concrete facing. Many were built in industrialised systems using simple components endlessly repeated without the relief of decoration or variety. From the late 1960s a more traditional approach became common. Forms were more complex and varied and materials such as brick and timber were reintroduced. There are also differences of scale both in the size of blocks and in the size of estates. Generally these variations in style and size are of limited significance. In terms of the problems created and the physical solutions available, the key differences are between the five basic types.

Throughout the text there are references to housing density. This is, essentially, a measure of the number of people living on a particular area of land, but its quantification is complex. The units used vary, sometimes based on numbers of people and sometimes on dwellings. In recent texts, land areas are usually translated from acres to hectares. The scope of what is measured also varies. It may be only housing (net residential density); it may be residential districts including open space, roads and services (gross residential density); it may be whole cities (development density). For these reasons the numerical expression of density commonly creates confusion. The use of density figures is therefore avoided as far as possible. It must be emphasised that building blocks of flats does not necessarily mean building at high densities. Multi-storey estates can achieve high density but many have considerable open space and are actually at quite low densities.

Nor is there an integral link between high density and housing stress. Some research, particularly that dealing with social issues, has looked at the housing estate legacy as a whole (Power and Tunstall, 1995; Taylor, 1995). Urban multi-storey estates are certainly not the only form of problem housing. There are many low–rise estates of social housing, particularly those on the periphery of large cities, which are in as great or greater need of attention than high density urban housing. Socially there may be clear similarities although, in many respects, the disadvantages of residents of peripheral estates are more severe than those who live in large cities. Physically there are very clear distinctions. The changes which can be made to estates of cottage housing are limited. In multi-storey blocks there are many options for physical transformation. The development of these options can critically affect the social structure of estates. The choices made can affect the way buildings are used and the process of managing them. They are critical to the success of regeneration.

The main themes

This book has three main themes. First, the historical record is examined to discover how so much urban multi-storey housing came to be developed and what it was about the process which subsequently gave rise to so many negative reactions (Chapters Two, Three and Four). Second, the varied attempts to remedy both technical and social problems are considered so as to define an approach which is likely to prove successful (Chapters Five to Eight). Third, the lessons from these examinations are projected forward to try to define a viable future for the extensive stock of multi-storey estates (Chapters Nine and Ten).

Modern multi-storey housing had its origins in the 19th century. The serious stresses created by rapid urbanisation gave rise to two key initiatives: the development of purpose-built flats for the working classes, and the introduction of legal procedures for slum clearance and redevelopment. The legacy of multi-storey flats was created by building on these initiatives in the 20th century, particularly in the three decades after the Second World War. To reach an understanding of how mass housing came to be built, the process is examined from three different perspectives: the influence of the slum clearance process; the impact of public policy and the funding regime; and the role of architectural theory. Through this investigation a multi-dimensional picture is constructed of the influences which shaped Britain's multi-storey housing stock.

From the historical material it emerged that while there was generally an aspiration to raise standards in social housing, there was long-standing concern over the cost of multi-storey flats. The cost issue came to receive increasing attention as more and more flats were built during the 1950s and 1960s. Chapter Three analyses the impact of these increasing economies. Economies of scale were sought through building large estates and by introducing prefabricated systems. Savings were made by using cheaper materials and components and by omitting valuable social and recreational facilities. Above all, the need for economies required that more and more flats shared the same lifts, stairs and corridors leaving the common areas wide open to unrestricted access. The overall impact of these cost reductions soon led to serious problems in use. Chapter Four chronicles the impact on the people who moved into the new estates, particularly the difficulties experienced by families with children. The interaction between cheap multi-storey flats and the low-income families they housed proved critical. Concentrations of children created high levels of vandalism and abuse of the common parts. This, in turn, helped to stigmatise multi-storey housing and accelerate its unpopularity. Dissatisfaction with the new forms of housing helped to stimulate collective action. 'Community action' was the organised rejection both of slum clearance and its product. It helped to bring an end to the building of multi-storey estates and introduced a new and more democratic approach to urban development.

Although no new estates were being built, social landlords were left with large stocks of multi-storey housing which was proving increasingly problematic. The second theme examines the attempts that have been made to deal with these problems. Initially the improvements introduced were small-scale or partial, dealing with specific issues of repair or management. From the early 1980s new funding arrangements made large-scale comprehensive improvements possible. Increasingly central government began to intervene with programmes specially designed to deal with the problems of multi-storey estates. These developments are described in Chapter Five. Chapter Six looks at seven specific types of intervention or 'facets of regeneration', which reflect the range of approaches developed to deal with problem estates. These can be divided broadly into 'managerial' approaches and 'technical solutions'. Managerial approaches addressed the structure of estate management or the social and economic needs of the residents. Technical solutions sought to solve problems by physical improvements or alterations to the design of estates. The ultimate technical solution was, of course, to demolish the estates entirely.

It emerges that none of these 'facets' can provide a satisfactory solution on their own and that an holistic approach is needed. Chapter Seven defines a model framework for regeneration which constitutes just such an holistic approach. The model focuses on various aspects of resident participation in decision making. This emerged as a critical shortcoming when the estates were built and became a key demand of the community action which followed. It has since become established as a critical component of improvement schemes for housing estates. The model also incorporates a range of technical, design and social components. Together these components form an interconnected framework which should provide the basis for successful estate regeneration. The effectiveness of the model was tested by applying it to a range of case studies of completed improvement schemes. The results of these tests are described in Chapter Eight together with the implications they have for the successful improvement of the most difficult types of multi-storey housing.

The third theme looks to the future. There is still a large stock of multi-storey housing which is substandard, defective or unpopular. The successful transformation of this stock depends on drawing appropriate lessons from the record of the past. Analysis, at the beginning of Chapter Nine, shows that the funding regime has had a critical influence on the built form of multi-storey housing and in shaping the improvement programmes designed to deal with its problems. Given the importance of the policy framework, the changes introduced by the New Labour government since 1997 are examined in some detail. These will provide the basis for future regeneration schemes. But successful schemes also require a new strategic approach. The development of housing strategy should be less centralised than has been the case, allowing local communities to assess their own needs and to create their own priorities. These priorities should not necessarily concentrate on the most obvious problems but on achieving maximum effect and on integrating multi-storey estates into diverse urban communities. In the final chapter, broader issues are addressed. These include the parallel problems of multi-storey housing which have developed in Europe and the contribution which the British experience might make to addressing these. They also include the more general contribution that multi-storey housing might make to generating more sustainable urban form.

Multi-storey housing has had a bad press. It has been regarded as a problematic form of housing and has been deeply unpopular compared with the attractions of the house and garden. But there are signs of a new perspective emerging. It is becoming recognised that the low density sprawl which characterised urban development for much of the 20th century is no longer sustainable. It is wasteful in its use of land and energy resources and creates insoluble transport problems. The attraction of high density cities is increasingly being recognised. The option of living in flats is winning growing numbers of new converts. The idea of the mixed community is being revived based on the evident success of some of the inner areas of cities both in Britain and continental Europe. Despite the low status it has acquired, the legacy of multi-storey housing has the potential to become a critical part of a more compact, high density urban form. It can make a significant contribution to generating a more diverse and attractive life-style which could eclipse the negative urban images of the past.

TWO

Forming the multi-storey legacy

Over a period of 20 years Britain's cities were torn apart in a sustained and powerful outburst of demolition and redevelopment. The bulldozers began their work – slowly – in the 1950s and reached the peak of their destructive power in the following decade. In their wake, many of the familiar Victorian buildings of the city centres were replaced with new modern shops or office blocks or with new roads. In the residential areas surrounding the commercial centres, old houses – most of them run-down and overcrowded – were cleared away in increasingly large swathes. In their place rose new estates of council housing – thousands upon thousands of blocks of flats culminating in tall towers or densely packed multi-storey slabs. The social and environmental consequences of this process quickly became apparent. The destruction of communities and the loss of familiar neighbourhoods provoked a response which helped to bring wholesale redevelopment to an end. It took a little longer for the shortcomings of the resulting legacy to be revealed.

Estates of multi-storey flats came to form a very substantial part of the inner areas of large cities. They were designed to provide a standard of housing greatly superior to the slums they replaced. In many respects, standards were much higher. But before long the problems of multi-storey living became increasingly manifest. Many of the inner-city estates quickly deteriorated through vandalism and abuse and have since become the focus of crime and serious social deprivation. Their problems have kept them high on the public agenda. Often the opprobrium they generate is reflected on the period when most of the estates were built – the 1950s, 1960s and 1970s. Some blame a high-handed and inflexible public bureaucracy; some the misguided aspirations of politicians; others the misplaced idealism of architects. In truth, the problems of multi-storey estates are but the latest manifestation of Britain's urban housing problems, the roots of which lie much deeper in history.

Multi-storey living is not an innovation of the 20th century. At the centres of large cities, even in pre-industrial times, buildings were commonly subdivided to house several families. This practice intensified as more and more people flocked to the cities in the rapid urbanisation of the 19th century. Over the century as a whole the urban population increased more than fifteenfold. By the early 20th century the cities of England and Wales alone housed more than 28 million people. This rapid growth resulted not only in much poor quality building but also in intensive multiple occupation of housing. The problems of health and hygiene caused by the increasing overcrowding generated considerable public debate. These concerns led to a series of initiatives which were to sow the seeds for the urban transformation of more recent years.

Nineteenth-century initiatives

There are many contemporary records of the appalling urban conditions of the early 19th century. Novelists such as Charles Dickens, Elizabeth Gaskell and Charles Kingsley highlighted urban life-styles. But one of the most comprehensive and vivid accounts is the wide-ranging study conducted by Friedrich Engels (Engels, 1844). He recorded the poor quality of back-to-back housing in his native Manchester and the insanitary cellar dwellings of nearby Liverpool; he visited Glasgow and condemned conditions in the dense and thickly populated 'wynds'; and London, where he observed dense overcrowding in the multiple-occupied buildings in the centre of the metropolis. Engels' purpose was to expose the evils of industrial capitalism. It was all 'grist to the mill' for the political aims of himself and his collaborator, Karl Marx. While Marx and Engels focused on long-term objectives, more immediate impact was produced by the sober and painstaking work of Edwin Chadwick.

Chadwick was Secretary of the Poor Law Commission. In 1838 he led a tour of London's East End following a typhus epidemic. From what he found he concluded that disease was not the fault of the poor but in fact resulted from inadequate sanitation and cleanliness. This led him to enquire more widely and, over the next four years, he conducted a nationwide survey largely drawn from the reports of doctors, clergymen and public officials. These were compiled into a comprehensive report (Chadwick, 1842). The report concentrated on health and life expectancy and Chadwick's main interest in housing was in sanitary issues. He criticised the poor construction of many of the back-to-back houses predominant in the industrial cities, but his chief concern was for the lack of through ventilation and inadequate drainage and water supply.

Unlike Engels, Chadwick had no revolutionary intentions but he was concerned that the conditions he had described should be redressed by legislation and regulation. His report proved controversial. His fellow commissioners took fright and refused to endorse such a radical document. Nevertheless, the government of the day did respond by setting up the Royal Commission on the Health of Towns. This led to the introduction of the first building regulations in London in 1844 and the spread of regulation throughout the country under the 1848 Public Health Act. Regulation was, in fact, relatively toothless until the more effective legislation of 1875. But the public debate generated during this period did lead to two key trends which were to prove highly influential – the development of a tradition of tenement housing and the initiation of slum clearance.

The tenement tradition

The concern over urban housing and health attracted the attention of the noted reformer, the Earl of Shaftesbury. He was instrumental in founding the Society for the Improvement of the Conditions of the Labouring Classes (SICLC) in 1844. The new Society saw its role as campaigning for the construction of new housing specifically for the working classes and to set new high standards for such housing. Henry Roberts was appointed Honorary Architect to make real these new standards. Roberts believed that healthy housing was produced by the application of sound construction principles and that self-contained dwellings were necessary both to preserve privacy and to prevent the spread of disease.

Roberts' most ambitious and influential project was the 'Model homes for families' in Streatham Street, Bloomsbury, completed in 1849 (Figure 2.1). Its form was to become an archetype for urban multi-storey housing and it set standards of accommodation extraordinarily high for the time. At five storeys, its height almost exactly matched nearby houses and this was probably considered an acceptable maximum height to walk up. The block was served by a single staircase and the flats were approached at each level by access galleries in the open air. Roberts considered this arrangement more healthy than internal common staircases. Each of the 46 flats was self-contained with its own scullery and a WC compartment with space for refuse storage. Space standards were high – Roberts set down 140-150ft^2 as the required standard for living rooms and 100ft^2 for the main bedroom. He also considered that separate bedrooms should be provided for children of opposite sexes. The architect paid particular attention to the standards of construction, believing that good housing should be sound and dry and have permanent ventilation to each room provided by chimneys or ducts. The building was rendered fireproof by an innovative system of 'tile arches' at roof level (Roberts, 1850).

The Society's aim was that the building of such housing would be funded by 'philanthropic capitalists' willing to invest in social housing at a limited rate of interest. 'Five per cent philanthropy' won some converts and a number of multi-storey developments were funded in this way. These efforts were overshadowed, however, by a more fully philanthropic initiative from the wealthy American financier George Peabody. In 1862 Peabody gave a large sum of money to found a trust to develop housing for the London poor. In stark contrast to the high standards promoted by SICLC, the Peabody Trust

Figure 2.1: **'Model homes for families', Streatham Street, Bloomsbury (1849). Designed by Henry Roberts for the Society for the Improvement of the Conditions of the Labouring Classes and still in use as social housing**

Source: British Library

opted for 'associated dwellings' – not self-contained flats but two- or three-room apartments with shared toilets and sculleries. Part of the reason was economy – the Trust wanted to make its endowment go as far as possible. It was also partly because common facilities could be more easily supervised and maintained in a clean and healthy condition. For the same reason the walls were left unplastered to minimise the risk of vermin and the tenants were forbidden to put up wallpaper. The spartan conditions within the Peabody Estates and the grim and barrack-like external appearance established a negative image for the Victorian tenement. This image became entrenched partly because of the proficiency of the Trust. In its first 25 years it completed more than 5,000 dwellings and went on to build many more. More particularly, in terms of housing standards, Peabody was a step backwards from the 'model' schemes. Leaving aside construction standards there was little physical difference between a Peabody block and private subdivided houses where the facilities were also shared. The difference lay in the management which had to be strict in order to maintain standards. The austere ethos of Peabody was largely adopted by other philanthropic trusts and became the hallmark of the tenement tradition (Tarn, 1973).

The advent of clearances

Slum clearance was pioneered, not by national government, but by urban authorities most seriously affected by overcrowded and insanitary housing. In 1864 the Liverpool Corporation put its own Act through parliament giving it powers to demolish property which its medical officer considered unfit for habitation. These powers were largely held in reserve although they were used to build 'St Martin's Cottages' – in reality not cottages at all but a rather dull development of four-storey tenement flats – which became the first council housing in Britain (Taylor, 1974). Similar powers were taken by Glasgow City Council in its own Act of 1866. Glasgow quickly applied its powers extensively in a major project to clear 88 acres of densely populated slums around the medieval centre. The cleared sites were sold to private developers and these city centre slums were replaced by commercial buildings or spacious flats for the middle classes. The poor, displaced by slum clearance, were not offered new homes but had to rehouse themselves by a process known as 'filtering', taking over areas of middle-class housing which had moved down market. These areas, in turn, became overcrowded and insanitary – new slums replacing the old (Horsey, 1990).

Despite its shortcomings, the Glasgow Act was widely admired for its effectiveness in clearing slum areas. Many of its provisions were incorporated into the national government's Artisans' and Labourers' Dwellings Improvement Act of 1875. This extended clearance powers to all cities larger than 200,000. Under the Act clearance could be initiated by the local medical officer. If the authority agreed that an area was insanitary it could prepare an improvement scheme. After an inquiry by the Home Secretary, a provisional compulsory purchase order could be issued which had to be confirmed by an Act of Parliament. The authority could then acquire the area – paying compensation by agreement or as decided by arbitration – and demolish the buildings. Authorities were not expected to build housing themselves but to act as facilitators to ensure that slum housing was cleared and replaced. The cleared sites were advertised for sale but, to avoid overcrowding other areas, there was a proviso that replacement housing should be provided for the same number of people who had been displaced (Gauldie, 1974).

Greatest use of the 1875 Act was made in London. The Metropolitan Board of Works completed 16 schemes, clearing more than 42 acres of slums. The replacement housing was built and managed by philanthropic housing trusts, Peabody being the most prominent and carrying out the lion's share of development (Figure 2.2). The requirement to replace the quantity of housing demolished meant that very high densities were necessary which could only be achieved by developments of five-storey tenements packed cheek by jowl. The dense and grim environment created by these early slum clearance

Figure 2.2: **The Whitechapel Estate, completed by the Peabody Trust in 1880, part of an early slum clearance scheme. The estate has never been comprehensively improved, although one block has been demolished to reduce the density**

schemes did not inspire admiration and served to entrench the negative image of the Victorian tenement (Tarn, 1973). In 1889 an elected body – the London County Council (LCC) – took over redevelopment in London and, under the control of the Progressive Party, resolved to do better than its predecessor. The LCC was helped by a new Act of 1890 (see p 25) which reduced the amount of new housing required in slum clearance schemes. But they also had high aspirations. Taking their lead from the new 'mansion blocks' of flats being built for the middle classes they determined that housing for the working classes should also reach high standards. Over the following 20 years the LCC completed more than a dozen slum clearance schemes. Most of these provided good standards of housing with striking designs (Beattie, 1980).

Numerically the achievements of 19th-century reformers were small. In London the housing societies built just 40,000 dwellings and the local authorities perhaps 10,000 more. A little social housing was built in industrial cities such as Liverpool, Manchester and Glasgow where the needs were greatest. Overall this new housing did virtually nothing to address the problems of an urban population which was still expanding, packed into cities which were densely crowded, heavily polluted and insanitary. But the initiatives taken had created new forms of multi-storey housing and had established the principles by which the slums could be renewed.

Outlines of the urban transformation

At the turn of the century urban conditions were as bad as ever. The gross shortage of housing and high levels of overcrowding in the cities were exacerbated by the impact of the First World War, when house building virtually ceased. In response to these shortages a major post-war housing drive was begun which marked the first state intervention in providing homes for low-income families (Swenarton, 1981). For the most part, this did not address poor urban housing directly but sought to relieve overcrowding by providing new estates of cottage homes on the edges of cities. During the 1920s, 700,000 council houses were built but they had barely made a dent in the intractable problem of the urban slums. Overcrowding had hardly fallen at all over the decade and in many cities the problems were still legion (Branson and Heinneman, 1971). In 1930 a new Housing Act was introduced which addressed the slums by providing a subsidy based on the numbers of families rehoused in clearance areas and required each local authority to produce a five-year plan for eradicating its slum housing. Because of the state of the national economy little progress was made until 1933, when the government switched all housing resources to slum clearance (Mowat, 1955).

The new emphasis on clearance necessitated replacing dense concentrations of housing and this could generally only be achieved through building multi-storey flats. Indeed, the legislation required that redevelopment be in flats of at least four storeys to make intensive use of land (Dunleavy, 1981, p 37). In cities where the tenement tradition had been established, the new policy simply meant accelerating the existing programmes. In London in particular, slum clearance had continued unabated throughout the 1920s. Now more clearance areas were identified and flat building gathered pace. By 1937 the LCC had built more than 15,500 flats while the London boroughs had completed more than 21,000 dwellings, almost all of them in blocks of flats. Quite a number were also built by the established housing trusts and newer, locally based, housing societies (LCC, 1937). In Glasgow the City Corporation built more than 54,000 dwellings between the wars. Initially, many of these were in cottage estates but the renewed emphasis in slum clearance brought a fresh concentration on flat building. Overall Glasgow completed almost 29,000 flats in traditional style three- and four-storey blocks (Horsey, 1990). The tenement tradition was revived in Liverpool, where the Corporation built more than 6,000 flats during the 1920s and 1930s, mostly in four- and five-storey tenements (Liverpool, 1937, 1951).

In these cities flat building had followed established patterns. But other cities now began to experiment. During the late 1930s Manchester built 9,000 flats in slum clearance schemes (Ravetz, 1974), but the most dramatic initiative in clearance and redevelopment was in Leeds. Leeds City Council developed a programme to tackle its Victorian legacy by building more than 34,000 new council homes. It was planned that many of these would be flats. By 1939 less than 1,000 had been built and these were all in one estate – Quarry Hill (Finnigan, 1984). This model development was supposed to have been followed by a further 5,000 flats, but the slum clearance programme in Leeds, as elsewhere, was cut short by the outbreak of the Second World War.

Under the clearance programme initiated in 1934 all major authorities prepared plans. Although many councils underestimated the extent of the slums, the collective programme proposed rehousing 1.25 million people. By 1939 housing for just over one million had been provided. The programme had fallen well short of its target and it was now being officially admitted that the problem had, in any case, not been fully appreciated. The Ministry of Health commented "... slum clearance is a continuing process ... further reviews have revealed more houses that can only satisfactorily be dealt with by demolition. The completion of the programme will keep local authorities occupied for some time yet" (Bowley, 1945, p 152).

The post-war drive

The Second World War had an even more disastrous impact on housing. As in the First World War, house building was suspended and no progress was made on the serious problems still outstanding in 1939. Added to that was the wreckage of the blitz. London, Coventry, Birmingham, Liverpool and Manchester all had large residential areas flattened by bombing. A total of 475,000 houses were destroyed or made uninhabitable and many more were seriously damaged (Burnett, 1986, p 285). After the war even more pressure was added to the housing shortage by the impact of delayed marriage and the 'baby boom'. All this made housing a central issue of public policy and a major new building programme was put in place by the incoming Labour government.

The bulk of this programme was realised in a revival of decentralisation policy – low-rise cottage estates. In London, however, inner-city developments continued – partly on sites cleared for development before the war; partly on sites cleared by the blitz. Before the war London's council flats had been characterised by the five-storey walk-up block. Many such schemes, planned pre-war, continued after 1945. But, in line with a general increase in standards, a new policy was emerging – walk-up blocks were to be restricted to four storeys. Many four-storey estates were developed in the post-war period but these schemes had to be developed at a lower density, housing fewer people. Higher blocks could be built if lifts were installed and models began to emerge which helped to set a new pattern for urban housing.

At Woodbury Down in Hackney, the LCC developed a 64-acre site with a scheme which included eight-storey slab blocks (LCC, 1949). The Borough of Finsbury commissioned three schemes which were, similarly, largely eight storeys high. At Churchill Gardens on the Thames Embankment, Westminster Council commissioned a prize-winning scheme of 10-storey blocks. Once spawned, the high blocks spread rapidly. By the early 1950s the LCC had built 10-storey point blocks at Alton East, Roehampton; a massive 11-storey slab block at Bentham Road in Hackney; and 11-storey blocks on the Akroydon Estate, Wimbledon (GLC, 1976).

The final assault on the slums

These metropolitan experiments with inner-city high-rise housing were largely against the grain of the period. Glasgow continued to build traditional four-storey tenements in such peripheral developments as Drumchapel and Castlemilk (Horsey, 1990). Everywhere else the new housing was in the form of cottage homes on greenfield ex-urban sites. The high priority given to housing was continued by the Conservative government which took power in 1951. For some time the new government continued the decentralisation policy and the substantial programme of ex–urban housing estates. But in 1956, as in 1933, an abrupt change of policy switched subsidy finance from general housing needs to a new concentration on slum clearance.

The impact of this policy has been detailed in Patrick Dunleavy's exhaustive study (Dunleavy, 1981). Local authority housing in England and Wales (as measured by tender approvals) increased from 137,015 in 1955 to a peak at 172,557 in 1966 and the proportion of flats changed significantly. In 1955, individual houses made up 71%; low–rise flats 23%; and high–rise housing (five storeys and above) just under 6%. By 1966, the proportion of houses had dropped to 47%, low–rise flats had risen to almost 27% but the numbers of high–rise flats had increased dramatically to nearly 26% of the total (Figure 2.3).

Figure 2.3: **Local authority dwellings approved for construction by building type**

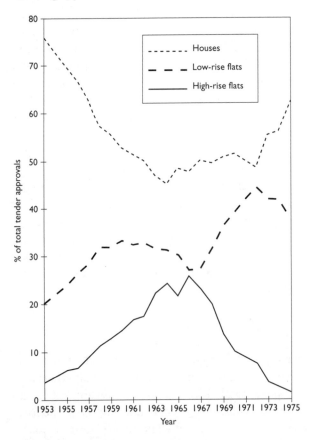

Source: After Dunleavy (1981, pp 40-1)

Dunleavy commented:

> Within the high rise category there was a marked trend towards increasingly
> tall blocks. From 1955 to 1965, blocks of five to nine storeys, often termed
> 'medium rise', made up between 4.5 and 5.6 per cent of all public housing,
> varying without any apparent pattern from year to year. Taller blocks, on
> the other hand, were an increasing proportion of public housing during
> this period. Blocks of 10-14 storeys expanded from 0.7 per cent of public
> housing in 1955 to 8.4 per cent in 1963. Blocks of 15-19 storeys expanded
> from 0.1 per cent of public housing in 1956 to 8.3 per cent in 1964. The
> tallest blocks of 20 storeys and more, expanded from 0.3 per cent of public
> housing in 1959 to 4.5 per cent in 1967. (Dunleavy, 1981, p 40)

Multi-storey housing, which had been confined to a few cities where flat
living had become established, now sprang up in most cities of reasonable size.
The great bulk of it, however, was concentrated in a handful of the largest
cities. Dunleavy's research shows that 86% of high-rise housing (five storeys
and above) was built in just five regions. Greater London built the lion's share
– 36.2%; Scotland (mainly Glasgow) – 21.5%; the North West (Liverpool and
Manchester) – 12.4%; the West Midlands (mainly Birmingham) – 8.2%; and
Yorkshire (Leeds and Sheffield) – 7.1% (Dunleavy, 1981, pp 44-8). Although
it cannot be demonstrated statistically, the great majority of multi-storey housing
is concentrated in slum clearance areas in the inner cities.

Throughout this period housing remained at the top of the national policy
agenda and the construction programme was constantly expanded, reaching
unprecedented levels in the 1960s. Innovations were made to try to boost
housing production. First was an increasing emphasis on industrialised building.
System building was already well established in Europe, particularly in Denmark.
In Denmark building cooperatives, supported by the state research institute,
had initiated measures to standardise building components and improve
productivity. This led to the development of systems using prefabricated
concrete panels. The achievements of these innovative systems were impressive
and standards were high. Such methods were widely emulated in other
European countries (Power, 1993).

In Britain, building systems were increasingly being adopted and promoted
by large construction companies. In all, between 750,000 and one million
dwellings were built using industrialised systems. Some of these were individual
houses but many systems used heavy concrete panel construction which could
be used most efficiently in multi-storey housing schemes (AMA, 1984). The
second means of accelerating output was through increasingly large clearance
and rebuilding schemes. Ever larger projects involving estates of 1,000 and
more dwellings were prepared. Thus, although new approvals of high-rise

schemes had virtually ceased by the end of the 1960s, many of the large schemes took seven or eight years to complete. As a result, the clearance programme reached its peak in the early 1970s. A total of 600,000 dwellings were demolished between 1955 and 1965 and one million more between 1965 and 1976 (Power, 1993)

The massive housing drive between 1955 and 1975 brought great changes to Britain's inner cities. As it progressed it became increasingly controversial. The process was criticised for the destruction of familiar environments and the dispersal of established communities. The product was condemned as barrack-like and inhuman and for the increasingly manifest social problems. Critics sought to attribute blame – variously the bureaucrats, the politicians and the architects were taken to task. Others have continued to defend the process as necessary and to view the product as a desirable improvement. Some light might be shed on this controversy by closer examination of the forces which brought it about. Three key influences are apparent:

• first was the established slum clearance procedure which provided *the means*;
• second, the fluctuations of public policy in development and finance which defined *the ends*;
• finally the influence of architectural theory which set out *the ideals*.

Slum clearance – the means

Bad housing had long been associated with concerns about health. This concern had two components. One focused on poor construction standards which created damp draughty housing with inadequate water supply and sanitary disposal. The other centred on overcrowding which put an intolerable strain on space and facilities and created a breeding ground for disease and vermin. By the inter-war period there were essentially two types of urban slums in Britain. One was the cottages built during the earlier part of the 19th century specifically for working-class occupation. In the industrial cities of the North these were back-to-back houses. In London and some of the older cities they were terraced houses built around narrow courts (Figure 2.4). These were small cramped houses, generally two-storey. Almost invariably they were of the most basic design and poorly constructed. There were no damp courses, the walls were cracked and crumbling due to inadequate foundations and the roofs generally leaked. What is often now forgotten is that many were infested with parasites, as Noreen Branson and Margot Heinneman recorded:

> Bedbug infestation was a major horror of slum life.... The bedbug lived on human blood but lodged not only in bedding, but in furniture, in cracks in walls and ceilings and behind the wallpaper. Self-respecting

people did not talk about it much, possibly because it was frequently suggested that the best defence against the bug was cleanliness, and to have bugs could be taken as a reflection on housekeeping standards. The truth was that once it had entered the fabric of the house no amount of scrubbing and scouring could dislodge it, and no quantity of floor polish could disguise its smell. Local sanitary inspectors fought a losing battle keeping it in check with fumigation. When the tide finally turned after the second world war, and the bedbug was on the way out, it was not scrubbing and scouring that did it, but the discovery of DDT and other new insecticides. (Branson and Heinneman, 1971, p 183)

Figure 2.4: **A court of slum cottages in Southwark (1923). Housing of this type was the first to be targeted by slum clearance in London and has long since entirely disappeared**

The other type of slum was the housing overcrowded by multiple occupation – houses or flats designed for single families but occupied by many. In large swathes of inner London there were areas of terraced housing designed and built for middle-class occupation. These were houses of three or four storeys or more, generally of quite distinguished design and comparatively well built. In some areas speculators glutted the market in the late 19th century and the houses never found buyers. In other areas the original occupants had moved out to greener pastures and the houses had 'filtered down' to poorer occupants. William Barnes, former Director of Housing in Camden, described such housing in 1920s, St Pancras:

> The typical terrace house was an eight room dwelling; on the second floor there would be a family of anything up to ten persons; on the first floor in the original drawing room and best part of the house, another large family; on the ground floor, still at the time called the 'parlour', perhaps an elderly couple, or a single old person in each room, perhaps again a family; in the basement, yet another family. Usually one WC and one wash-house, both in the back yard, served the needs of the entire house. (Barnes, 1973, p 11)

Multiple occupation was responsible for much of the overcrowding recorded in surveys. In Scotland, where the problem was much worse, filtering down took a much more extreme form. In Glasgow, the Gorbals/Hutchesontown area had been redeveloped in the late 19th century with wide streets and generous stone-built tenements designed for the middle classes. Gradually these had been 'made down' with more and more families multiple-occupying a single tenement flat. Eventually many were made down to 'single ends' – one-room lettings. By the 1940s single ends were recorded as housing as many as eight or nine people. A single staircase which originally contained eight flats housing perhaps 35-40 people had come to provide shelter for two or three hundred (Worsdall, 1991).

Small wonder that such conditions eventually stimulated decisive action to demolish and rebuild. The basic legislation facilitating redevelopment had remained unchanged since the late 19th century and by the time effective slum clearance got under way, in the mid-1930s, the procedures were well established. Perhaps these are best illustrated by the pattern of events in London where there was long and continuous experience of slum clearance.

The pattern of London clearances

Slum clearance had begun in London under the 1875 legislation. On its foundation the LCC inherited many of the sites cleared by the Metropolitan Board of Works. Several pioneering schemes were completed by the turn of the century. But slum clearance did not stop. A pattern was created which continued almost unbroken. The Tabard Gardens Scheme in Southwark shows how this worked. The scheme was prepared in 1910 using powers provided by the 1890 Housing of the Working Classes Act. The clearance procedure was that provided by the 1875 Act where the public health officer declared the housing unfit and a compulsory purchase order was made. The Tabard Street Improvement Scheme was confirmed by the Local Government Board in 1912. The first block was started in early 1915 and complete two year later. Work was then suspended because of the war. It re-started at the end of 1919 and the remaining six blocks were completed in 1925. In 1930-33 the estate was extended by the acquisition of adjoining housing and in 1937 part of the area remained to be developed with a further five blocks.

Before clearance and redevelopment, the Tabard Street area was densely packed with poorly-built two-storey cottages fronting narrow streets. These were replaced by five-storey walk-up blocks of flats enclosing courtyards and, at the centre of the site, a public open space (Figure 2.5). The blocks were developed in phases over a considerable period of time. Tabard Gardens set a pattern both in process and form and over the course of the 1920s and 1930s was followed by a dozen other similar schemes in a rolling programmes of slum clearance. By the mid-1930s the LCC had built a streamlined machine for slum clearance. Procedures for designation and clearance of unfit housing areas were well understood and standardised type plans had been adopted for their redevelopment (LCC, 1937). While the LCC concentrated on large redevelopment schemes, slum clearance was also carried out by the London boroughs. These projects were on a much more modest scale – generally small estates of up to 100 flats.

Once again war was to force a hiatus in building. But, as before, the slum clearance schemes suspended during wartime were revived and continued. The war had also created new priorities. Bombing had taken a severe toll, creating both homelessness and sites for new housing. The first was tackled by extending housing development to open land in the inner suburbs, such as at Roehampton or Wimbledon. And for several years, development of the blitzed sites, particularly in the East End, absorbed much of the resources available for house building. When slum clearance began again there remained a large amount of 19th-century cottage terracing, poorly built for working-class occupation, for which clearance was the only realistic option.

Figure 2.5: **'Before' and 'after' plans of the Tabard Gardens Estate, Southwark, a slum clearance scheme which spanned 30 years**

a) Tabard Street, Minto Street and Law Street Areas – Before clearance

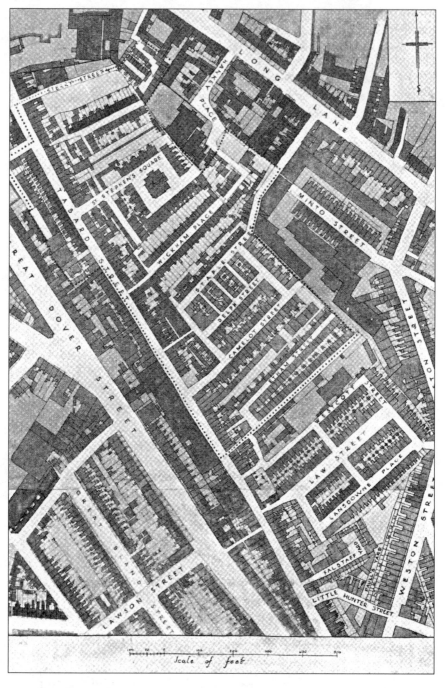

b) Tabard Garden Estate

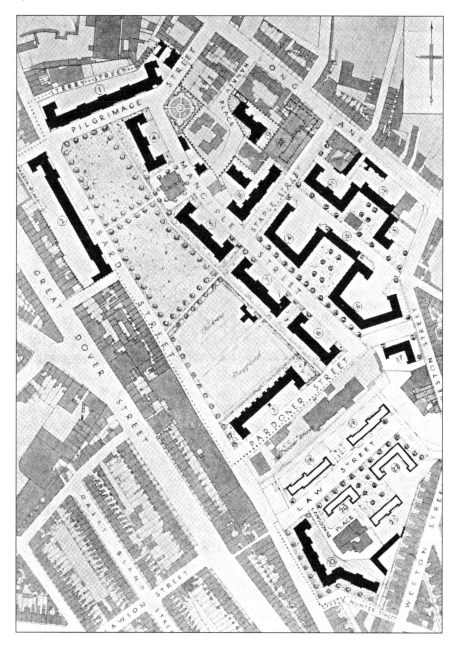

Source: From LCC (1937) © London Metropolitan Archives

Much of this was accurately focused. In North Kensington, during the 1960s, redevelopment concentrated on the areas of mean cottages developed in the early 19th century, leaving intact the substantial stuccoed terraces built for the middle classes, even though many were, by then, run-down and multiple-occupied. In Islington, however, it was a different story. By the late 1960s, the Greater London Council (GLC) (successor body to the LCC) was tearing down 15 acres of elegant four-storey Regency-style terraces in the Packington Square area to make way for a new system-built multi-storey estate. Meanwhile, a few streets away, exactly similar houses were being bought up by speculators and rehabilitated for the middle classes. The 'gentrification' of Barnsbury is legendary and had regrettable social consequences (Power, 1973). But it showed beyond question that redevelopment of overcrowded housing was not the only option.

The national picture

Slum clearance in London had developed almost continuously and acquired an accelerating momentum, which became, in the end, almost unstoppable. Meanwhile the pattern in other British cities was much more staccato. The clearances which had taken place in the late 19th century had not continued beyond the First World War. Redevelopment began again in the mid-1930s and was re-started much more widely from the mid-1950s. While each renewed initiative stemmed from policy changes, the procedure remained largely unchanged. If it had fallen into disuse in some areas there was plenty of experience available from its continuous application in London. The public health officials retained their extensive powers, granted under the 1875 Act, to declare unfit whole areas of housing; to condemn the houses for demolition; and to prepare compulsory purchase orders. True, these orders were subject to government scrutiny and eventually to public inquiry. But all too often they escaped critical evaluation.

In fairness, until the early 1960s, these powers were generally applied judicially. The great majority of the houses demolished were the urban working-class cottages. These were, unquestionably, poorly built and provided miserable homes – damp and vermin infested. But by then the great majority of the mean cottages and back-to-back houses had already been demolished. The slum clearance machine became increasingly incapable of distinguishing between housing that was irremediably inadequate and that which was neglected or simply overcrowded. Clearance began to eat into the 'tunnel-back' housing built under the improved standards of the 1875 Public Health Act, which may have been poorly maintained and run down but was not fundamentally unsound. In Glasgow, the notorious Gorbals was entirely demolished, yet its main problem was quite appalling overcrowding and the disrepair which results from overuse. It now seems that it might well have been possible to redeem many of the existing buildings which were of basically solid construction. In London, the last urban cottages had been cleared by the mid-1960s and the slum clearance machine began to take out the late-Victorian terraced housing which has since proved so desirable to the aspiring middle classes. It was as if the entirely understandable concern with housing and health had created an insatiable monster which, in its quest to cleanse the slums, lighted on ever more improbable targets.

Public policy – the ends

At the level of central government there were shifting and interconnected strands of planning objectives, policy priorities and financial provisions which together had a major influence in shaping the pattern of urban housing. It began when the state first intervened on a significant scale. The 'Homes fit for heroes' programme of 1919 was stirred by popular demand – or, at least, by fear on the part of the government of popular rejection. And this was enough to stimulate the provision of generous funding. But how to do it? Early planning theory was heavily influenced by rejection of the industrial city and promotion of the Garden City model, which emphasised lower densities and closer correlation between housing and the natural environment (Howard, 1898). It was to achieve these ends that the Tudor Walters Committee, set up in 1917 to examine housing standards, looked to cottage estates as the solution rather than urban renewal. It sought a decisive contrast with the crowded cities and recommended traditional houses at exaggeratedly low densities (Burnett, 1986, p 222ff). Almost all public subsidy in the 1920s was put into peripheral council estates of cottages. Where the public sector led, the private sector followed and began to create its own slightly more decorous version of peripheral cottage estates in the new middle-class suburbs.

Concern over continuing urban slums created the conditions for the provisions of the Labour government's 1930 Housing Act but its implementation relied on a dramatic shift in policy by the subsequent administration. At the end of 1932 the National government – a coalition of Conservatives and part of the Liberal Party – introduced a Bill to shift almost all subsidy from general housing needs to slum clearance:

> Sir Hilton Young, Minister of Health ... did not argue that the shortage of working class houses was over; he argued that the way to overcome the shortages was to abolish the subsidies. The demand for private houses was almost saturated, he said, and private enterprise was thus seeking a new outlet. Prices had fallen and so had interest rates – why then had private enterprise not provided the smaller houses so badly needed? The

answer was that private enterprise could not compete with subsidised municipal housing. 'If you wish to provide the supply of houses that we need the most obvious course is the withdrawal of the subsidy'. (Branson and Heinneman, 1971, p 184)

The efforts of the public sector were, then, to be concentrated on the urban slums which were to be redeveloped as flats. The building of houses was left to the private sector. In the event, private enterprise did provide lots of housing – but it was not for the working classes. During the 1920s and 1930s, three million houses were built by speculative builders, all of them for sale to the growing army of owner-occupiers. Great belts of unplanned suburban development spread around the major cities. By the end of the 1930s the problems of servicing the sprawling suburbs and the rate at which they were eating into the countryside was causing increasing concern. These concerns were a major stimulus to the introduction of the post-war planning system with its comprehensive controls designed to bring order to development.

A key component of the new system were the urban plans prepared during the 1940s. The most influential of these was the Greater London Plan completed in 1944. Abercrombie's Plan sought to constrain urban sprawl by imposing a Green Belt and to concentrate overspill development in a ring of new towns. Within the Green Belt a hierarchy of residential densities was defined – 200 persons per acre (ppa) in the innermost area stepping down to 136 ppa, 100 ppa, 75 ppa and a suburban zone at 50 ppa which required only 10 or 12 houses per acre. Similar principles were applied to plans for most major cities, particularly Glasgow, for which Abercrombie produced an almost identical plan in 1946 (Cullingworth, 1976). The extremely low densities at the periphery were, undoubtedly, due to the persistent influence of Garden City ideals. Even a modest increase in density would have produced far more efficient use of land with virtually no loss of amenity (Dunleavy, 1981, p 74). The high densities at the centre were partly due to established practice in slum clearance, partly to a desire to retain as much as possible of the urban population in situ. Nevertheless its was well established that such high densities made the building of flats inevitable.

Despite the prescriptions in these plans, the bulk of new public housing development in the 1940s was in cottage estates on the urban fringes. Urban redevelopment, although continuing to receive a special subsidy, played a subsidiary role. The Conservatives, who replaced Labour in government in 1951, maintained a very similar policy for some time. The change of policy of 1956, switching resources to slum clearance, was accompanied by a new subsidy structure which favoured high-rise housing:

> The old expensive-site subsidy paid per dwelling was replaced by a much smaller one per acre and ... a new progressive storey height subsidy. Under this flats of four, five and six storeys qualified for very large increments to the basic house subsidy.... Above six storeys the subsidy rose by a fixed increment for each additional storey in the block. A flat in a six-storey block received 2.3 times the basic subsidy paid on a house, and this rose to 3.0 at fifteen storeys and 3.4 at twenty storeys. (Dunleavy, 1981, p 37)

This regime not only made tall blocks possible, it made them financially desirable. In 1955 blocks over 11 storeys were virtually unknown. By the mid-1960s they comprised 20% of all public housing. Some schemes of very tall blocks were built, such as the dramatic but daunting cluster of 31-storey blocks at Red Road in Glasgow (see Figure 2.11); or the equally tall Trellick Tower in West London. But it was not only tower blocks which benefited. Multi-storey schemes of all sorts were encouraged; however, it was not to last.

From the early 1960s, high-rise housing was increasingly criticised and this public questioning coincided with the return to government of the Labour Party which had traditionally favoured the Garden City approach. Within the Civil Service, the excessive costs of high-rise housing were increasingly questioned (Merrett, 1979). In 1965 the new government severely curtailed the height subsidy, retaining it only for four-, five- and six-storey buildings (Owens, 1987). In 1967 a more fundamental change in the funding regime was introduced – the Housing Cost Yardstick. The new system brought the high-rise era to an end. As the official voice of the GLC put it: "To [the] social concern and increasingly adverse publicity was added the impact of the introduction of governmental cost controls on housing, the cost 'yardstick', which favoured low rise development and made the point blocks ... financially impossible" (GLC, 1976, p 69).

Although the new financial regime ended the bias towards high rise, it retained the focus on slum clearance. It included variations by region and increased subsidy for urban areas. There was also a special subsidy for redevelopment sites, most of which would be in the inner cities. Most importantly, the subsidy was increased as density increased in a range from 40 to 240 ppa, with the yardstick at high densities about 50% higher (*The Architects' Journal*, 1967, 1969). The new system did not sponsor high rise but it maintained the support for high density housing which was still regarded as essential in the inner cities. This support now favoured high density low-rise designs, four to eight storeys high, rather than the discredited tower blocks. This now became the predominant form of multi-storey housing.

That redevelopment continued on such a massive scale was largely the result of pressure created by 'the numbers game'. From the end of the Second World War housing had been at the top of the public policy agenda. The post-war

---

Labour government came to power pledging to build 240,000 houses a year. It never quite achieved this high ambition but by the time the Labour Party left office in 1951, 900,000 new homes had been built. The high priority given to housing was continued by the Conservative government which took over. Indeed the priority was amplified by a new higher completion target of 300,000 homes a year (Power, 1993). The political competition continued unabated and culminated in the 1964 General Election when the Conservatives set a new target of 400,000 homes a year, only to be outbid by the victorious Labour Party with a promise of 500,000. This was a massive commitment which strained the infrastructure of the building industry to an almost intolerable level and was largely responsible for a significant reduction in standards. It also meant that, despite the Labour government's misgivings about the quality of multi-storey housing and its attempts to ameliorate its impact, it was obliged to maintain a large-scale slum clearance programme in order to meet its political promises. In the late 1960s, in order to realise these ambitious promises, the government approved a lot of very large-scale redevelopment schemes which ensured that slum clearance continued well into the 1970s.

Architectural theory – the ideals

It has become fashionable among contemporary critics to blame the whole phenomenon of multi-storey housing on the Modern Movement in general and Le Corbusier in particular. Such critics include Alice Coleman (1985), Peter Hall (1988), Rod Hackney (1990) and The Prince of Wales (1989). Apart from the fact that this ignores the influence of public policy, it is a gross oversimplification. Architectural ideas were, undoubtedly, influential, but they came from a variety of sources and became interwoven over a considerable period.

Until the Second World War the design of multi-storey housing had hardly moved beyond the model set by Henry Roberts in 1849. Almost all blocks were five-storey walk-ups and most were balcony access (Figure 2.6). In style many still followed the pared down classicism favoured by Roberts. Some adopted the Queen Anne style introduced by the early LCC architects, which became increasingly common in social housing schemes built in the 1920s and 1930s. From the mid-1930s, however, new influences from Europe began to infiltrate British housing design. With the new emphasis on flat building for the slum clearance programme, delegations from British authorities began touring housing schemes in France, Germany, Austria and Scandinavia, seeking inspiration. One of the consequences was a new approach to space standards. The older tenements were cramped and even in the early 1930s were provided with tiny kitchens and bathrooms. In 1937, following a continental tour by Lewis Silkin MP, Chairman of the Housing and Public Health Committee,

Figure 2.6: **China Walk, Lambeth, slum clearance scheme (1934). Typical of the balcony access tenement blocks built in the inter-war period**

the LCC introduced a 'new type plan' with generous utilities and storage, fitted kitchens and private balconies (Figure 2.7).

One particular scheme which impressed the municipal tourists was the new town developed in 1928, as overspill for Paris, at Drancy-la-Muette. Here they saw the first 'sky-scrapers' – tower blocks, served by lifts, 15 storeys high containing small flats for single or childless people rather than families. These may have been the shape of things to come, but of more immediate interest were the technical innovations at Drancy. The scheme was built by a partly industrialised method – the Mopin system – which comprised a steel frame clad in precast concrete panels. It also had the highly innovative Garchy system in which refuse from each flat was flushed away from a container under the sink and piped to a central incinerator (Denby, 1938, p 233). The scheme greatly impressed visitors from Leeds – Reverend Charles Jenkinson, Leader of the Council and his Director of Housing, architect R.A.H. Livett. Key elements of the project were immediately adopted for their pioneering scheme at Quarry Hill, which was the first British estate to incorporate such technical innovations as industrialised construction, centralised refuse disposal and passenger lifts (Ravetz, 1974a).

Figure 2.7: **'New Type Plan' new model flats introduced by London County Council (1937)**

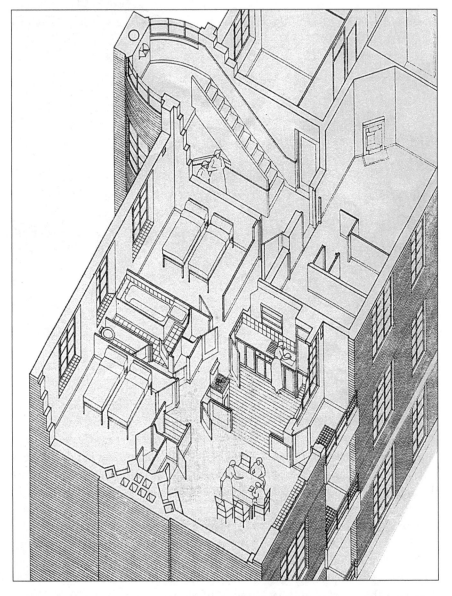

New type of plan   Axonometric view of a three-room dwelling

Source: LCC (1937) © London Metropolitan Archives

The model community

While British housing designers were able to learn various lessons from the Continent on design and construction, the projects which provided most inspiration were the workers' flats built in the 1920s by the socialist municipality of Vienna (Figure 2.8). Here it was neither the design nor construction which impressed – these were generally quite conventional. Nor was it the standards within the flats – which were small by comparison with the best in Europe. It was the generous social facilities. Elizabeth Denby recorded:

> … the smallness of the dwellings was offset by their being surrounded by ample space … and by the municipality providing the tenants with everything necessary for a full communal life, such as infant schools, clubrooms, gymnasiums, laundries, playgrounds and gardens. That is to say, the city council concentrated on the needs of the children, and on the encouragement of companionship and the general health of tenants. The layout of the tenement estates was spacious, orderly and quiet. The flats are generally built around vast common gardens, laid out with playgrounds, paddling pools. Some of these common gardens have an extraordinary, park-like effect…. (Denby, 1938, pp 157, 160)

The Viennese flats were another influence on Quarry Hill but they were also part of a broader inspiration. The idea of communal living had featured strongly in utopian literature – from Plato to Sir Thomas More to William Morris – and here, apparently, was a working model of the ideal society. The housing projects in Vienna had virtually nothing to do with the Modern Movement. They were motivated by social objectives and the appearance of the buildings was of little consequence. But the ideal of the model community did inspire key figures in Modernism.

One such figure was Berthold Lubetkin. Lubetkin was Russian-born and studied in Moscow until 1922 where he became enthused with ideals of the revolution. Lubetkin moved on to Paris and then London, but he was very familiar with the ideas behind the 'communal house' – such as the six-storey block in severe Modernist style built in Moscow in 1929. Designed by Ginzburg and Milinis, the block contained a gymnasium, library, roof garden and communal canteen (Jencks, 1973, p 86). Lubetkin, working with a group of British architects in the practice Tecton, built his first scheme of model flats in Highgate in 1935. This project, 'Highpoint', contained spacious flats with generous communal facilities – but it was designed as a speculative development for wealthy occupants. Lubetkin's ideal was to build such housing for the workers. He was appointed to do just that by the London Borough of Finsbury but his ambitions were stilled by the war. The projects were revived in 1945

Figure 2.8: **Karl Marx Hof, Vienna (1926-30). One of the most impressive of 16 model estates, totalling more than 10,000 flats, built by the socialist municipality of Vienna (1924-33)**

and over the next few years Lubetkin completed three estates of multi-storey flats – Spa Green, Bevin Court and Priory Green. These schemes combined the highest standards of design with generous facilities and proved highly influential models (Allen, 1992).

Just as Vienna had no connection with Modernism, there is no evidence that Le Corbusier had any significant influence on the design of social housing during the inter-war period. His early built projects were largely individual houses, but in 1952 he completed a project which both adopted the communal house ideal and provided a significant model for the design of multi-storey housing. The *Unité d'Habitation* in Marseilles provided housing for 1,600 people in a single-slab block 16 storeys high which included nurseries, a gymnasium, outdoor recreation facilities on the roof and, half-way up, an entire floor designed as a shopping centre. The *Unité* also broke new aesthetic ground in façade treatment and the use of exposed concrete finishes (Jencks, 1975, p 137ff).

Open planning – the Zeilenbau *idea*

While the Modernists adopted the model community they also brought a new interpretation to the long-standing association between housing and health. Miles Glendinning and Stefan Muthesius, in their book *Tower block* (1994), recorded the criticism by early Modernists of older forms of terraced housing and flat design. Their rejection of these as dark and dingy led to an almost obsessive concern to maximise daylight and sunlight. One consequence was the large areas of glazing and the room-width strip windows which dominate the appearance of Modernist buildings. More fundamentally, it affected the whole approach to site planning and layout. The term *Zeilenbau* stems from German practice in the 1930s where housing blocks were laid out in strict parallel lines. The technical arguments for this approach were primarily developed by Walter Gropius (Gropius, 1931). He believed that, in order to make the most of sunlight, blocks of flats should be strictly aligned from north to south regardless of the surrounding street pattern. Height was also important – a height of eight to twelve storeys would limit the number of buildings and maximise sunny grounds between the blocks. The first project in Britain to exhibit these characteristics to the full was the Churchill Gardens development on the Westminster embankment, designed by the architects Powell and Moya for a competition in 1946 (Figure 2.9). The scheme comprised a dozen or more large slab blocks, ten storeys high, set in parallel rows on a north–south axis, almost entirely disregarding the existing street pattern.

Figure 2.9: **Churchill Gardens, Westminster (1946). The scheme was the first in Britain to follow the *Zeilenbau* principle. All the large blocks are orientated strictly on a north–south axis, disregarding and destroying the building's relationship with the street**

The idea of tall blocks of flats, bathed in light and air and set in sunlit open parkland, was not exclusive to *Zeilenbau*. It was the core of Le Corbusier's Radiant City – an idea first espoused in the 1920s (Le Corbusier, 1923). Le Corbusier was a strong influence on the LCC of the 1950s. The 11-storey slab blocks, set in parkland, of the Loughborough Estate in Lambeth, were clearly influenced by the *Unité d'Habitation* – although, crucially, without the community facilities. These were to be the prototype for similar blocks in the more famous Alton West Estate. But here there was a mixture of forms – slab blocks, low-rise maisonettes, bungalows for elderly people. And 'point blocks' – square in plan and 10 storeys high (Figure 2.10). These were inspired not by Le Corbusier, but by the early models at Drancy-la-Muette and by similar blocks – the *punkthus* – in Stockholm (Glendinning and Muthesius, 1994).

Once introduced, tower blocks, easier to plan and orientate than the slab blocks, grew ever more numerous – and ever taller (Figure 2.11). Site planning, once freed from the street, grew ever more open. The inter-war approach to site planning in flat development paid great attention to space creation and to addressing the main lines of the established street pattern. The new approach, inspired by the quest for light and air and the desire for open parks, paid no attention to urban space. Where the inter-war estates created well-designed streets and open spaces, the tall blocks of the 1950s simply sat in spaces which

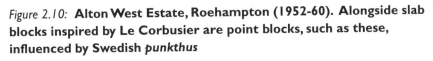

Figure 2.10: **Alton West Estate, Roehampton (1952-60). Alongside slab blocks inspired by Le Corbusier are point blocks, such as these, influenced by Swedish** *punkthus*

were ill-defined, windswept and of no practical or aesthetic value. The new approach to site planning and building form had destroyed the urban street, physically and socially.

Streets in the sky

In the traditional urban street, lined with houses, people's windows overlooked the common space. They got to know their neighbours by sight and, at best, formed productive relationships. At worst, they could follow and observe the activity of the street, an antidote to isolation and a check on anti-social behaviour. The tall block ended all that. Windows looked out into thin air. Flat doors faced onto Spartan corridors or landings where observation was impossible and chance encounters unlikely to blossom. This limitation to multi-storey living was quickly apparent. As early as 1952, in an unsuccessful competition entry, the architects Alison and Peter Smithson put up the idea of "streets in the air" (Glendinning and Muthesius, 1994, p 116ff).

Figure 2.11: **Red Road, Glasgow. Part of the large cluster of tower blocks exceeding 30 storeys (completed 1968-69)**

The first realisation of the concept, however, was in the Park Hill scheme in Sheffield, completed in the early 1960s (Figure 2.12). Access was concentrated onto wide high-level decks which were open at one side to fresh air. Multi-storey blocks were linked together so that each deck served a large number of flats. The decks were expected to be busy with pedestrians, encouraging social interaction, and the original idea was that they would also carry small electric vehicles for milk and postal deliveries (*The Architects' Journal*, 1964a, 1965).

Park Hill excited high praise from architects at the time. It is hard, now, to understand how this concrete cliff of stacked houses – as grim and barrack-like as any Peabody building – could generate aesthetic approval. Some did admire its dramatic visual qualities but what created most interest was the

Figure 2.12: **Park Hill, Sheffield completed early 1960s. The first large scheme to realise the 'streets in the sky' concept. Pedestrian decks link all the blocks together, bridging across at several levels**

Source: © Royal Institute of British Architects

realisation of the concept of 'streets in the sky'. This countered the criticism that the urban street had been destroyed. At the same time, the need to link the blocks together meant a return to joined-up buildings and regeneration of the idea of space creation. Park Hill was, in part, a high-rise scheme, but the concept of the high-level street was soon adapted to relatively low-scale schemes. As the environment created by high blocks came more and more into question, deck access estates, five or six storeys high, became an increasingly common solution to high-density inner-urban redevelopment.

The context of the legacy

The era of flat building as a solution to urban housing problems came to an effective end in the late 1960s when the last major schemes were commissioned. Many identify the demise of multi-storey housing with the Ronan Point disaster of 1968. Five people were killed and many more injured when part of a tower block built of concrete panels collapsed as a result of an explosion. In truth, by then, flats were becoming more and more unpopular and the focus of increasing problems. Policy makers had realised that the high cost of multi-storey housing did not represent value for money and the funding regime had already been changed. As Stephen Merrett succinctly put it: "The evidence suggests that the Ronan Point disaster ... largely served to administer the *coup de grace* to a very very sick man rather than the disaster itself initiating the malady" (Merrett, 1979, p 126). It certainly marked the demise of the tower block. High-density estates of relatively low blocks of flats continued to be built for a few years but these were to be the end of the line for large-scale multi-storey social housing.

In the competition between house and flat, the house has emerged the clear winner. The great bulk of the housing developed in Britain in the 20th century has been individual houses and gardens. Despite some flat building in the inter-war period, the great majority of social housing was in peripheral cottage estates. In addition to the one million council houses many more houses were built for owner-occupation around the major cities. After the Second World War this pattern continued. New social housing was concentrated in new towns and town expansion schemes while the bulk of housing for sale was built by developers on ex-urban greenfield sites. In addressing the problems of the urban slums, decentralisation was the predominant remedy whether achieved through public housing or the choice of house purchase. Where, at the start of the 20th century 80% of the population were city dwellers, at its close perhaps only 30% lived in what were the Victorian cities. This massive shift created serious divisions. Generally it was the better-off who moved to live in the newer suburban and ex-urban housing. The old Victorian cities have come to house a greater number of the poorer and disadvantaged and are now known as the 'inner cities'. This social division is matched by striking physical contrast. The concomitant of relieving the slums through decentralisation was the replacement of much of the old housing by multi-storey blocks.

In the great divide between inner city and suburb, the multi-storey estates remain as an enduring legacy of the housing problems which began in the 19th century. Before the Second World War more than 150,000 flats were built in slum clearance schemes. But these figures are dwarfed by the accelerating progress of the post-war housing drive which peaked in the 1960s. By 1975 1.7 million flats had been built in British cities, mostly in England and Scotland (Dunleavy, 1981, p 41; Glendinning and Muthesius, 1994, pp 1–6). At its peak, the multi-storey legacy totalled more than 1,850,000 flats. Some of these have since been knocked down. No official figures are available but the number demolished – or scheduled for demolition – is small, perhaps only 30,000-50,000. The great majority of the multi-storey flats built, therefore, still stand. They are home to five million people or more. These estates have special problems, partly due to their social character and partly due to their form. Understanding how they came to be built is the first step in solving those problems. The next step is to analyse the factors that led to their decline.

THREE

Politics, economics and housing form

The history of Britain's urban housing problems explains the location of the multi-storey legacy in the inner cities. It also explains the overall forms that it took – the walk-up tenement blocks of the inter-war period necessitated by the requirements of slum clearance procedure; the tall blocks of the 1950s and the 1960s, a response to planing policy but shaped by the subsidy system; and the high-density low-rise estates of the late 1960s and early 1970s which grew out of review and revisions to policy and funding. What it does not explain, however, is the poor quality of much of the multi-storey housing produced in the boom period and the physical shortcomings which lie at the root of many of the problems of inner-city estates.

It is clear that, from the beginning, there was a conflict over quality and standards in multi-storey housing. By the start of the housing boom, in the early 1950s, this conflict had resolved into two distinct traditions. On the one hand was the 'utilitarian' tradition. This grew from the concern over housing and health and sought to ensure that low-income families were provided with housing that was sound, clean and dry but not embellished with visual quality nor given good facilities or public amenities. It was to be provided as cheaply as reasonably possible. On the other hand was the 'idealistic' tradition. This promoted the idea that flat living was a desirable end in itself and that people should be given the dignity of high quality homes. The concentration of people in high-density buildings created both the opportunity and the need to provide generous communal open space and facilities for recreation and childcare. The idealistic approach recognised that multi-storey housing, done well, was not a cheap option.

During the years of high housing output, when the bulk of the multi-storey legacy was built, these traditions created a serious contradiction. Many of the policy makers, providers and designers were inspired by the idealistic tradition. The reality of funding, however, and the sheer scale of the ambitions in terms of housing numbers, meant that the priorities of the utilitarian tradition largely dominated. Although the conflict over the quality of the flats themselves was largely resolved in favour of high space standards this created pressure for economies elsewhere. The nature and the quality of the access systems suffered, as did the quality and standards of construction. The quality of the public environment was downgraded and the amenities reduced to a minimum. That all this was allowed to happen was a result of the conflict between the two traditions – a divergence of attitude and approach which was essentially political.

The political framework

Addressing a conference in 1995, the then Prime Minister John Major condemned multi-storey estates: "There they stand, grey, sullen, concrete wastelands, set apart from the rest of the community, robbing people of ambition and self respect" (Meikle, 1995). In an attempt to blame their progeny on his political opponents he condemned such buildings as "monuments to the failed history of socialist planning". The Prime Minister may have been discomfited by the following day's newspapers. Over the headline 'The house that John built' *The Guardian* pictured one multi-storey "grey concrete wasteland" which Mr Major himself had approved when chair of the Housing Committee in the London Borough of Lambeth (Meikle, 1995). The story made good political slapstick but the Conservative leader's view reflected contemporary political perceptions. Today it is conventional to associate multi-storey housing estates with the urban Labour councils who are struggling to manage them, while the leafy suburbs of cottage homes seem almost the epitome of Conservatism. All the same, the reaction of the press was a reflection of a more accurate political reality.

Multi-storey housing owes its origins to enlightened Conservatives in their efforts in the 19th century to address the horrors of insanitary housing. They started a tradition of 'one nation' social concern which was to sustain Conservative administrations until the early 1970s. Nineteenth-century socialists, on the other hand, were united in their condemnation of the industrial city. Rather than reform them they sought escape. Their aim was to resettle the oppressed workers in new smaller communities in the purer air of the countryside. This line of thinking generated the Garden City movement which was so influential in the cottage estates of the 1920s and the new towns founded in the 1940s. There has been a strong presumption in British socialist tradition towards decentralisation, low densities and the cottage home ideal. All this is not to say that the political Left played no part in the development of multi-storey housing. When in power at local level socialists have been eager to pursue slum clearance but they often sought higher standards than their Conservative counterparts and looked to socialist innovations abroad for inspiration.

One nation Conservatism

While 19th-century socialists such as Engels were busy denouncing the urban horrors created by capitalism, it was left to establishment figures to try to do something about them. Edwin Chadwick, who alerted Parliament to the serious public health problems, was a national public official. Lord Shaftesbury, who initiated the first model housing, was a prominent parliamentarian and a leading figure in the Conservative Party. George Peabody, who funded the first philanthropic intervention, was a prominent banker. These reformers were united by a desire to improve the living conditions for the urban masses but divided on the best means to achieve this. A conflict of opinion which had first emerged in the Royal Commission on the Health of Towns in 1844 was to rumble on for more than half a century.

On the one side there was architect Henry Roberts, who argued that self-contained flats of generous space standards were necessary both for the achievement of human dignity and to minimise health risks. On the other side of the argument were those who believed that clean and dry housing of sound construction was the main objective. Overcrowding and health standards could be controlled by strict management. Economies could be achieved by minimising space standards and finishes and providing kitchens and toilet facilities shared by several families. While some of the smaller housing providers adopted Roberts' approach, the philanthropic Societies, led by Peabody, opted for the cheaper solution. They quickly established what might be called a 'utilitarian tenement' solution to urban housing problems.

The spread of this approach was stimulated by the founder of 'one nation' Conservatism. Benjamin Disraeli had sat on the Health of Towns Commission and was familiar with urban problems. In 1875 – Disraeli's *annus mirabilis* of social reform – his government introduced two Acts which were to have far-reaching consequences. The Public Health Act shaped the pattern of urban housing for half a century and laid the basis for the regulation of building to the present day. The Artisans' and Labourers' Dwellings Improvement Act set up the procedure for slum clearance which has remained essentially the same ever since. Under the powers of this Act an expanding programme of slum clearance was carried out which further consolidated the utilitarian tenement tradition in the development of new social housing. In the main the authorities who carried out this redevelopment were controlled by councillors of a conservative disposition. Most significant was the London County Council (LCC) where the Moderate (ie Conservative) Party took power in 1907 and held it until 1934 (Burnett, 1986, p 186). During this period 10 major slum clearance schemes were initiated by the Council (LCC, 1937). The experience in local government formed the background to the concentrated slum clearance programme introduced by the largely Conservative national government. It was to spread the tenement tradition through many of the industrial cities.

Socialists in power

For the most part the Left did not come to power in urban authorities until well into the 20th century. Once in control, socialists took a different approach to urban working-class housing – seeking a more idealistic solution than the utilitarian tradition established by the Right. The pioneers were the sole Left wing urban administration of the 19th century – the Progressive Party which controlled the LCC from 1889 to 1907. The housing they produced differed radically from the utilitarian tenements. There were higher standards of space and privacy, including a high proportion of self-contained dwellings. Standards of architectural design deliberately emulated the 'mansion block' apartments built for the wealthy and were inspired by the ideals of the Arts and Crafts movement. Their estates were not just housing but included schools, laundries, shops and green open space.

This approach was raised to new heights by the socialist administration which ruled Vienna from 1919 until the early 1930s. In the workers' flats in Vienna standards of communal provision reached new levels – lavish communal open space provided with playgrounds and gardens, well planted and well maintained; clubrooms for meetings and recreation; laundries and bathhouses to promote cleanliness; gymnasiums to keep the body healthy. Above all there were the kindergartens, which became the envy of Europe. Elizabeth Denby encapsulated this idealism:

> It was ... recognised in Vienna that shelter is not enough, that human beings need companionship and recreation, need beauty in environment, need the help that can be given to parents ... by taking their children into nursery schools ... by putting first things first, Viennese housing may ... be claimed as the greatest housing achievement of the century. (Denby, 1938, p 253)

A large claim, but during the 1930s, Viennese housing did provide a model to be emulated for the socialist administrations coming to power in Britain. It was a notable influence following the Labour victory in Leeds in 1933. It was also visited by the Labour administration which took control of the LCC, for the first time, in 1934 at the start of 30 uninterrupted years in power.

The Viennese housing was a libertarian ideal which elevated the lives of those who moved there from the overcrowded 19th-century slums. In many respects the communal houses developed in Russia provided the same range of facilities. But in the hotbed of ideas generated in the revolution there was a more sinister element of compulsion. In a drive towards communal living, private space was to be minimised. Everyone would eat in communal dining rooms, wash in communal bathhouses and spend their recreation hours in communal clubrooms, libraries or gymnasiums. The dark totalitarian aspect to such a concept of social housing was later savagely satirised by George Orwell in his novel *Nineteen eighty-four* (Orwell, 1949). But during the 1920s and 1930s this approach to collective living still had the attraction of novelty. Such ideas chimed with those of Le Corbusier who had visited the new Soviet Union. He was no libertarian, and believed in strict hierarchy and rigid standardisation. According to Peter Hall, Le Corbusier believed these virtues would be achieved through centralised planning, a form of syndicalism "having some close affinities to the left wing variety of Italian Fascism":

> ... now, everyone will be equally collectivised. Now, everyone will live in giant collective apartments called *Unités*; every family will get an apartment not according to the breadwinner's job, but according to rigid space norms; no one will get anything more or less than the minimum necessary for efficient existence. And now everyone – not just the lucky elite – will enjoy collective services. Cooking, cleaning, child care are all taken away from the family. (Hall, 1988, p 210)

Clearly not a view tempered with sympathy. In reality there may be two sides to the same coin. The provision of nurseries to help families and to promote good educational standards can be seen as diminishing and damaging the family. A fairness in providing housing according to people's needs can be seen as rigid regimentation. In the idealistic model of social housing there is a fine line between the liberating influence of high standards and the oppression that can easily flow from their overzealous application.

Despite these pitfalls the schemes developed in Vienna and elsewhere in Europe provided an inspiration to socialist municipalities in Britain. They not only inspired Quarry Hill but also influenced the approach to slum clearance in London and Liverpool (Orwell, 1937, p 65). The ideas of the communal house were a strong influence on Lubetkin and were realised in the estates he designed for the London Borough of Finsbury. The ideals in the European projects also influenced such schemes as Kensal House – developed by the Gas, Light and Coke Company, in 1938, as a prototype for slum clearance (Gaskell, 1986). In the post-war period they were to form the basis for several schemes which came to be regarded as models to be emulated.

Utility versus idealism

By the mid-20th century, two clear traditions had been established in urban multi-storey housing. The older was the utilitarian tenement tradition. This was the concept of housing as a public service – a counter to the overcrowded and unhealthy conditions in the private sector. It went, in the main, to the 'deserving' poor who would pay their rent and could generally be trusted to behave themselves. Its genesis was very much a product of the class structure; good housing provided out of *noblesse oblige* in a social system where the difference between 'us' and 'them' was clearly defined – villas for us, barracks for them. It would never have occurred to Lord Shaftesbury that he or his class should actually live in the model homes provided by his Society, good as they were. While the best providers aimed for high standards, for the most part the utilitarian tenements were put up as cheaply as was consistent with the needs of management. Solid dry and clean shelter was the aim without frills and with scant consideration of provision for communal needs.

On the other hand the idealistic tradition took an egalitarian view. This was the concept of housing as a social right – public housing available to anyone who wanted it. Because it was to be available to all it should be of a high standard which anyone would be happy and proud to live in. It is no coincidence that the exemplars for such housing were the flats built for the wealthy – the Victorian mansion blocks, or the high-quality flats built in Highgate and the borders of Regents Park. Shelter was not enough – housing of high quality was the aim. And it should not just be housing but should provide all the social and recreational facilities necessary for a healthy, happy and successful life. The contrast could hardly be greater and it was evident in the models on the ground. The tenements – plain, grim, repetitive, set in bleak sheets of tarmac on estates devoid of communal facilities. The model housing – designed to the highest architectural standards, given generous green spaces and provided with the facilities necessary for a full communal life.

Post-war – the decline of quality

For some 10 years after the Second World War, housing policy seemed to develop in a logical and progressive fashion. The Labour government placed great emphasis on moving people out of the congested cities. The New Towns played a major part, but authorities were also able to develop sites outside their own boundaries. Borehamwood in Hertfordshire, for example, was originally a huge 'out county' estate developed by the LCC (LCC, 1949). Most important was the fact that there was a choice. Plenty of housing was becoming available outside cities. No one was forced to accept a flat in a multi-storey block. Within the inner cities redevelopment was taking place on a modest but steady scale. New high standards were being achieved in the design of flats. In the promotion of these new standards it seemed as if the utilitarian tradition was being eclipsed.

This trend largely survived the change of government in 1951. But it altered abruptly with the Conservative government's shift of policy in 1956. In a desire to succour the private sector, urban authorities were denied suburban and ex-urban sites. All resources were to be concentrated on slum clearance and this meant an accelerating programme of flats. The large-scale redevelopment which was to follow was actually carried out by urban local authorities. Many of these – probably most – were Labour-controlled. The shape of policy, however, and the details of its implementation, were very much under the direction of central government. Patrick Dunleavy detailed the degree of control:

> The Ministry's extensive influence over public housing construction policy derived from housing legislation, the setting of subsidy scales, the programming of local authority building by a system of annual allocations, the exercise of cost controls over schemes in the course of granting or denying loan sanction approval, and the specification of design standards or desiderata. (Dunleavy, 1981, p 9)

The relatively small numbers of flats produced in the 1940s and early 1950s to the new higher standards were a comparatively expensive form of housing. While urban renewal was a small proportion of the public housing drive, the need to spend relatively high unit costs on multi-storey housing could be recognised and accommodated. With a concentration of flat building there was inevitable pressure to reduce unit costs to a level closer to ordinary houses. This meant economies in design. Conceivably, cuts could be made in the space standards within flats. Given the long-running debate over standards and the historical concern with overcrowding and health this would have undoubtedly seemed retrograde. With firm pressure to maintain standards within the flats, there were relatively few options in the search for savings.

The main way savings were achieved was by increasingly stringent economies in the access systems which were to become the root of many of the subsequent problems. To achieve an increasingly ambitious programme, economies of scale were explored which included the introduction of industrialised construction techniques. As a last resort, projects were stripped of desirable amenities by cutting out 'non-essential' expenditure. All this meant a damaging dilution of the quality of the multi-storey models and a reassertion of utilitarian priorities. The Labour government of 1964-70 reviewed the policy which certainly had some impact on the form of multi-storey developments. However, that government had committed itself to a production programme which was almost absurdly ambitious. The pressures of this programme meant continuing economies and a failure to raise overall quality.

The debate over standards

The issue of standards goes back to the origin of tenement housing. For a long time the key question was about shared facilities – self-containment versus 'associated dwellings'. As late as 1930 associated dwellings, with shared toilets and water supply, were still being built by housing societies and some local authorities (Barnes, 1973). Generally, however, by the inter-war period, the issue had been resolved and most municipal tenements comprised self-contained flats. But standards were generally low and flats were small by today's standards. Kitchens and bathrooms were often tiny and sometimes the bath was actually in the kitchen.

Providing adequate space to eliminate overcrowding and ensuring cleanliness through good washing facilities were central to the issue of housing and health. Improving these standards became a major concern for reformers. The Tudor Walters' Report of 1918 was a significant step forward. It set generous new standards for working-class housing. The Report was chiefly concerned, however, to promote cottage housing. It had very little to say about flats, noting that "...large blocks of tenements four or five storeys high are currently erected in great towns and particularly in Scotland", but concluding:

> ... although it was admitted that modified types of such buildings might
> be necessary in the centre of areas already partly developed with this
> class of dwelling.... Such blocks of tenements are not dealt with in this
> report, but the accommodation to be provided and many of the
> considerations as to economy of construction referred to would apply
> equally well to those buildings. (LGB, 1918, para 84)

There was, however, no obligation to apply such high standards and it was left very much to the discretion of the local authorities and housing societies. The more progressive administrations were keen to improve standards. When Labour took power at the LCC in 1934 the Council was still building, alongside its self-contained flats, a lower standard tenement with shared facilities, unplastered walls and low ceilings. The Labour Council immediately abandoned these "type B dwellings" (Yelling, 1992, p 156). Within three years it had introduced the "new type plan" with unprecedented standards of space and amenities (see Figure 2.7).

Universal standards for flats were first established by the Dudley Report prepared for the Ministry of Health in 1944 (Table 3.1). Like its predecessor, this second major report on housing standards concentrated on houses, for which it established new space standards based on room sizes. But it did recommend that these standards be applied to flats and that each flat be provided with a private balcony, "... where the baby can sleep in the open air and where flowers or vegetables can be grown in window boxes" (MoH, 1944a).

Table 3.1: **Comparison of recommended overall sizes for flats in successive government reports (figures in square feet)**

Size of flat	1944 Housing Manual	1949 Housing Manual	Parker Morris Report (1961)
1 person	–	300-350ft²	328ft²
2 persons	432ft²	500ft²	490ft²
3 persons	561ft²	–	622ft²
4 persons	692-712ft²	700-750ft²	765ft²
5 persons	740-792ft²	850ft²	865ft²
6 persons	–	900-950ft²	915ft²
7 persons	–	1,000ft²	–

The Dudley Report was accompanied by the *1944 Housing Manual* which fleshed out these standards and also provided model layouts for blocks of flats (MoH Ministry of Works, 1944b). These standards were further refined and developed by the *1949 Housing Manual* (MoH, 1949), which contains what is probably the most comprehensive investigation in official literature into the design and layout of blocks of flats. Standards were raised once more by the Parker Morris Report of 1961 (MoHLG, 1961). For the first time standards were set for car parking with one space per dwelling recommended as the minimum for new residential developments. Again this report was chiefly concerned with houses. Flats were essentially treated as stacked-up houses. Very similar standards of space and amenity were applied. There was some discussion on lift provision and the need for sound insulation. Unlike the earlier housing manuals, however, the new report had nothing to say on the planning or form of multi-storey blocks.

As in most paths of progress, two steps forward are followed by one step back. The high standards of the Tudor Walters' Report, enthusiastically adopted by the Liberal government of Lloyd George, were cut back by the succeeding Conservative government in 1923 (Burnett, 1986, p 232). In the same way those pursued by the post-war Labour government were trimmed by the incoming Tories (MoHLG, 1952). The high standards of the *1949 Housing Manual* were rejected in favour of consolidation of the lowest levels established in 1944. Where the Dudley Report had recommended sizes giving a tolerance of about 10%, the new report, *Houses 1952* (MoHLG, 1952), cut back standards to the minimum (Table 3.2). The government did, however, make these standards mandatory for flats and their application in new developments was enforced through the cost control system (MoHLG, 1958, p 153).

Table 3.2: **Comparison of recommended room sizes for housing in 1944 and 1952 (figures in square feet)**

	1944 Housing Manual	Houses 1952
The kitchen living room house		
Kitchen living room	180-200ft^2	180ft^2
Sitting room	110-120ft^2	110ft^2
Scullery	35-80ft^2	50ft^2
The working kitchen house		
Living room separate dining space	180-200ft^2	180ft^2
Living room plus dining space	235-245ft^2	225ft^2
Working kitchen	90-100ft^2	90ft^2
The dining kitchen house		
Living room	169-180ft^2	160ft^2
Dining kitchen	110-125ft^2	110ft^2
Bedrooms		
First bedroom	135-150ft^2	135ft^2
Other doubled bedrooms	110-120ft^2	110ft^2
Single bedroom	70-80ft^2	70ft^2

The Labour government review of 1965 adopted the standards of the Parker Morris Report for new local authority housing. Like the Report itself, however, the main concern was to set higher standards for individual houses. The space standards were adopted for flats as were the requirements to provide central heating and improved electrical installations. This raised the quality of the flat interiors to very high standards. The requirement for 100% car parking was also applied to flats and a special subsidy provided to pay for it. The obligation to invest more in the flat interiors and in more car parking, however, placed even greater pressure to find economies elsewhere in the design and development of multi-storey housing.

The economics of access systems

The conflict between utility and economy did not revolve solely around the issues of self-containment and space standards. From the earliest models two types of access systems emerged in tenement housing – 'balcony access', where flats are reached from galleries served by a single staircase; and 'staircase access', where flats are entered directly from each stair, two or three at each level. The division between advocates of each type was partly philosophical. Henry Roberts strongly believed the open access balcony to be more healthy than an enclosed staircase and used this arrangement in his influential model scheme in Bloomsbury. But the 'balcony access' system is also inherently cheaper. Staircases are more costly to build than balconies and the more dwellings which can be served from a single staircase, the cheaper the design. This was also a major consideration in the design of 'associated dwellings', where many rooms with shared facilities could be reached from a single stair. Despite their desire to raise standards, the Progressives in the LCC of the 1890s were constantly dogged by this problem. Staircase access was considered desirable but economic difficulties necessitated more flats served from each stair so that hybrid plans emerged which had some shared facilities. For reasons of design economy, the balcony access block became the predominant form of tenement housing built in London and Liverpool up to the mid-20th century. Only in Glasgow was staircase access the norm. This was probably because most tenements were actually designed for middle-class occupation. The relatively small numbers of working-class tenements followed the same pattern, although they had shared toilets.

Staircase access generally came to be regarded as superior. Lewis Silkin's report on his European tour of 1936 noted that blocks of flats on the Continent were 'almost universally' provided with staircase access and many had secured entrances at ground level (LCC, 1936). When Silkin's LCC introduced its 'new type plan', staircase access was preferred. Reasons cited included the elimination of overshadowing caused by the access balconies and the loss of privacy due to balconies passing in front of some the windows of flats (LCC, 1937). An evident advantage is that, with a relatively small number of flats reached from each staircase, tenants come to know each other and can readily challenge intruders. Also, although many of the early staircase access blocks had open entrances, it is relatively easy to provide a secured main entrance door. For all these reasons staircase access flats became the preferred type and are commended exclusively in the detailed type plans included in the *1949 Housing Manual*.

In the drive to raise standards in flat development, there was also recognition that the standard tenement 'walk-up' of five storeys was too high, particularly for young children or elderly people. The Dudley Committee was impressed with the lifts installed in the recently completed Quarry Hill Estate. They recommended that all blocks above three storeys should have lifts. During the late 1940s these new standards strongly influenced flat design. Dudley's recommendations were not fully followed but, in inner London, the five-storey balcony access estate was generally superseded by four-storey staircase access blocks. Even where lifts were provided the preference for staircase access was maintained (Figure 3.1).

Figure 3.1: **Woodbury Down Estate, eight-storey blocks developed by London County Council in the late 1940s. Their planning illustrates the contemporary preference for staircase access serving two flats per floor even where lifts were provided**

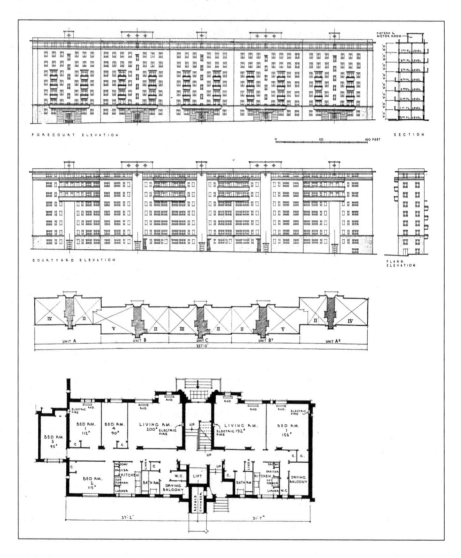

Source: LCC (1949) © London Metropolitan Archives

Staircase access was, itself, a more expensive option than balcony access. The new policy of providing lifts made it much more expensive still. In an eight-storey block with staircase access, as at Woodbury Down, each lift served only 16 flats – effectively only 12 if the lowest two floors are discounted. The benefits of such high standards were considerable although there was the risk that if the lift broke down everyone had to walk. For reasons of economy taller blocks became the norm, most often with paired lifts to provide back-up, although for some time a height of 100 feet (11 storeys) was the practical maximum (Owens, 1987). A government report – *Flats and houses 1958* (MoHLG, 1958) – compared the costs of various types of block. The costs of three- and four-storey blocks of flats and maisonettes without lifts were analysed. The costs of 11- and 12-storey slab and tower blocks with lifts, and a variety of access arrangements, were also studied (MoHLG, 1958).

The most striking comparison reveals the cost of building high (Table 3.3). The extra cost of the 11-storey blocks as compared with three-storey blocks was a minimum of 45%, rising to as much as 63%. Some of this extra expense was for refuse chutes, fire escape provisions and structural requirements, but the bulk of it was the cost of the lifts. This is illustrated by comparison of 11-storey tower blocks of different layout. One group had four flats per floor with each lift serving a total of 20 flats. The other group had eight flats per floor, each lift serving 40 flats. When the number of flats served by each lift was doubled, the extra over cost of building high was reduced to 31%, a considerable saving.

Table 3.3: **Comparative costs of low-rise and high-rise flats**

	Cost per unit	Ratio
three-storey flats, no lifts	£1,450 average	100
11-storey flats with lifts 20 flats per lift	£2,100 to £2,360	145 to 163
11-storey flats with lifts 40 flats per lift	£1,900	131

Source: From figures given in MoHLG (1958)

It was also evident that savings could be made by reducing the proportion of the external walls (Figure 3.2). Comparison of balcony access layout with a central corridor arrangement shows the latter has a much larger floor area and a lower cost per dwelling. This saving comes largely from spreading the cost of the expensive external walls over a larger floor area – a cost factor known as the 'external wall/floor area ratio'. But it also meant that the same size access corridor could serve a larger number of flats. As the search for economies intensified it became evident that savings could be made if more and more dwellings were served from the same access system. One of the features of Le Corbusier's *Unité d'Habitation* was its design economy (Figure 3.3). Here a central walkway served two-storey maisonettes stepping both up and down. There was thus only one corridor for every three floors. The scheme combined the fiscal virtues of a deep plan with a very large number of dwellings served by each access corridor.

Figure 3.2: **Balcony access and corridor access. The central corridor allows a much deeper plan and serves more flats providing a considerable cost saving**

PART PLAN

PART PLAN

Figure 3.3: **Unit plan and part section of Le Corbusier's *Unité d'Habitation*, Marseilles (1952). The scheme combines the fiscal virtues of a low external wall/floor ratio with the economy of an access corridor serving a large number of dwellings**

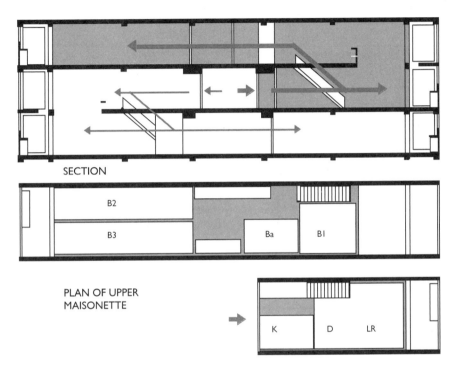

SECTION

PLAN OF UPPER
MAISONETTE

This concept was developed in Britain in 'scissor block' planning (Figure 3.4), and the approach was pioneered by the LCC (Owens, 1987). It involved split level flats stepping up or down by half levels from the front of the block to the back. This meant that access corridors needed to be provided only on alternate floors. In a later development in Glasgow by former LCC architects Robert Matthew Johnson Marshall (RMJM), the interval between corridors was increased to two-and-a-half floors (*The Architects' Journal*, 1964b). The 'scissor block' design made savings in corridor space but within each block it was still necessary to provide two lifts and staircases. By linking blocks together the lifts and staircases could be shared and their numbers reduced by up to half. From the mid-1960s onwards schemes were built where more and more slab blocks were joined together by bridges – 'linked slab' estates.

Figure 3.4: **'Scissor block' planning: (left) diagrammatic section showing scissor block planning principle developed by the LCC reducing corridors to alternate floors, each serving flats above and below. (right) Later scheme completed in the Gorbals in 1964. Frequency of access corridors reduced further and now placed two-and-a-half floors apart**

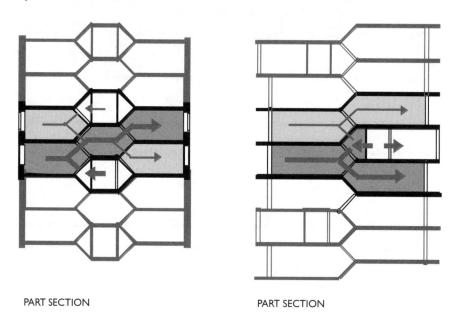

PART SECTION   PART SECTION

These principles reached their logical conclusion in the 'deck access' estates developed from the 'streets in the sky' idea. Many blocks could be linked together by a pedestrian deck which gave access to three or more levels of flats and maisonettes. The decks were generous in size and open to fresh air, unlike the corridors of linked slabs, but they served more flats. Also, because the deck access estates were not high rise – generally four to six storeys – there was far less dependence on lifts. Fewer were needed and those that were provided could each serve several blocks.

Minimal access and the impact of subsidy

The keys to reducing the cost of access were to increase the number of dwellings served by each lift and to reduce the amount of communal corridor space. From 1956 the application of the storey height subsidy made it almost inevitable that housing blocks would rise higher and higher. High blocks had the twin advantages of lower unit costs in providing lifts and more subsidy for the addition of each storey. This reached its maximum advantage in the very high blocks where each lift might be made to serve as many as 70 or 80 flats. When this was combined with planning arrangements such as the 'scissor blocks', where several levels could be served from each corridor, further savings could be made. The combination of height subsidy and economies in the access systems not only made possible the construction of high blocks, they made this form the most attractive to housing authorities and this explains the concentration on high flats which peaked in the early 1960s.

The Labour government's review of the subsidy system is credited with bringing an end to high-rise housing. The ending of the height subsidy certainly made it less attractive. But the Housing Cost Yardstick still favoured high-density schemes which ensured the continued concentration on multi-storey housing in urban redevelopment. In some respects its introduction exacerbated the financial constraints on design. It was accompanied by mandatory application of the higher standards of the Parker Morris Report. These were strictly applied through tight rules enforced through the vetting of each scheme by officials in central government. At the same time strict cost limits were applied which constantly fell behind inflation. All this created pressure for economies which largely had to be made in the form and construction of the blocks. The complexity tested the ingenuity of housing designers to the limit and beyond.

Overall the Housing Cost Yardstick was a more flexible system than what went before. It was instrumental in ending the high-rise era and, under its provisions, some good schemes were produced. But also many bad ones. The new system did not end the constraints which had demanded economies in access systems. These were responsible for the provision of access arrangements which served more and more flats; used by so many tenants that they could not possibly recognise intruders; unsecured against public access and wide open to abuse. The lifts provided were of poorer and poorer quality – slow, unreliable, subject to frequent breakdown and finished in the grimmest utility materials. The stairs were stark, bare concrete. The internal corridors in slab blocks were long oppressive rows of doors without natural light or ventilation. At least the walkways in deck access estates were not denied light and air, but they were equally featureless and cheaply finished.

The utilitarian product

The requirements of the funding system had made necessary incremental changes which cheapened the access systems and made them of poorer and poorer quality. The pressure created by a rapidly expanding housing programme and the concentration on slum clearance also had other effects which made multi-storey housing increasingly utilitarian. The search for economies of scale led to the construction of ever larger estates, more and more of which were built using monotonous industrialised systems of questionable calibre. At the same time, the constraints on funding often meant the elimination of 'non-essentials' – the facilities and amenities which had been crucial to the success of the idealist model of multi-storey living.

Economies of scale

One way to achieve economies of scale was the adoption of ever-larger construction contracts. Very large redevelopment contracts, it was considered, could achieve economies both in design, through repetition, and construction, through minimising overheads, even when using conventional building methods. The greatest economies, however, were seen to lie in the adoption of industrialised building. The mass production of components fabricated in factory conditions, and the reduction of site work prone to disruption by the weather, was expected to procure significant savings. The benefits would be greatest in multi-storey developments where the potential for repetition was greatest. Even more advantage could be derived from building large schemes which would require a long run of components and perhaps even justify the construction of an on-site factory.

From the early 1960s industrialised methods were promoted by the government and by the late 1960s formed the basis of a significant proportion of multi-storey schemes. In fact the financial benefits were largely illusory. One study put the cost advantage at less that 3% (AMA, 1984). Patrick Dunleavy's figures put the advantage at about 5%, briefly rising to 10% at the peak of production in 1968 (Dunleavy, 1981, p 86). It is not clear whether this minimal advantage was understood at the time although there were also certain indirect cost advantages. Industrialised developments could undoubtedly be completed more quickly. This could produce savings in 'on costs' and make a significant contribution to the achievement of the ambitious housing production targets. This, alone, may have presented political attractions.

Whatever the reasons, the adoption of industrialised methods had critical implications for the quality of multi-storey housing. The requirements of mass production needed large numbers of identical components. It also required that the components be as simple as possible to minimise production difficulties. The result was very large estates with the same forms monotonously repeated, each block constructed of components with the minimum of variety and completely lacking adornment. Worse still, untried methods were put into large-scale use without the test of time which would have allowed the accumulation of knowledge about their performance. The risk of this strategy was tragically revealed in the collapse of Ronan Point, but later investigation disclosed a whole range of less critical technical shortcomings.

Eliminating 'non-essentials'

A key feature of the idealistic model of urban multi-storey housing was the provision of generous communal facilities and amenities. In the drive for economy top priority was given to the standards of space and amenity within the individual dwellings. If necessary, non-essentials such as community facilities could be cut down or eliminated altogether. Early model schemes did include such facilities. Kensal House provided club rooms, a nursery school, play areas and allotments (Gaskell, 1986). Spa Green in Finsbury included a nursery and generous landscaped communal gardens (Allen, 1992). But, as the housing drive gathered pace, as soon as cost problems arose, the immediate response was to eliminate some of the social facilities. Most often such common amenities were minimal and, almost always, accorded the lowest priority. The massive Red Road scheme in Glasgow is good example. When the estate was completed in 1966, it was provided with extremely limited recreation space and no play equipment or enclosed space for young children. The nearest health clinic was more than a mile away. There was one shop and no more were built. The nearest public transport was a bus stop half a mile away (Jephcott, 1971, p 66). The Broadwater Farm Estate in North London, completed in 1973, was similarly poorly served. The original scheme included shops, a pub, a launderette and surgeries for a doctor and dentist. All fairly basic facilities, but all cut out as the first targets of cost savings (Hackney, 1990, p 130).

The same was true of environmental quality. Hardly any British housing estate was set in grounds which matched up to the "extraordinary park-like effect" which Elizabeth Denby observed in Vienna. The key exception was the LCC's celebrated scheme at Alton West, Roehampton. The scheme was not completed until 1960 but its genesis dates from the early 1950s. Roehampton became a model, widely admired, largely because of the attractive mature landscape in which it was set. No other scheme was to match it. The best that most could offer was an open, windswept grassed space dotted with a few trees; the worst a bleak expanse of hard paving. Architectural quality, too, was sacrificed in the incessant drive for economies. The celebrated and generous entrance and staircase which Lubetkin provided at Bevin Court in Finsbury was made unrepeatable by the drive to eliminate 'non-essentials'.

What made all this doubly ironic was that although cost savings reduced social facilities and the quality of the environment, under the Housing Cost Yardstick dedicated funding was available to provide car parking. Nor was this optional: 100% car parking was a mandatory requirement. This may have been appropriate for low-density schemes of individual houses. For high-density multi-storey estates it was not. Car ownership rates were low in the inner cities and have remained so. Land was at a premium. As a result many multi-storey estates were provided with expensive underground or multi-storey car parks for which there was little demand. At best these were largely redundant and at worst they were to become a serious liability.

The accumulation of economies

Through economies the cost of multi-storey housing was reduced. Dunleavy's research shows that over the period 1960-68 the relative costs of housing over five storeys declined by about 20% before stabilising (Dunleavy, 1981, p 85). Very little of this steady reduction can be attributed to the advantages of industrialised building. Most of it must be due to savings in housing form, the cheapening of construction and finishes and the elimination of communal amenities. By the 1960s most multi-storey housing was of dismal quality. The blocks were monotonous, repetitive and completely lacking visual quality. The public areas were finished in the most basic materials. The buildings were set in featureless acres of grass or paving and provided with huge areas of unnecessary car parking. The estates were almost entirely devoid of communal facilities. Social housing had been stripped to its bare and unappealing essentials. In short, the Victorian tenement had re-emerged.

Mixed development – the hidden option

Perhaps it need never have happened. An alternative option lies hidden in history. The post-war planning system was inspired as much by concern at the chaos of suburban sprawl as by distaste for the industrial city. Drawing on her experience in Europe, Elizabeth Denby was a keen advocate of the benefits and vitality of city life. But she proposed flats only for those who wanted them and was keen to see urban development emulate the squares and terraced houses with gardens which characterise English cities of the pre-industrial era (Denby, 1938, pp 209-64). A similar view was taken by the leading planner Thomas Sharp. In his best-selling book *Town planning* (1940) he presented a devastating critique of the waste of land and resources embodied in the acres of semi-detached houses encircling the major cities. He advocated denser urban development and cited the squares of London and the terraces of Exeter and Durham as his models. Flats would have a place, but a subsidiary one.

Both Denby and Sharp wanted to see more compact urban development which would, for the most part, comprise terraced houses with gardens. Flats would be built but only for those who were attracted to the benefits of this way of living. Such a model would have been appropriate for the redevelopment of all but the most densely populated urban areas. This concept seemed to find favour with the Dudley Committee of 1944:

> We are aware of the keen controversy of the house versus the flat. Our evidence shows that flats are unpopular with large sections of the community, particularly families with children. It also suggests that the principal reasons for this unpopularity are noise; lack of privacy; the absence of a private garden; the difficulties of supervising children at play; and the necessary rule against keeping pets.... On the other hand ... a considerable proportion of the population are not members of families with children and here there is often a preference for flats.... Our own view is that while flats are open to many objections for families with children, they are less objectionable for other persons. There is a need, therefore for a mixed development of family houses mingled with blocks of flats for smaller households. (MoH, 1944a, paras 33-5)

The idea of mixed development was a strong strain in the debate about housing development in the 1940s. Much more recently Ruth Owens carried out a well researched study of the subsequent development of the idea (1987). The post-war planning system imposed the need for high densities, particularly in the urban centres. It was known that high densities could be achieved by building dense terraced houses or tenement flats. Both these housing forms had attracted opprobrium, the former regarded as slums and the latter as grim and barrack-like. There was a propensity to look to models which provided more open and airy accommodation. Houses in the form of cottages, flats on the idealistic model. To achieve high densities and at the same time more open planning, blocks of flats of at least five storeys were seen as inevitable. With the need to reach new standards by providing lifts it was a short step to the widely built 11-storey blocks.

However, mixed development did have an influence. In Leicester the Council achieved higher densities by mixing houses with blocks containing only one-bedroom flats. By far the greatest number of schemes labelled 'mixed development', however, were carried out in London, mainly by the LCC. These comprised not houses and flats, but tower blocks containing one- and two-bedroom flats coupled with four-storey blocks of maisonettes for larger families (Owens, 1987). The principle of separating small and large households seems to have had some influence on housing policy in Birmingham. The 463 high blocks built in the city contained, almost exclusively, one- and two-bedroom flats (Dunleavy, 1981, p 259). Elsewhere there was less interest in mixed development. The 26- and 31-storey tower blocks at Red Road, Glasgow, consisted entirely of three-bedroom family flats (Jephcott, 1971) and in the tall blocks built in Liverpool in the period 1964-68 there was a predominance of two- and three-bedroom flats (Owens, 1987).

The mixed development concept did play a role in limiting the numbers of families in high blocks but its impact could have been much stronger. By the late 1960s it had become evident that high blocks were not necessary to achieve high densities. Britain's urban renewal could have been achieved with lower-scale development in the manner of the traditional city. It would have cost less and achieved higher quality. The principles of mixed development – families on the ground, multi-storey flats for those who choose them – provides an important alternative model to the utilitarian legacy of multi-storey housing that actually emerged.

FOUR

Social stigma and community action

At first, the new multi-storey flats seemed to confer considerable benefits on their occupants. Compared with their old homes they were spacious, bright and clean with modern kitchens and bathrooms. Soon, however, the problems of multi-storey living became all too apparent, particularly for families with young children. Furthermore, the downside of the economies which made cheap multi-storey housing possible created increasing problems. The poor quality lifts frequently broke down, trapping many on the upper floors. The common stairs and access ways, neither public nor private, became vandalised and abused, further downgrading the already utilitarian public environment. The lack of communal facilities rapidly became a source of dissatisfaction. Within a few years of their completion, many multi-storey estates became 'hard-to-let', rejected by those for whom they were supposed to provide a release from bad housing.

At the same time, Victorian terraced housing was being revalued. There was growing awareness of the value of community life in old residential areas – and many, it seemed, were quite happy with their homes. Resistance to slum clearance grew. More and more local groups formed to fight comprehensive redevelopment and campaign for more sensitive and small-scale solutions. Faced with increasing management problems on multi-storey housing estates and with increasing resistance to them being built, public policy was forced to retreat. The building of high blocks and large-scale developments came to an end. There was an increase in rehabilitation and small-scale new housing. With this change came a new approach in which the views of local communities and those who would occupy new buildings became the key to successful housing solutions.

Living in multi-storey housing

In the early days of flat building a degree of choice was on offer. Most council tenants got their homes after a period on the 'waiting list' while their needs were prioritised through a points system. Those who wanted to stay near friends and family and in the inner city usually had to accept a flat. But those who wanted a house could usually get one, albeit some distance away on a peripheral estate or in a new town. As slum clearance became the main focus of housing policy the choices got less and less. The chief aim was to rehouse those living in clearance areas. As fewer and fewer houses were being built this increasingly meant moving to a flat. Even so, for a long time, not everyone affected by demolition was offered the chance of new housing.

In her book *Hovels to high rise* (1993), Anne Power pointed out that many were excluded. Generally, single people and childless couples did not merit enough priority for rehousing. Newcomers were also excluded so that they would not be rehoused ahead of those who had waited longer. For this reason those in furnished lettings, which were regarded as transient tenancies, were denied rehousing. Those excluded from rehousing rights when an area was demolished were forced to move to other run-down districts of cheap housing. For obvious reasons these areas became the focus of migrant communities:

> Councils delayed certain slum clearance and redevelopment areas in order to avoid dealing with areas of immigrant concentration. The delayed areas attracted greater and greater minority populations, in ever worsening conditions as a solution to exclusion from better areas. The blighted areas were used by councils to rehouse families from more advanced slum clearance areas who had to be moved but were 'unsuitable' for new flats – generally so-called 'problem families'. 'Dumping' on redevelopment areas became common from the 1960s. Trapped immigrant households, long standing ... elderly tenants unwilling to move, and 'problem families', were forced together. (Power, 1993, p 195)

Eventually, however, even these blighted areas were mostly redeveloped. This pattern of clearance and rehousing partly explains the social structure of multi-storey estates. The earliest estates housed people who had a degree of choice and were generally happy to live in flats. By the 1960s there was, increasingly, little choice. This is confirmed by Pearl Jephcott's seminal study of multi-storey housing in Glasgow carried out in the late 1960s. This study found that the population of high blocks had much the same age and household structure as the city as a whole and was probably representative of the general urban population (Jephcott, 1971). The more recent estates, however, were often used to rehouse those displaced from blighted areas. As a result, estates completed in the 1970s often contained disproportionate numbers of families with children and of the poorest, most vulnerable tenants – those with the greatest social problems. This served to exacerbate the problems of multi-storey living which were already becoming all too evident.

The reaction of tenants to living in flats depended greatly on their social circumstances and family structure. Pearl Jephcott found that those households making a success of high-rise living were those whose interests did not centre on the home; who had plenty of personal resources; and who were relatively better educated and well-off. These were generally single people, middle-aged couples without children or other adult households. This helps to explain why multi-storey housing works well in the private sector. But given the pattern and policy of rehousing such people are very much in the minority in public housing.

Elderly people and those handicapped by infirmity or disability are commonly housed in the public sector. Among these groups there has been a mixed reaction to multi-storey living. Pearl Jephcott found that, while many elderly people were initially disorientated by a move to a high flat, many adapted well. They liked the relative peace and security offered by living off the ground. They also tended to be more sociable than other groups, developing strong links with their neighbours. Similarly, handicapped people responded well to the security of flat life and benefited from a level and accessible environment. Other evidence is more mixed, with some surveys suggesting that elderly people would opt first for a small house and garden (Adams and Conway, 1974). While it was clear that many adults could live happily in multi-storey flats it was equally evident that such housing provides an unsuitable environment for children.

Families with children

From as early as 1961 research had shown the concern of mothers for the safety of young children on balconies, staircases and lifts, and this has been underlined by periodic tragedies involving children falling from high blocks. Studies have also shown that young children living in flats are able to play outside less and that indoor play is restricted because of space and the need to keep noise to a minimum. This has created stress and illness in mothers both because of the restrictions of supervising a child in a flat, and the pressures and difficulties of the increased need to take a young family out for recreation (Gittus, 1976).

For the older child there are less dangers, but multi-storey housing has created an environment which is quite different from the traditional street. Pearl Jephcott commented:

> ... the new form of housing segregates the generations and cuts off the child from his home. In traditional housing dozens of reasons lead him to make brief appearances there. He runs in to shelter from a squall, to fetch a toy, to go to the toilet, to wheedle 2p when he hears the chimes of the ice cream van – all of which mean that he is fairly often in touch with his grown-ups. In a high flat this is less likely because of the bother of the lift. The adult is equally reluctant to have to use it. And as regards anybody having a glance now and then to see if he is all right, the child can slip under the block, round the corner and vanish from sight more

easily than in a street. Nor can the grown-up admonish by a tap on the window and administer justice 'who slapped who?' The child's casual contacts with people other than those of his own home have also lessened. No one leans on a sill or pops out to look at a pram, no couples have a half hour's blather at the gate, no father mends a fence, no gran sits on the step minding a toddler but also available for talk with the 8-year-old. (Jephcott, 1971, p 87)

While living in flats created restrictions and dangers for young children – and serious problems for their parents – for the older child it provided an alien environment, one in which the normal social controls were weakened. Under the best of circumstances this would have created tensions. In the particular forms of housing developed to meet the needs of economy and low cost it proved little short of disastrous. In the old urban areas children were accustomed to established zones of control. In the home it was their parents; in the school their teachers; and in the streets the authority of the law and the surveillance of neighbours and passers-by. The new forms of multi-storey housing created areas which were a sort of 'no man's land', where no authority or responsibility was established.

Children could roam the common areas – lifts, stairs, corridors and walkways, underground car parks – unchallenged and unobserved by adults. These areas became increasingly subject to abuse and vandalism. This may have started as relatively innocent mischief – joyriding in the lifts, swinging on doors and gates, inscribing a remote and inviting blank wall. But many children had moved into the estates from clearance areas where demolition sites and derelict buildings provided abundant opportunities for destructive play. The damage being done to the common areas of many estates quickly accelerated to a serious and costly level.

In the early 1970s the Home Office commissioned a major study of vandalism. During 1973-74 Sheena Wilson surveyed damage on 38 London housing estates. While vandalism was associated with poor maintenance and repair, the most significant factor was child density. The incidence of damage was correlated against the numbers of children aged 6-16. It was found that vandalism increased as a direct relation to the numbers of children per dwelling. Concentration of children was also significant. Where there were more than 20 children in a block, vandalism was likely to be high. The study also confirmed that child density was commonly lower – and vandalism less – in tower block estates built in the 1950s (Wilson, 1978). This is probably a reflection of the preponderance of smaller flats in London tower blocks.

The Wilson study looked only at three types of vandalism which could be quantified – damage to lifts, broken glass and physical damage to doors, railings and the like. A more recent study concentrated on graffiti and found, unsurprisingly, that this was most prevalent on the least visible and least accessible common areas of estates (Hamid, 1990). One of the most common forms of abuse – the fouling of lifts and stairs – seems not to have attracted research, although it is a source of great concern to tenants. This is commonly attributed to vagrants or passing drunks but observations suggest that the principal culprits are young children unable to reach their own homes and the groups of teenagers who congregate in the common areas.

Other abuses for which children and teenagers are commonly blamed include the setting of fires, dumping of rubbish and throwing down objects from upper levels, sometimes with disastrous consequences (Wainwright, 1996). Whether or not this is all the work of children there is little doubt that their abuse of common areas created a syndrome. As a result of the absence of adequate surveillance and control, the communal parts of estates became degraded and devalued. They subsequently became the focus of much more serious crimes, some of which may have been committed by those who had grown up in the estates and acquired increasingly bad habits from an early age.

The extent of failure

All this is not to suggest that the problems of multi-storey housing are entirely the fault of the tenants. There is no doubt, however, that a key issue was the failure to recognise the general problems likely to arise from housing a large number of children in high blocks and the particular problems caused by disadvantaged households where parental control is likely to be weaker. But all these issues surrounding use and abuse were exacerbated by poor social provision and technical inadequacies. The shortcomings created by the economies which had been introduced to make multi-storey housing 'low cost' soon became apparent.

Those moving into the new estates were disadvantaged by the shortage of local shops and communal provision. The lack of facilities disproportionately affected the young and the old. Better provision for children and teenagers might have ameliorated the multi-storey environment and provided displacement of their destructive activities in the common areas. It is significant that Sheena Wilson's research found that levels of vandalism were lower in blocks provided with landscaping and open space. While elderly tenants generally adapted well to living in flats, they were most likely to be disadvantaged by a lack of health facilities and local shops. And to improve the quality of their lives there was a clear need for facilities such as lunch clubs and day centres. They were also the most adversely affected by access problems within the blocks.

The lift was a *sine qua non* of multi-storey housing. Yet the economy measures which required that each lift serve more and more dwellings meant that they were in almost constant use. Such demands would test even the most robust machinery, yet these lifts were generally of the cheapest possible quality. Add to this the impact of vandalism and it was small wonder that the lifts frequently broke down. Problems with the lifts were among the most serious concerns of tenants in high blocks. The frequent breakdowns not only stranded tenants on upper floors but increased the fear, and the likelihood, of being trapped in a lift car. But the social impact of technical shortcomings did not end with the lifts. There were frequently problems of noise transference particularly where flat plans interlocked or where walkways were sited above bedrooms. There was dampness and condensation which helps to account for the high incidence of respiratory infections among flat dwellers, particularly children (Adams and Conway, 1974). This problem was partly caused by poor insulation but it was exacerbated by the breakdown of extract fans which were supposed to withdraw steam from internal bathrooms. It could have been ameliorated by good heating but in many high blocks electric underfloor heating was provided which the tenants could not afford to run. Instead many used paraffin heaters which made condensation problems worse. On many of the more recent estates communal heating was provided which relieved dampness but the large ducts through which the systems ran frequently became infested with vermin.

On some estates the problems of use and technical failure combined to disastrous effect. One such was the massive Hulme development in Manchester. Architect Rod Hackney described a visit in the early 1970s:

> The outside areas were unkempt, frightening, windswept places strewn with litter, glass and broken furniture, and fouled by the dogs that people kept in their flats to ward off intruders. Inside there was a prison atmosphere. The concrete had become stained and unsightly, some flats had been burnt out as a protest against the council....

> Rain and wind battered the blocks and blew through the tunnels created by the long passageways. Graffiti, usually spelling out pure anger, frustration and aggression, covered the walls. Urine and excrement fouled the lifts and walkways. Teenagers often used those walkways as racetracks and screamed along them on motorbikes....

> Lighting was inadequate and bulbs were not replaced. Heating systems failed with predictable regularity; they took ages to repair because of the long wait for ordered parts. Condensation and dampness were unavoidable because the solid concrete walls rarely dried out. Burst water pipes on upper floors wreaked havoc and lifts, once broken, remained inoperable for weeks. There was widespread rat, cockroach and flea infestation.

> Rats seemed to thrive by eating plastic pipe insulation and were abundant in Hulme. Cockroaches live in the ventilation systems. Fleas spread behind wallpaper and timber skirtings. (Hackney, 1990, p 41ff)

This report may be coloured. Even if accurate, Hulme was an extreme case where a multitude of failed systems interacted to severe effect. Nevertheless, many multi-storey estates – perhaps most – experienced some of these problems. A government survey conducted on estates in London, Liverpool and Leeds during the 1960s recorded a similar range of shortcomings. And it noted growing dissatisfaction – over two thirds of families with children living in multi-storey flats would have preferred a house (MoHLG, 1970a). Faced with inadequate homes and a degraded external environment many voted with their feet. Those who could, got rehoused or rehoused themselves. The worst estates acquired a stigma. Increasingly people refused to move into them and they became 'hard-to-let'.

For the most part tenants served themselves, as best they could, in their desire to escape from the worst multi-storey estates. But on one estate, at least, as early as 1973, the occupants came together to campaign for a better deal. Haigh, Canterbury and Crosbie Heights were 14-storey slab blocks in Liverpool, each containing 70 maisonettes. Nicknamed the 'Three Ugly Sisters' the blocks had seriously degenerated only six years after they were built. Residents complained about useless lifts, dark and slimy staircases, long periods without water and electricity and grossly inadequate social facilities. They organised a survey and petitioned the council for the immediate removal of all families with children under the age of 15; the comprehensive upgrading of common entrances, lifts, staircases and landings; improvements to the surrounding areas; and the introduction of tenant management. Councillors said they were ahead of their time. They were indeed – their protest prefigured many that were to follow. It was an early demonstration of tenant disillusionment with the multi-storey ideal (*Community Action*, 1973).

The revelation of community

Slum clearance had always had its critics. The limited efforts of the 19th century had been opposed by those who felt repair and rehabilitation would be less disruptive. In the 1930s George Orwell criticised the destruction of community life and the isolation and poor services on the new estates (Orwell, 1937, p 66). But the most influential study was the work carried out by Michael Young and Peter Wilmot. During 1953-55 they compared life in Bethnal Green with that on a new estate 20 miles away on the fringes of East London. The research brought to light the importance of kinship networks in established urban communities. Life in Bethnal Green revolved around a complex pattern of connections with relatives, friends and acquaintances established over years of living in close proximity. Once on the new estate, however, people became more isolated. They faced long distances to travel to work. They enjoyed much less social life and had greatly reduced contact with relatives. This resulted in a lack of social support in child rearing and during times of illness or personal crisis.

Family and kinship in East London (Young and Wilmot, 1957) became highly influential. In the early 1960s, it was followed by a government study of an area of old terraced housing near the centre of Oldham. The St Mary's district was condemned and scheduled for demolition but the study found a vibrant community life:

> ... people in St Mary's were gregarious; they met each other frequently and chatted in the local shops, in the streets, in the common yards and on the doorsteps. There was a high degree of social recognition, even when not associated with personal acquaintance and many small shopkeepers and residents had an intimate knowledge of the daily movements of people living in the same street.

Many families living in the area were related, partly because young people leaving home were easily able to find housing nearby. Relatives lived close together and visited each other frequently:

> Most of the contact between relatives ... was purely social, but relatives evidently helped each other when necessary. A few old or single men living alone were particularly dependent on the care of female relatives who cooked and cleaned for them, and some daughters helped their elderly mothers who were living alone.... In an emergency, the nearness of relatives was a great advantage. One young woman had lost her husband suddenly in tragic circumstances. She moved into her parents' home in the next street while she recovered from the shock, and her children continued to attend their usual school. (MoHLG, 1970b, p 25)

St Mary's, Oldham was revealed to have a vital community. Not only that, there was not overwhelming dissatisfaction with the houses themselves. About a third of those interviewed did complain of dampness or the inconvenience of outside toilets, but an equal number liked their homes or had no complaints about them. Despite that, St Mary's was demolished and its residents dispersed into council estates or private accommodation up to two-and-a-half miles away (MoHLG, 1970c).

A strong sense of community could be found even in the most deprived areas. In a fictionalised account published in 1992, Glaswegian Jeff Torrington described the colourful life of the old Gorbals. The action takes place over a few days in the 1960s as the hammers tear down the old buildings and the inhabitants are dispersed into new tower blocks or peripheral estates. The central character stands on a roof terrace and surveys the scene:

> I stood there mentally re-erecting the Gorbals of old, running my hands so to speak through the pile of grey jigsaw which depicted fragments of lost streets, shops and buildings....
>
> Cold though it was I was well compensated for my gooseflesh by a panoramic view of the Lost Barony of Gorbals, What set the red nerves twitching was the utter contempt for the working classes which was evident no matter where the glance fell. Having so cursorily dismantled the community's heart, that sooty reciprocating engine, admittedly an antique clapped out affair but one that'd been capable of generating amazing funds of human warmth, they'd bundled it off into the asylum of history with all the furtive shame of a family of hypocrites dumping Granny in Crackpot Castle.
>
> Much imbued by the so-called merits of functionalism, the planners and architects had taken wardrobes and tombstones to be their thematic design models, and had set to work with that civic slapdashery which erecting homes for the pre-Holocaust working classes tends to invoke. (Torrington, 1992, p 316)

The studies in Bethnal Green and Oldham had identified the links, both active and passive, which develop over time between the people of a residential area. Slum clearance destroyed these networks, but Jeff Torrington suggests the built environment had value, too. Community did not just consist of social relations; it had a physical dimension which rested in the buildings and streets with which people were familiar.

The idea of neighbourhood

The neighbourhood concept had been one of the tools of post-war planning. In the planning of large developments the design of residential areas had been based on the size of population required to support a primary school. Each school became the focus of a geographically distinct new 'neighbourhood'. These became the smallest planning units in the design of new towns and other new housing. But, while it was a key to the development of new residential areas, there was no understanding that such a concept could be applied to the extensive and amorphous established residential areas of large cities. Following on from his work in East London, Michael Young was engaged by the Royal Commission examining local government reform in the late 1960s. His task was to carry out a 'community attitudes' survey. The survey found that even in urban areas people did identify with a 'home area' and could define it relatively accurately on a map (Redcliffe-Maud, 1969).

These findings were confirmed by similar work in Sheffield by William Hampton and Jeffrey Chapman. The home areas were relatively small in terms of population and, although there was considerable variation, most fell within the range of 6,000 to 10,000 people (Hampton and Chapman, 1971). Their geography might be defined by barriers – railways were the strongest, although major roads or waterways might prove similar barriers. Or it might surround a focus – a shopping centre or a station. The work on home areas was used as the basis of a campaign to establish neighbourhood councils in urban areas which might become the lowest unit of local government – an urban equivalent of Parish Councils. Michael Young went on to found the Association of Neighbourhood Councils to promote this concept.

Its more immediate significance was that, for the first time, it established that city dwellers had a concept of living in a community which had clear physical limits. When this was combined with the social networks through which many derived support, and which governed their social life, the large city could be reinterpreted as a pattern of urban villages. If people could identify their own communities in this way they might be moved to band together to defend them.

Community action

The social atmosphere of the late 1960s was charged with revolt. Throughout Europe and the United States young people challenged their political masters. During 1968, mass protests in Prague, in Paris and in Chicago attracted worldwide attention. All of these were to fail in their immediate objectives, but they served to generate an atmosphere of rebellion; to demonstrate that there was an alternative to passive acceptance of the impact of public policy. During the 1960s, urban Britain had been transformed by reconstruction. It was not just slum clearance and housing redevelopment. Swathes of old cities had been demolished to make way for urban motorways. A lot of the older and often architecturally estimable buildings in the central areas had been swept away and replaced with modern commercial blocks. Now people began to resist such destruction.

By the late 1960s some large cities – notably Birmingham – had already built large motorways through their inner urban areas. Many others had similar proposals. The largest and most destructive were in London where the Greater London Council (GLC) proposed to built two 'ringways' – major urban roads circling the centre. The inner 'ringway' would have thrust an elevated urban motorway through some of the most densely populated areas of inner London. Thousands of homes would have been lost and many more blighted by the noise and disturbance of the resulting traffic. A major campaign was launched across the capital in which local action groups were coordinated by three 'umbrella' groups. In 1973 the protesters succeeded in getting the motorway plans scrapped (Towers, 1975a). During the same period, protests were launched against motorways in Lincoln, Southampton and Manchester. In Cardiff, proposals for the Hook Road – a six-mile stretch of motorway close to the city centre – were defeated by public protests (*Community Action* 1972/73a).

In the same way that public protest was brought to bear on motorways it also focused on plans for increasing commercial development. The cauldron of this confrontation between mammon and community was London and the earliest manifestation was in its heart. Covent Garden was a mixed area of run-down commercial and residential buildings. Most activity centred on the fruit and vegetable market and, when this moved to a new site in South London, the GLC saw an opportunity for major redevelopment. Their plans included office blocks, hotels and conference centres all served by motorway-scale roads. Little heed was given to the existing community. When they were published in 1971 the proposals sparked a storm of protest and over the next two years a campaign was waged which eventually produced a change of policy. A new plan emerged with more social housing, more rehabilitation and redevelopment reduced to small-scale schemes which maintained the character of the area (Christenson, 1979; Anson, 1981).

The commercial pressures which were bearing on Covent Garden were hungry for development opportunities. They were beginning to spread beyond the commercial heart of London – the City and the West End – and into surrounding areas. Many of these were similar to Covent Garden – run-down areas ripe for development. The strip of land along the south bank of the Thames was a prime target for development of new offices and luxury housing. Community groups sprang up to try to counter such moves – the Battersea Redevelopment Action Group in South West London and the North Southwark Development Group which focused on a number of sites opposite The City, most notably Coin Street (*Community Action*, 1972/73b). Meanwhile, north of the central area a major battle was fought over a run-down area of Camden – Tolmers Square (Wates, 1976). What all these groups had in common was that they were fighting for the preservation of existing communities; for the provision of rented housing and social facilities; and for rehabilitation rather than redevelopment. They were ranged against powerful forces seeking to exploit these sites for profit. But the same objectives and the same tactics were soon used to contest plans which ostensibly had a more beneficial social purpose.

Neighbourhood resistance

The community in Bethnal Green seems to have faced obliteration without dissent. The multi-storey estates which were supposed to have provided better homes may not be among the worst of such housing. But the few streets of terraced cottages which escaped the bulldozer have since become prized and highly valued by owner-occupiers from the professional classes. Similarly St Mary's, Oldham, did not resist destruction and dispersal. But by 1969 attitudes were changing. St Ann's, Nottingham, was a similarly poor community in similar Victorian terraced streets. Faced with the threat of comprehensive redevelopment, a Tenants' and Residents' Association (SATRA) was formed under the leadership of the journalist Ray Gosling. Basing their case on a government report (MoHLG, 1966) they argued for selective renewal – rehabilitation of the best and small-scale piecemeal redevelopment of the worst (Coates and Silburn, 1970). SATRA lost their fight but at least their redevelopment was houses not multi-storey flats. And they had opened a path for others to follow. Neighbourhood resistance grew throughout Britain's urban areas:

- *Glasgow:* most of the tenement housing of the Gorbals had already been demolished but, by 1969, residents of the 300 flats in the Shawfield area were pressing for rehabilitation. Shortly afterwards the City Council declared 250 tenements in the Old Swan area suitable for improvement but by 1973 residents were complaining of lack of progress and too many people being moved out of the area (*Community Action*, 1972/73c).
- *Manchester:* wholesale clearances had taken place since the Second World War, with about 65,000 houses demolished. By the early 1970s, however, this was being challenged by a number of groups. One of the first was the Whittington Association seeking to save 300 terraced houses in an area three miles south of the city centre. Their efforts were met with the sort of obstruction typical of the time – they were refused access to council documents and official reports, and they were not allowed to address the Health Committee. Instead their case was 'put' by the Chief Public Health Officer – the very man who was recommending that their homes be demolished. By 1974 several neighbourhood associations had campaigned to preserve their districts with greater success. Most notable was Ladybarn where, after a Public Inquiry, 183 houses were saved, of 291 originally scheduled for demolition, and a selective renewal scheme was adopted (*Community Action*, 1972/74).
- *Birmingham:* the city had carried out extensive redevelopment during the 1960s but, by the end of the decade, was beginning to face pressures for an alternative approach. In one inner-city area, stimulated by an influential

sociological study (Rex and Moore, 1967), the community association produced its own proposals for renewal. The Sparkbrook Community Plan also proposed selective renewal with large-scale rehabilitation and limited new development (*Community Action*, 1972). By 1972 Birmingham had declared nine General Improvement Areas (GIAs) but these were in relatively prosperous areas and missed out the inner ring of run-down terraced housing. In 1974 in the deprived inner area of Saltley, the residents of George Arthur Road mounted a campaign against demolition which resulted in the declaration of a Housing Action Area (HAA). By 1977, slum clearance had virtually ceased and 105 GIAs and 35 HAAs had been declared (*The Architects' Journal*, 1977b).

- *London:* although there had been considerable slum clearance in London there were many areas of run-down Victorian housing untouched either by redevelopment or improvement. From the late 1960s the overcrowded and insanitary housing conditions in North Kensington had been the focus of local campaigns. Some of the pressure was for preservation and improvement but some housing was considered irredeemable. In 1970 the neighbourhood association produced a community plan for 400 multiple-occupied houses in Swinbrook. The plan pressed for redevelopment but on a scale in character with the area and in a manner which would preserve the community (Towers, 1975b). A few miles across North London, housing conditions in Islington were as bad as anywhere. A great deal of redevelopment had taken place but the North Islington Housing Rights Project was pressing for rehabilitation and cooperative management. In 1973 it mounted a campaign for the improvement of 382 houses in Alexander Road. Backed by a compulsory purchase order the area became one of the first to be comprehensively rehabilitated (*Community Action*, 1973/75).

The widespread resistance to clearance and redevelopment not only posed a challenge to public policy; it required a wholesale change in attitude and approach to housing design and development. In the old order decisions were made for whole districts in remote town halls. Designs for large new developments were worked up in architects' offices without reference to those who would live in them. Large construction contracts were let for demolition and reconstruction. In the new climate, this cumbersome machinery simply would not work. It could not provide the more sensitive approach now required. Gradually, new methods emerged from the work of building designers who had become involved in supporting community-led campaigns.

Community architecture

For the architects and town planners who provided the technical support to community organisations in their resistance to insensitive redevelopment it was obvious what was wrong with the system. It was also relatively easy to work up alternative proposals sensitive to the interests of existing communities. What was less obvious was how these alternatives could be realised. Few had begun to understand the necessary changes in organisation and the new approaches to design and technical issues which would be required. Gradually new methods were tried and tested in the improvement of the residential environment. They fell into three broad areas – the rehabilitation of old housing; user-sensitive design in the development of new housing; and a community-based approach to the provision of social facilities.

Rehabilitation

If old areas were to be modernised and existing communities preserved, it could not be done using the old methods. Certainly, blocks of housing could be compulsorily purchased and improved using large contracts. But where this was done, it too often meant the original residents were dispersed. Preserving the community and ensuring that people had control over their own housing required a different process. New possibilities were opened up by the 1969 Housing Act which allowed the declaration of GIAs with enhanced improvement grants. Initially GIAs were only thought appropriate for areas of owner-occupation rather than multiple-occupied and rented housing.

One of the earliest experiments in a community-based approach to rehabilitation was the Neighbourhood Action Project set up by the housing charity Shelter in the Toxteth area of Liverpool (Shelter, 1972). SNAP (Shelter Neighbourhood Action Project) was set up in 1969 to test the viability of a GIA in a deprived inner urban area. By the end of its two-year life the project had succeeded in rehabilitating just over half the houses in its area, but it had encountered two major obstacles. One was the cumbersome procedure involved in getting improvement grants processed. The other was the problem of ownership – absentee landlords showed little interest in improving their property. Two pioneering projects addressed these difficulties in different ways:

- *Macclesfield:* Black Road is one of the most celebrated community-based improvement schemes. In 1972 the architect Rod Hackney organised 32 of his neighbours to resist the demolition of their 19th-century cottages. Eventually they succeeded in getting them declared a GIA and the Residents' Association became instrumental in implementing the improvements. Initially 70% of the houses were tenanted but by organising loans and mortgages all but a handful of residents were able to buy their homes. The Residents' Association also acted as a channel for obtaining Improvement Grants and was the key to organising the building work. Because of escalating costs, much of this was done on a self-build basis. Black Road proved highly successful but essentially a model most appropriate for areas of small-scale family housing (Hook, 1975; Hackney, 1990).

- *Glasgow:* a pioneering scheme which did provide a model for multi-storey housing was the tenement improvement at Taransey Street, Glasgow (Figure 4.1). The Glasgow tenements were in a myriad of ownership. Within each block there could be a complex mix of owners, tenants and sub-tenants. These complexities had made compulsory purchase extremely cumbersome and bedevilled early attempts at rehabilitation. In 1970, architect Raymond Young, working from his own tenement home, persuaded the City Council to declare the Taransey Street a Treatment Area (the Scottish equivalent of a GIA). Young helped the residents to set up a housing association. The association was able to buy up enough housing to start improving and converting eight to twelve flats at a time on a rolling programme. Free technical support was provided by Assist – a unit set up within Strathclyde University (Hook, 1973).

While these two projects took place in different administrative environments and involved quite different forms of housing they both relied on the catalytic effect of an umbrella organisation to resolve problems of ownership and the organisation of funding and building work. Both also relied on the presence of a resident architect who provided unpaid support at the start of the project and both schemes proved influential models leading to a succession of similar projects.

User-sensitive new housing

By the late 1960s, various approaches to the design of high density urban housing had been tried – and most had been found wanting. One scheme which has achieved enduring success has been the Byker development in Newcastle designed by the Swedish-based architect Ralph Erskine. Commenced in 1970 and developed over 10 years or more, Byker's most celebrated feature is the 'wall' – a long and continuous block of housing, up to eight storeys high, which sinuates along the north eastern edge of the site (Figure 4.2). The wall was originally conceived to protect the area from a proposed motorway but it served two key purposes in the design of the development. First, it allowed a large amount of housing to be built on a small amount of land. This meant that several terraces of old houses could be cleared, starting a rolling programme of demolition and redevelopment which enabled the existing community of 12,000 to be rehoused on site. Second, the wall achieved what the proponents of multi-storey housing had always intended. At ground level there are family maisonettes with their own gardens; but there are no children in the flats above. All the occupants are elderly and adult households – precisely those categories shown to respond best to multi-storey living. The 'wall' raised the density sufficiently that the remainder of the site could be developed largely as two–storey family housing.

Figure 4.1: **Taransey Street, Govan, Glasgow. The first area of tenements to be rehabilitated by a community housing association**

Figure 4.2: **The Byker 'wall' redevelopment, Newcastle upon Tyne – the multi-storey element of a predominantly low-rise development. The 'wall' was the key to ensuring the existing community could be kept together**

Source: © British Architectural Library, RIBA, London

Byker's other key innovation was participation. Ralph Erskine's partner lived on site and all the design was done in a local office. Residents were invited to take part in the design process through a series of ad hoc contacts and informal meetings. Participation not only helped to shape the housing to the needs and wishes of its future occupants, it also developed a strong sense of proprietorship and commitment which has contributed to the long-term success of the scheme (Ravetz, 1976; Erskine, 1984).

The Byker scheme was influential in the development of Swinbrook in North Kensington (Figure 4.3). Local residents had campaigned for new housing and for the preservation of the local community. When the GLC took on the redevelopment they set off with a comprehensive interview survey followed by a series of large and small group meetings. This wide-ranging participation process led to a scheme which redeveloped the area in four-storey terraces of flats and maisonettes on a similar scale to the old housing. Rebuilding was carried out over a long period in small phases so that all those who wanted to could be rehoused nearby, close to relatives and familiar neighbours (Towers, 1995, p 67ff).

Figure 4.3: **Swinbrook, North Kensington. As a result of a prolonged resident campaign the area was redeveloped as four-storey flats and maisonettes on the existing street pattern**

By the time these schemes were complete, large-scale redevelopment had become a thing of the past. But the principles of community rehousing and participation continued on a more intimate scale. Resident groups in small areas of irredeemable old housing were able to band together in cooperatives to build new housing for themselves. From the mid-1970s housing cooperatives were set up in many places. Mostly, these were very small in number and faced considerable difficulty. In Liverpool, however, the cooperatives prospered. More than 30 carried out their own developments supported and sponsored by an umbrella organisation. The cooperatives were able to appoint and instruct their own architects. The housing they produced exhibits a considerable variety which reflects the precise requirements of the user groups and their aesthetic values (Wates, 1982; McDonald, 1986).

Community-led social facilities

Lack of adequate communal facilities was a key concern in many new housing developments, as it was in many deprived inner-city areas. One solution was for local groups to take matters into their own hands. North Kensington was an early focus of this self-help approach. The Notting Hill Summer Project of 1967 was a key initiative in community activity. One of its innovations was a play programme which set up several short-term schemes including two adventure playgrounds which eventually became permanent institutions. North Kensington had its share of new housing which, as elsewhere, was built without social provision. In the Kensal New Town Estate residents banded together to raise funds to build a rudimentary community centre for themselves and also set up their own children's playground. Across the road, Trellick Tower had just been completed. No outdoor space had been provided for the new block but, alongside, part of the site had been left cleared and derelict. A few years later, a local artist, Jamie McCullough, raised a shoestring budget and a volunteer labour force and turned it into a community open space. Thinking it was likely to have a short life they called it Meanwhile Gardens. It is still there 20 years later, thriving and well used (Towers, 1995, p 55ff).

Doubtless these pioneers would have preferred that proper communal provision had been made for them. Certainly they had good reason to expect better funding and better quality facilities. Elsewhere, community-led campaigns have often resulted in projects of high standards funded by local or central government. But the necessity for local groups to seek their own provision has had two major benefits. First, it has been innovative. It is doubtful if such departures as urban farms, ecological gardens or training workshops would have emerged without the activity of community groups. Second, community management has helped to ensure that the facilities are responsive to local needs, properly used, and adequately maintained.

New priorities

Community architecture pioneered new approaches to design and development. In the improvement of urban residential areas it developed important new principles: first, it makes it a priority that the existing community be preserved. Initially this means that local people must have the opportunity to develop their own proposals. They must be able to take part in the planning process or be given support to prepare their own community plan. If they wish their housing to be preserved and it is technically feasible, then this wish should be supported. If rehousing is necessary then it should be carried out on a phased rolling programme so that relatives and neighbours can be rehoused together.

Second, new housing, or improvements to existing housing, should meet the needs and wishes of those who are to live in it. In the past, tenants were presented with a *fait accompli*, and given little or no choice. Important lessons can be learned from the negative responses to existing forms of housing. But the key to achieving better solutions is participation in design. The future users should be invited to take part in the design of their homes at every stage through group meetings, detailed discussion by representatives and by individual customising of the interiors. This means designers must be open to discussion and accessible, preferably based on or near the site. It also means that support must be given to facilitate participation and this may best be done through establishing a locally based organisation – a residents' association, a cooperative or a housing association.

Finally, the success of community-led initiatives shows the importance of locally based decision making. Many of the mistakes of the past arose because the decision-making process was over-centralised. The least successful housing took its form almost entirely as a result of central government policies and funding structures. Local communities know their own needs best and their initiative and priorities must be supported through decentralisation of decision making and management.

A new approach to urban development

By the early 1970s, public housing policy and practice was under mounting pressure on two fronts. On the one hand, it was more and more obvious that multi-storey housing, which had made up the bulk of new urban housing for 10-15 years, was not popular and was posing difficult management problems. On the other hand, the process of slum clearance and redevelopment was hampered by highly vocal, increasingly well organised, protest movements which were becoming more and more successful in stopping the bulldozers. Faced with these pressures, a change of course became inevitable.

Wholesale clearances gradually came to an end and with them the large multi-storey redevelopment schemes. For some time big multi-storey estates continued to be built, but most of these were conceived at the height of the 1960s' boom and took 10 years or more to realise. The new approach generally took the form of selective renewal advocated by many campaigners. The worst housing was still redeveloped but generally this was concentrated in small pockets. What replaced it was new housing of modest scale providing a mix of houses and small blocks of flats for those without children. There was more and more rehabilitation. Terraces and streets which 10 years earlier would have been condemned without question were now recognised as redeemable. Even the large Victorian houses – multiple-occupied and overcrowded and which had become the epitome of housing deprivation – were now restored and converted to modern self-contained flats.

Some of this work followed the new priorities which were being set by community architecture. A good deal of rehabilitation, particularly of small family houses already occupied, was carried out in cooperation with residents. A few schemes of new housing consciously sought to involve future occupants in the design process. In the main, however, the old methods prevailed. New housing was now designed by architects mindful of past failure and anxious to avoid more public opprobrium but there was still no attempt to seek the views of users on these more modest designs. Much of the rehabilitation work was done the same way – designed and organised by architects and surveyors in the secrecy of town halls. The result was that communities were still disrupted by the improvement process, albeit less drastically. Strangers were still thrust together when rehoused, whether in newly built or rehabilitated accommodation.

The change of approach to housing development was one to be welcomed even though it did not go nearly far enough to create housing which truly reflected the needs and wishes of its occupants. But it still left untouched the legacy of the past – the multi-storey estates disregarded and disrespected by their occupants which were increasingly in need of attention. These estates housed large communities whose interests could not be ignored. Given their disaffection, it was essential to seek the residents' support if improvements were to stand a realistic chance of achieving lasting results. It was here that a democratic and accountable approach, desirable in all housing development, was to become an essential ingredient of success.

FIVE

Redeeming the estates

By the mid–1970s the multi-storey legacy was substantially complete. There were more than 1,850,000 local authority flats, the great majority of them in inner areas of large industrial cities. Around 300,000 consisted of tenement-type blocks built before the Second World War or shortly afterwards. More than 600,000 were in high–rise tower blocks and slab blocks built in the 1950s and 1960s (Glendinning and Muthesius, 1994, p 1ff). There were up to 350,000 flats in high-density 'medium-rise' estates built from the late 1960s onwards (Dunleavy, 1981, p 41ff; DoE, 1993a). The remainder comprised low-rise post-war blocks of various types. Much of the oldest stock was run-down and substandard. Some of the newer blocks were exhibiting technical problems, particularly the 500,000 or more which were built using industrialised systems. Many estates were degraded by the problems of use and social stigma.

As local authorities began to turn their attention to their troublesome legacy of multi-storey estates, a range of disparate approaches were taken, partly as a result of an unsympathetic funding regime. Some councils sought to dispose of the problem altogether. For those that didn't, many were content simply to repair and maintain while others introduced modest improvements which proved partial and inadequate. Eventually, the most effective approach to improvement was provided by the application of more generous funding and the adoption of the new priorities established by community architecture. The preservation of established communities, participation of tenants in the design and development process, and decentralisation of decision making became the key to successful estate modernisation.

From the mid-1980s, improvements to housing estates became increasingly dependent on programmes funded and controlled by central government. Programmes such as Estate Action and Housing Action Trusts had their roots in political priorities and, initially, were resented and resisted by local authorities and tenants organisations. In their engagement with reality, however, government programme managers were forced to compromise. The single-minded pursuit of policy gave way to a more pragmatic approach. Nevertheless, centralised funding reduced the power of local authorities and restricted the establishment of community-based priorities. Smaller and older estates were neglected while major funding was channelled into modernising the most high profile problem estates. The focused approach which developed from the late 1980s was not only highly selective, its effectiveness was increasingly open to question.

The changing framework

A decisive shift took place during the 1970s away from large-scale clearance and redevelopment towards preservation and rehabilitation of older housing. However, the legislative framework and the subsidy system still reflected the old priorities. The Housing Cost Yardstick, introduced in 1967, remained the main focus of government subsidy and control. Under this procedure detailed submissions to the Department of the Environment (DoE) were required and schemes were subject to tight control over both cost and design. The Cost Yardstick applied only to new build schemes which were becoming more modest in scale and uncontroversial in design. In any case they represented a diminishing proportion of housing investment as more and more money was channelled into refurbishment.

Rehabilitation had, increasingly, been supported by Improvement Grants, first introduced in 1949. It had been given a major boost by the introduction of General Improvement Areas (GIAs) in the 1969 Housing Act. Under the stimulus of the increased grants, renovation had mushroomed from 124,000 homes in 1968 to 4,554,000 in 1973. Further stimulus was given by the introduction of even more generous grants in Housing Action Areas (HAAs) introduced in 1974. Much of this work was carried out by individual householders or by housing associations but local authorities had the power to acquire and improve unfit houses. A total of 40% of houses improved in 1973 were council houses (Cullingworth, 1979, p 74ff).

In 1975 a new government policy initiative laid emphasis on 'gradual renewal'. This broke away from the approach of GIAs and HAAs which was based on comprehensive treatment of a defined area. Instead attention should be focused on pockets of substandard housing and a selective approach adopted which reflected the needs of residents. Local authorities were encouraged to consider the selective acquisition of dwellings to arrest environmental deterioration and ensure improvement. Some councils responded enthusiastically, purchasing run-down houses on a considerable scale, if necessary by compulsion. Improvement of these houses was covered by general subsidy arrangements provided they were more than 30 years old.

Subsidy for new building and for rehabilitation left untouched the bulk of the estate housing constructed in the 1950s and 1960s and which was presenting increasing management and maintenance problems. Any repair or improvement could only be funded by councils' own resources and this led to diverse and often partial responses when dealing with the problems of multi-storey housing.

The need to address these issues was given greater urgency with the introduction of new housing legislation.

The 1980 Housing Act reflected the new political priorities of the incoming Conservative government. The most prominent feature of the new Act was the much greater incentive it gave to council tenants to exercise their 'right to buy'. It was immediately evident that it would be better-off tenants who would take up this 'right' and that they would buy up the most desirable parts of the housing stock. In the main it would be houses rather than flats which were sold off. This would leave local authorities with a smaller stock in which multi-storey housing estates formed an increasingly significant proportion (Bulos and Walker, 1982a). Another key feature of the legislation was the introduction of revised subsidy arrangements which were, eventually, to provide the means to implement more comprehensive solutions to the problems of multi-storey blocks.

Government continued to exercise overall control of housing capital investment through an annual block allocation of permitted expenditure – the Housing Investment Programme (HIP) – but a new approach to scheme approval was introduced known as 'Project Control'. Within the HIP allocation, under the old arrangements, government approval had been required for individual projects on a detailed basis. The new system of Project Control swept away the procedures with the stated intention of freeing local authorities from the "web of detailed bureaucratic controls" contained in the old system (Garland, 1981). Instead of submitting design drawings and costings – as had been necessary under the Housing Cost Yardstick – authorities were required to submit only a single sheet of statistical and cost information for each project. The new system provided a unified approach and was essentially the same whether the project involved new build, rehabilitation or capitalised repairs.

The information required compared two sets of figures. One was the market value before construction work plus the cost of the work. The other was the market value after construction. The clear intention was to subject local authorities to the discipline which a private developer might apply in calculating the viability of acquisition, construction and sale value. The new system was met with scepticism, not to say hostility, by housing professionals. For one thing, while it simplified procedure for new build schemes, it increased government control over repair and rehabilitation. More seriously, the whole idea of market testing was considered inappropriate. John Jeffries' comment was typical:

> The weakness of the procedure is that it places a heavy reliance on the comparison between cost and market value. Since the location, type and design of public sector housing for rent should be determined by housing

need, not just marketability, the comparison has limited relevance. (Jeffries, 1982)

In the event the system was implemented in a flexible manner. Profitability was not regarded as an absolute priority. Over the years, as if in recognition of social objectives, costs were allowed to exceed returns by 5%, 10% and even as much as 20%. Project Control provided a relatively simple procedure through which local authorities could establish their own priorities. It gave enough flexibility to allow the development of modernisation schemes for estates of older flats which were sufficiently generous and far-reaching to be effective.

Diverse responses to the multi-storey stock

Within the shifting framework of legislative and subsidy controls it is unsurprising that there was no clear view on how to address the mounting technical and managerial problems of multi-storey blocks. Local authorities adopted a variety of approaches in dealing with their existing estates. Some sought to dispose of the problems – by demolition or partial demolition or by selling off their problem estates. Others sought to keep the difficulties under control by repairs or piecemeal improvements. The most successful approach, however, involved the comprehensive modernisation of multi-storey housing.

Demolition

The first major housing estate to be torn down in Britain was the pioneering 'model' estate of the late 1930s – Quarry Hill in Leeds. As early as 1953 the estate had become stigmatised, and there were reports of vandalism and vermin infestation. Its deterioration should have provided an object lesson at a time when the flat building boom had hardly started. During the 1960s the estate's problems worsened when serious technical deficiencies were discovered. Water penetrating the precast panels was causing the steel structure to rust – a problem which was later to afflict many of the industrialised blocks then under construction. Large-scale expenditure on major repairs could not put things right and the estate was demolished in 1978 (Mitchell, 1990). Quarry Hill survived more than 40 years, but other estates have done less well.

Oak and Eldon Gardens were two 11-storey blocks constructed in 1957–58 in Birkenhead. Vandalism and abuse had made the blocks hard-to-let by the 1970s and they were demolished in September 1979. But perhaps the most remarkable case was the Darnley Estate in Glasgow. A development of 240 flats in long deck access blocks was started in 1973. By 1978 the scheme was still not finished and the problems in estates with similar access systems were abundantly evident elsewhere. Faced with the prospect of another two years' construction the council cut their losses and demolished the blocks before they were even complete. In their place they built terraced houses with gardens (Bulos and Walker, 1982b).

Short of complete demolition some authorities sought to rid themselves of multi-storey problems by height reduction. Lopping a few storeys off the top of blocks reduced them to manageable proportions. Sometimes this involved cutting down blocks to three storeys and turning them into modernised walk-up flats. Sometimes blocks were reduced in height and converted into terraces of family houses. Schemes involving diminishing and converting multi-storey blocks were carried out in Middlesborough, Liverpool and elsewhere (*Housing*, 1984a, 1985; Sim, 1993, p 85).

Disposal

Some local authorities, unwilling to contemplate the wholesale loss involved in demolition, sought to sell off their problem blocks. One of the earliest was Martello Court in Edinburgh. This 21-storey block was built in 1965 and quickly degenerated through serious vandalism and abuse. By 1977 more than half the flats were empty and the remaining 40 tenants insisted on being rehoused. The council sold the block to a local developer who installed electronic security, improved the flats and sold them off. The council retained an interest by underwriting the funding and, in return, the flats were sold to existing council tenants (Bulos and Walker, 1982b).

In 1978 a similar course was followed by the London Borough of Wandsworth, although in pursuit of policy rather than as an expedient. St John's Estate was a five-storey inter-war tenement development built around three courtyards. One courtyard had already been improved for the existing tenants. It was the aim of the radical new Conservative council to reduce the housing obligations of the authority. Tenants were forced to move from the rest of St John's Estate and the remaining flats sold to Regalian Properties for £4 million. The flats were converted to small dwellings and sold on the open market. Most of the new owners were first-time buyers and none of them had children (Rowland, 1983). In the following few years similar tenement blocks in Liverpool and Salford were sold off for conversion and re-sale by specialist 'Urban Renewal' arms of national house builders, such as Barratt and Wimpey (*Housing*, 1984b, 1988).

Repair

Most councils were still faced with long waiting lists for housing, particularly those in urban areas, and were reluctant to contemplate the loss of their stock by demolition or sale. For the most part they concentrated on maintaining their multi-storey blocks by repair and improvement targeted at particular problems. These might be the replacement of rotting windows or leaking roofs, the improvement of insulation to roofs or the exposed external walls of tall blocks (*Housing*, 1983a, 1983b, 1983c). It might involve the installation of secured entrances and electronic surveillance to blocks affected by vandalism and crime (Smith, 1982). On older estates improvements were needed to the flats themselves. Mostly these concentrated on 'package' improvements carried out with the tenants in residence. These could be completed quite quickly. The Greater London Council (GLC) developed a package which could be installed in four days comprising replacement of kitchen and bathroom fittings and services and the installation of central heating and hot water (*Housing*, 1981).

While it was possible to carry out such work relatively cheaply and tie it in with the general maintenance programme, the improvements offered were selective and partial, leaving untouched many basic problems. Repairs did not address problems of space standards or of the mix of dwellings which might be inappropriate for the existing tenants. Installing security systems on their own did nothing to resolve technical shortcomings. Package improvements did not address problems with access or a degenerated external environment. Because of their partial approach, piecemeal improvements often failed to arrest the cycle of decline in multi-storey blocks. What proved more successful was a comprehensive approach to improvements which addressed all the problems simultaneously.

Modernisation

The most celebrated example of the comprehensive approach was at Lea View Estate in the London Borough of Hackney. Lea View was a five-storey tenement estate built in the 1930s. Over the years the building had deteriorated and become increasingly vandalised and hard-to-let. In the late 1970s the tenants campaigned for improvements and the council appointed architects Hunt Thompson to carry out a pilot scheme. Taking a lead from the new approach pioneered by community architecture, the architects set up an office on the site and embarked on a wide-ranging process of consultation with the tenants. Over an intense three-month period of discussion it became evident that the tenants would not accept piecemeal improvement and that only a scheme which tackled all their concerns would do.

The scheme that emerged addressed the problem of repairs by replacing the old steel windows with timber and by adding new pitched roofs. It dealt with the problems of access by providing new lifts to most of the upper floor flats. It tackled the problem of flat size and mix by replanning the blocks to remove large families from the upper floors and rehouse them in ground level maisonettes with their own gardens. It improved the external environment by turning all entrances to the street and creating secure communal gardens in the old courtyards. The transformation in the appearance of the estate was dramatic (Rowland, 1983). The scheme created a national reputation for its designers but it did not provide a prototype. Perhaps because of the high cost involved, no other estate in Hackney was modernised in the same way and many have remained largely unimproved. Meanwhile, in the neighbouring Islington, a comprehensive programme was under way which did succeed in transforming most of the Borough's older estates.

Islington – a practice study

From the late 19th century, the inner London Borough of Islington had a legacy of housing deprivation – some in the poor quality cottages built to house the urban working classes; most in the multiple occupation and overcrowding of large houses. From the 1920s onwards the worst slums were cleared and replaced by tenement housing built both by the local council and the London County Council (LCC). This programme of rebuilding continued unbroken in the post-war period. Considerable redevelopment took place in the 1950s, generally of modest-scale multi-storey estates. In 1964, the Borough was merged with Finsbury and inherited the celebrated Lubetkin schemes as well as some larger-scale estates. Several large estates were built during the 1960s and by the end of the housing boom Islington Council owned about half the housing in the Borough. The great majority of it was multi-storey flats although, among these, there was a very small proportion of tower blocks (Islington Housing Department, 1989).

In the 1970s the council's housing stock was supplemented by the acquisition of hundreds of multiple-occupied Victorian houses – known as 'street' housing to distinguish it from purpose-built flats. In earlier times these old buildings would have been cleared and redeveloped. But, as elsewhere, programmes were in hand to deal with this run-down housing more selectively. Most of the council-owned 'street' housing was rehabilitated and converted into self-contained flats, although there was some redevelopment in infill sites. Meanwhile, public investment in improvement was attracting owner–occupiers to follow suit. Most of the older housing remaining in private hands was eventually modernised with the support of improvement grants. With the problems of Victorian and early 19th-century housing coming under control the shortcomings of the legacy of housing estates became increasingly obvious.

Tackling the older estates

Islington had a share of multi-storey estates of the 1960s but, because slum clearance had been carried out continuously over a long period, a high proportion of its housing was in older blocks of flats. Many of the older tenement estates, built in the 1930s and 1940s, had deteriorated seriously. Space standards were poor and many blocks were overcrowded; services were worn out and most flats lacked adequate heating; the environment of many estates, always bleak, had degenerated through disrepair and vandalism. In the post-war estates, space standards were generally higher but many of the estates built during the 1950s suffered with technical problems, inadequate services and a poor environment.

In the development of improvement proposals for these estates the funding regime, as so often before, made a critical difference. Government subsidy was available only for the improvement of housing more than 30 years old. This rule was intended to apply to old houses so that they could be refurbished as an alternative to slum clearance. Islington, with its large stock of tenement blocks, succeeded in applying it to old flats. Starting in 1978 two programmes were developed – the Estate Action Programme for housing built before 1948; and the Post 1948 Programme for estates built between 1949 and 1958. The former could receive capital subsidy allowing far-reaching improvements; the latter had to be funded from the council's own resources which severely limited the scope of work. Council officials tried to persuade the DoE that the 1948 cut-off was arbitrary and inappropriate and that the 30-year rule should be relaxed (Islington Council, 1979). They did not succeed.

Islington's Estate Action

In 1978, there were a considerable number of estates in Islington which were more than 30 years old. Some were owned by philanthropic trusts such as Peabody, Sutton and Samuel Lewis. Some were still owned by the GLC. A total of 37 such estates belonged to Islington Council. The housing committee commissioned a series of feasibility studies. These were subjected to cost benefit analysis which showed that six of the estates had deteriorated too severely to be worthy of investment. These were demolished. The remaining 31 – about 4,000 dwellings – were put into a rolling programme for modernisation. In shaping the programme important lessons were learned from the mistakes of slum clearance and the demands of community action. Over the decades since they were built strong kinship networks had developed on these estates. It was considered important to preserve the existing community and engage the tenants positively in their own future. A housing manager was based, in a newly established office, on each estate. The role of this 'Estate Action Manager' was to liaise with tenants and organise their participation in developing the improvement scheme for the estate. One block on each estate was emptied and that was the first to be improved. Tenants were preallocated modernised homes in the empty block so that modernisation rolled through each estate block by block. Most tenants were rehoused on their estates and communities were kept together.

As it developed over several years the Estate Action programme ensured that very far-reaching improvements were made to the oldest estates:

- Flats were converted and replanned to Parker Morris space standards. In the best schemes upper floor flats were restricted to one or two bedrooms to ensure that children need not be housed above the ground. Family accommodation was provided by combining ground and first floor flats to make maisonettes with their own gardens and individual entrances (see Figure 8.7).
- Interiors were comprehensively improved with new electrics and other services and individual central heating; new kitchens and bathrooms were provided and the flats redecorated, all with choices made by the prospective tenants.
- The estates were often transformed with new windows, new pitched roofs and renovated or rendered brickwork.
- Access systems were revamped with new lifts to five-storey blocks and electronic intercom security to each staircase. In contrast with the utilitarian tradition new lifts were of robust and reliable quality, well lit and finished with decorative panels and flooring. Staircases were refinished with attractive decoration and floor tiling.
- The external environment was improved with landscaping, seating and well equipped play areas. Where the layout of the estates allowed, communal gardens were created, secure and private to each block.

These changes are illustrated in Exemplars 1 and 2 overleaf.

Figure 5.1: **Hillrise Mansions, Islington.**
(*above*) **Phase 1 of the improvements; (*right*)**
new entrance to one of the maisonettes

Exemplar 1: Hillrise Mansions, Islington

Hillrise Mansions, an estate of 100 flats, was completed in 1938. It was a late example of the five-storey balcony access tenements extensively built in inner London. The estate was scheduled for modernisation at an early stage of Islington's Estate Action programme. Work to Phase 1 was one of the first schemes to require approval under the government's new Project Control system introduced in 1981. At its inception the new regime restricted funding for improvement to notional 'market value'.

Funding for the improvement scheme allowed the installation of lifts and the conversion of dwellings to Parker Morris space standards. This included combining flats vertically to make maisonettes at ground level with new entrances through their own private gardens.

The flats were entirely refurbished with new kitchens and bathrooms, new central heating, new electrical and water services. Some sound and thermal insulation was included and flats were entirely redecorated. Restriction on the funding level meant that not all desirable improvements could be carried out. There was not sufficient finance to pay for the addition of a new roof. Nor was there enough money to replace all the windows. While new double-glazed timber windows were fitted to living rooms and bedrooms, those to kitchens and bathroom could not be replaced within the budget.

Note: Improvement scheme by Islington Architects Department.

Figure 5.2: **Bentham Court, Islington. (*left*) Unimproved block and (*below*) similar block after modernisation**

Exemplar 2: Bentham Court, Islington

Bentham Court was built in the immediate post-war period, its design based on the staircase access system which was then in favour. These four-storey estates were accorded a lower priority in Islington's Estate Action programme than the older five-storey balcony access estates and their improvement began later. Phase 1 of the modernisation of Bentham Court was not initiated until 1985 and by then it was granted a relatively generous budget. Financial constraints were eased by the fact that it was not necessary to install lifts, nor would this have been practicable. But the scheme was also helped considerably because, by this time, the spending limits of the government's Project Control system had eased to allow budgets to reach 115-120% of the notional 'market value'.

This meant that the scheme could include all the improvements made to Hillrise Mansions – conversion of flats to Parker Morris standards; combining flats to make maisonettes at ground level; new kitchens and bathrooms, new central heating, redecoration. But also much more. A new pitched roof was added, new double-glazed windows were installed throughout, and the flats were provided with extensive thermal insulation. The appearance of the blocks was improved with cleaned and rendered brickwork and the addition of striking new entrances.

Note: Improvement scheme by David Ford Associates.

The shifting funding regime

In contrast to the comprehensive improvements on old estates the Post 1948 Programme was relatively limited, restricted, as it was, to funding drawn from the council's repair and maintenance budget. Initially only standard package improvements were carried out – new kitchens and bathrooms and the installation of central heating. Tenants remained in their flats while building work was carried out, suffering considerable disruption and discomfort. Inevitably this approach failed to tackle fundamental issues such as adjusting the dwelling mix and household structure on the estate. Often it failed to address problems with the access system and security in the blocks. Most seriously, it could be counterproductive – the installation of central heating for instance. Where there was no money to improve insulation and ventilation, or to replace old windows, the new heating often made condensation and dampness worse than before.

The introduction of the new Project Control procedure in 1981 proved a beneficial change. Under the new system all housing was treated the same and could be improved using subsidised funding subject to simple 'value for money' criteria. Initially it was expected to restrict funding for major improvements such as the Estate Action Programme. As the system settled down, however, a flexible approach recognised the needs of social housing. Funding, even for Estate Action schemes, became increasingly liberal allowing far-reaching changes to be achieved. More importantly, it allowed subsidised funding to be applied to the more recent estates. Some of the later schemes carried out on 1950s estates went far beyond package improvements with new windows and new roofs added; access systems secured and upgraded; landscaping and communal gardens added on an extensive scale. It was also possible to offer tenants rehousing. Most returned to their flats after improvement work but the new flexibility made it possible to resolve instances of poor planning or to permanently move tenants who were inappropriately housed. The extra funding also made it possible to return to some of the limited earlier schemes and make good the shortcomings, although tenants were often cynical about the repeated building work to their homes.

The modernisation programmes were council-led but on every estate policy and procedure ensured that tenants were fully involved in the decision-making process. Some complaints and a certain amount of conflict were inevitable. But on most estates feedback and post-completion surveys showed a high level of tenant satisfaction. Sometimes tenants were more proactive. On one estate – Hornsey Lane – tenant representatives campaigned for improvements under the Estate Action Programme and also succeeded in getting a new community centre and nursery built. After improvements were complete tenants sought a closer involvement in management to protect the gains on their estate. Negotiations took some time but, eventually, an Estate Management Board (EMB) was set up – one of the first in London. The EMB, controlled by elected tenant representatives, took over responsibility for cleaning and grounds maintenance, day-to-day repairs and some aspects of tenancy compliance (Spray, 1992).

The improvements carried out to Islington's older estates were highly successful. Before the programmes began many of these estates were in extremely poor condition and 'hard-to-let'. After improvement they were turned into very good quality housing, meeting the highest contemporary standards, generally providing a very attractive residential environment and high levels of tenant confidence. Some good individual schemes were carried out elsewhere. No other housing authority, however, seems to have been able to carry out a similarly far-reaching programme in which such a large number of estates were modernised to a consistently high standard.

The larger estates

Having addressed the older estates, Islington Council wanted to extend the programme to more recent multi-storey housing. The new funding regime also made it possible to introduce improvements to the larger estates built during the 1960s. Some of these had technical problems such as spawling concrete or leaking flat roofs. These had to be dealt with under repair budgets. But until the mid-1980s there had been no funding for improvements. Generally the flats on these newer estates were designed to high space standards and improvements to the interiors were not considered necessary. The access systems, however, were generally unsecured and the common areas of poor environmental quality.

The Estate Action schemes and the later improvements to 1950s estates had proved, in the main, to be highly successful, maintaining a high quality over time and easing management problems. The same principles were subsequently applied to larger more recent estates. Access systems were provided with electronic security, lifts and staircases were refurbished with decorative finishes, and landscaped communal gardens were provided. What had been effective on small estates, however, could not be transposed to a larger scale. Electronic intercom security works well on a block with up to 20-25 flats. On larger blocks it proved, time after time, inadequate. Control systems were wrecked by vandalism almost before they were commissioned. Entrance doors were smashed and lifts and staircases abused. The spiral of decline which so disfigured these estates proved impossible to arrest. It became clear that the approach which had successfully transformed small blocks and smaller estates could not be applied to the large housing complexes of the 1960s and 1970s. A fresh approach was evidently needed.

The government programmes

Central government had, for a long time, taken an interest in problem estates. As early as 1974, the DoE had surveyed local authorities about estates which were 'hard-to-let' – that is, estates where there were large numbers of empty dwellings; where there were high levels of transfer requests; a high rate of refusal of offers; high rent arrears; or a combination of all four. The survey established that the majority of the problem estates were in urban areas, three quarters were flats and over half were less than 10 years old. From 1978 the DoE collected annual returns of the number of dwellings that were 'hard-to-let'. In 1979 the government set up the Priority Estates Project (PEP) to work with local authorities in setting up and monitoring more sensitive management on unpopular estates (Power, 1985, p 552ff). For several years, central government seemed content to remain at arm's length. It made no efforts to promote 'best practice' or publicise successful approaches such as that in Islington. Nor did it develop proposals of its own to deal with increasingly serious problems associated with 'hard-to-let' estates. It was to be some time before government intervened directly in the regeneration of such estates.

Estate Action

In 1985 the Urban Housing Research Unit (UHRU) was set up at the DoE. The Unit's aim was to target unpopular estates and to seek their improvement by channelling funds for refurbishment; applying localised management initiatives pioneered by PEP; and encouraging the intervention of the private sector (Brimacombe, 1991). Initially UHRU's remit was confined to urban housing authorities and thus mainly targeted multi-storey estates. In 1987 its name was changed to Estate Action and its programme extended to all the housing authorities in England which brought in a wider range of housing (DoE, 1996). Initially the approach was flexible and a wide variety of projects could be funded. These might include repairs or environmental improvements; the installation of a security system for the common areas; or the introduction of an estate-based management scheme. Early schemes were criticised as partial approaches which left untouched many problems which stigmatised unpopular estates (Nevin, 1990).

The most controversial element, however, was the emphasis on bringing in the private sector. The government's 'Right to Buy' policy was proving successful in transferring council houses into private ownership but it was making virtually no impact on flatted estates, partly because tenants found it difficult to raise mortgages particularly for system-built flats. Ministers were eager to seek ways to transfer more public housing to the private sector. John Stoker – head of the DoE Estate Action team – summed up the approach:

> Estate Action is very keen to encourage authorities to supplement [targeted financial support] by looking wherever possible to the private sector as part of the package to turn an estate round. Over 20 of our schemes contain private sector involvement. So far these have followed the now well trodden path of an authority disposing of an empty block or part of an estate to a house builder or developer who refurbishes and sells the properties often to first time buyers. (Stoker, 1987)

Blocks of council flats, however, particularly those on large multi-storey estates, provided limited attraction to private developers. Ricardo Pinto of the London School of Economics surveyed 81 local authorities. He found that only 14% of schemes involved disposal to the private sector in 1986/87 and this had diminished to 10% in 1988/89. He concluded "If the government's primary intention in forming EA was as a vehicle for generating interest and enthusiasm for privatisation of council property, this has not occurred" (Brimacombe, 1991).

Once again – as with Project Control – a policy designed to apply the rigours of the free market had to settle for something less. Faced with the reality of private sector disinterest the priorities were diluted to refocus on achieving 'diversity of tenure'. The involvement of housing associations became an acceptable substitute for private developers as partners in the regeneration of housing estates. It was made an iron rule of Estate Action that, while local authorities were permitted to carry out refurbishment of their estates, any new building or redevelopment must be done by a housing association.

Apart from pressure to seek diversity of tenure the early priorities of Estate Action concentrated on three key areas. The first was management. PEP had demonstrated the value of more responsive and accountable management systems. These were best achieved through 'estate-based management' and a local office became an essential component of every scheme. A second key ingredient was tenant participation in developing the schemes. This was recognised as a prerequisite to successful improvement and afterwards to effective long-term management. The third area was the physical changes. Essentially schemes were required to concentrate on the exteriors of the buildings. This might include some elements of repair. More importantly it meant looking at security. This might mean securing communal open space or creating more private gardens. But there was a critical focus on securing the access systems which had become so degraded by abuse. Estate Action officials were particularly keen on promoting 'concierge' systems where access was controlled by a receptionist often backed up by surveillance cameras (DoE Estate Action, 1989a).

The concentration on the external environment meant that key issues such as the quality of the flat interiors or the dwelling mix could not be addressed. Nor could social issues be considered. Eventually, through feedback and criticism, the partial approach of the early schemes was perceived to be inadequate. From the early 1990s Estate Action schemes were encouraged to seek comprehensive solutions to the problems on each estate. A new system was introduced for assessing the whole range of problems; generating options; and evaluating them through rigorous cost benefit analysis (DoE Estate Action, 1989b). In addition to the original aims of physical improvements and better management there was a strong emphasis on social objectives. There was a new commitment to consider the provision of facilities such as community centres and employment projects such as estate-based training and enterprise initiatives. In this comprehensive form embracing both physical and social issues, Estate Action became the principal source of funding for the regeneration of multi-storey estates for much of the 1990s (DoE Estate Action, 1991).

Housing Action Trusts

Frustrated in its attempts to reduce the quantity of estate housing under local authority control the government introduced two new measures in the 1988 Housing Act. One was the 'alternative landlord' scheme which would have allowed outside organisations to bid to take over the management of estates, subject to tenant approval. Although this caused considerable consternation at the time, private companies expressed scant interest in managing council estates, although the threat of transfer did help to stimulate the activity of tenant organisations. The other innovation was the provision to set up Housing Action Trusts (HATs). Under this proposal housing estates would be transferred from local authorities to the control of trusts whose board members would be appointed by the government. The trusts would improve the housing, over a period of about five years, and then pass it on to new landlords outside the public sector. Originally, six HATs were proposed comprising 16 different estates grouped together – altogether about 25,000 homes (Burrows, 1989, p 51ff).

HATs were controversial from the start. Originally, tenants were to be given no choice as to whether their estates became part of a HAT. It was only a rebellion in the House of Lords which forced the government to accept that the designation of a HAT would be subject to a ballot of its tenants (Meehan, 1988). Secondly, where Estate Action had targeted funds at the worst estates, this did not seem to be the case with HATs. Several of the designated estates were described as popular or well kept; some had recently had large amounts of money spent on improvements; while others had already been granted Estate Action funding (Grant, 1988). The suspicion grew that the government was picking off estates that would appeal to prospective private landlords rather than addressing the most serious problems. The most controversial aspect, however, was the prospect that HAT residents would lose their rights as council tenants.

This consideration weighed heavily when it came to the ballots. In the first vote, in April 1990, tenants on four estates in Sunderland voted overwhelmingly against being incorporated into a HAT. Sensing defeat from opposition expressed in local surveys, the government withdrew its proposed HATs in Leeds, the London Borough of Lambeth and Sandwell in the West Midlands (Dwelly, 1990). Concessions were clearly needed if the programme was to be salvaged. More money was promised and, crucially, the government conceded that tenants could opt to return to council control at the end of the HAT improvements. This was not enough to save the Southwark HAT. In October 1990 the residents of North Peckham and Gloucester Grove Estates in South London voted decisively 'no', apparently unwilling to trust in the government's change of heart (Frew, 1990). But the new, more generous and flexible approach did prove attractive to others.

Early in 1991 Hull City Council 'volunteered' the creation of a HAT on the North Hull Estate – a development of cottage homes in need of improvement but hardly a high profile problem area. The Hull HAT was quickly followed by a similar voluntary HAT in the London Borough of Waltham Forest where tenants on four tower block estates had campaigned for redevelopment. This breakthrough was achieved through the promise of a house and garden for every tenant. It was followed by a HAT in Liverpool which incorporated all this city's tower blocks. In 1993 HATs were set up in Tower Hamlets in London and at Castle Vale in Birmingham (*Building Design*, 1993). The Declaration of the Stonebridge HAT in West London brought the turbulent programme to a conclusion. Of the original six authorities designated for HATs only one – Tower Hamlets – eventually prevailed and that was based on a different area from the initial proposal.

New challenges

From the mid-1980s, government funding for estate regeneration projects was surrounded by a considerable uncertainty for local authorities. Councils could develop schemes over a lengthy period which involved complex negotiations and submission in the format laid down by the DoE. But they could never be certain of approval and this was often withheld until very late in the day, all of which made efficient implementation a serious problem. During the 1990s, however, this uncertainty was greatly increased.

In 1992 the government introduced City Challenge. A fund was established for urban regeneration and local authorities were invited to prepare schemes in partnership with the private sector and community organisations. The bids were assessed in competition with each other. Those successful would receive substantial funding while the failures – often similarly needy areas – would get nothing. In order to compete, local authorities had to commit considerable funds to developing proposals. This investment was at risk and had to be written off in the event of failure – a considerable penalty.

Nevertheless, in 1994, the same principles were extended to a wide range of government capital programmes. The Single Regeneration Budget (SRB) was introduced to cover England and Wales and a similar scheme, Programme for Partnerships, for Scotland. The SRB absorbed more than 20 separate programmes which had previously been run by five different government departments. Once again the emphasis was on partnerships and on the uncertainty of a competitive bidding process (DoE Information Leaflet, 1994a). One of the largest programmes absorbed by SRB was Estate Action which ceased to exist as a funding source for new projects, although many large schemes remained in the pipeline.

With the introduction of these challenge funds, government seemed to have abandoned its support for the improvement of multi-storey estates and at the same time renewed its determination to transfer housing from the control of local authorities. Where estates did receive funding, schemes usually involved demolition and redevelopment with the new housing transferred to other agencies. Under City Challenge the redevelopment of Hulme in Manchester was finally funded – something for which the tenants had campaigned for years. The new housing was to be built and managed by two large housing associations, although the City Council was allowed to manage the regeneration (JRF, 1994). Under SRB the process was taken further.

The experience of the Peckham Estates illustrates how far the ground rules had changed in a short time. After the tenants' rejection of HAT status in 1990 some of the estates were granted Estate Action funding. But a City Challenge bid to regenerate the remainder was rejected and further Estate Action money was refused because proposals did not generate sufficient diversity of tenure. Instead the only hope for funding lay in the SRB. In what became the biggest SRB project, £60 million was granted for redevelopment by a consortium of development companies (Countryside in Partnership plc, United House and Laing Homes) and small housing associations. About 3,000 flats were to be demolished and replaced by about 2,000 houses. The majority of these would be social housing but 40% were to be designated for owner-occupation or shared ownership (Hill, 1995).

As if in recognition of the shortcomings of SRB, in 1996 the system was changed again. Two new challenge programmes were introduced under which estates could benefit. One was the Estates Renewal Challenge Fund (ERCF). This aimed to promote transfer of local authority estates to a 'registered social landlord', which might be an established housing association or a 'housing company' – a new locally based organisation jointly controlled by the local authority, community representatives and the tenants of the estate. ERCF granted a subsidy to the new landlord to cover the difference between revenue costs and rent income. The scheme was another aspect of the government's determined efforts to remove social housing from local authority control. Its advantage may be that the new landlords may be able to raise private capital more easily for much needed improvements. The other new scheme was Capital Challenge. In this the government aimed to submit all capital funding for local authorities to the rigours of competition. Bids could be made for any scheme – transport, employment, urban regeneration, and so on – but among the winners announced in December 1996 were several projects for the improvement of multi-storey estates. These included a scheme for the extensive Marquess Estate in Islington which involves partial demolition and redevelopment by a housing association.

The dominant centre

Since the regeneration of multi-storey housing began, in the late 1970s, the process has been decisively shaped by the funding regime and the attitude of central government. In the 1970s the funding structure was dominated by the historical emphasis on new build housing. Only by a creative use of procedure could money be diverted to existing run-down estates. The new Conservative government pledged to release local government from bureaucratic controls and the system of Project Control it introduced proved relatively simple and straightforward. It allowed councils to develop their own long-term programmes with confidence and to establish their own priorities subject only to a central overview of 'value for money' criteria. This regime was to hold good for seven or eight years.

The founding of UHRU in 1985 was partly as an experimental unit focusing on government policy priorities and on tackling the problems of the worst estates. This was probably a valuable initiative because many authorities were unable or unwilling to address the most serious problems. As the amount of work funded under Estate Action grew it became an increasingly significant element of housing finance. This was partly because its expanding budget was created by diverting money from the Housing Investment Programme previously allocated directly to local authorities. Partly, too, because it comprised an increasingly large share of a smaller and smaller budget – government housing expenditure fell, in real terms from £12.3 billion in 1979/80 to £3.8 billion in 1988/89 (*The Guardian*, Report, 12 March, 1992, p 21). The expansion of Estate Action was the realisation of the continuing desire of the government to diminish the housing role of local authorities.

This process reached its height in 1988. The introduction of 'alternative landlords' and HATs were only part of it. At the same time the funding allocated to housing associations was greatly increased with the result that they became the main providers of new social housing. In 1988 local authorities were still building more houses than housing associations. By 1993 they were building none at all (Parkes, 1993). Denied the funding to build new housing, local authorities were left with barely sufficient to repair and maintain their existing estates. Any funding required for their improvement had to be drawn, under increasingly stringent rules, from government-directed programmes. A government which began, in 1979, by decentralising housing policy had, barely 10 years later, recentralised it to a hitherto unprecedented degree.

The effects on Islington

By the end of the 1970s Islington had a large and diverse housing programme composed, in almost equal parts, of new development, rehabilitation of old street houses, and modernisation of the housing estates of the 1930s, 1940s and 1950s. In estate improvement it had established a priority based on age and condition. And it had demonstrated that older smaller multi-storey estates could be modernised to make very good housing indeed. These programmes thrived under the 'value for money' criteria introduced by Project Control. By the mid-1980s estate improvement had become a dominant part of the housing work – partly because opportunities for new build and rehabilitation had diminished.

By this time, too, reductions in housing capital funding had begun to bite into the programme. Islington was only able to maintain its estate improvement by 'creative accounting' – using funding loaned direct from the money markets to supplement the capital sanctioned by central government. Nevertheless, the authority remained within the rules and all projects had to pass the financial criteria imposed by Project Control. As the new rigour of 1988 began to bite, however, Islington's programme was decimated. At one time it had stood at over £80 million per annum. By the end of 1990 it had been reduced to maintenance and repair, a few environmental improvements funded by the Inner City Partnership programme, and improvements to two large 1960s' estates funded under Estate Action. The demise had been swift and sudden. On five of the larger inter-war estates the last phases were left unfunded so that a few remaining blocks of very run-down housing could not be modernised. Two blocks were transferred to housing associations. But three remained unimproved – functioning as substandard temporary housing – an enduring symbol of determined and insensitive centralisation.

The scope of estate improvement

The Islington programmes demonstrated the effectiveness of concentrating improvement funds on older estates. Regrettably there has been limited improvement on similar estates elsewhere and probably no other local authority embarked on such a comprehensive or intensive programme of modernisation. Glasgow has carried out a good deal of modernisation of its older tenements. But in many cities such as Liverpool, run-down inter-war tenements have often been demolished (Mars, 1987). Alternatively, such blocks were sold off cheap to private developers who have successfully modernised them for owner-occupation. In inner London boroughs, however, there are thousands of tenement flats built between the wars or during the 1940s. Most of these have received only modest improvements or none at all. Many are among the poorest housing in terms of condition and standards. It has been clearly shown that such estates can make excellent housing and that their modernisation represents good value for money. There remains, for the future, a major programme of estate improvement work which is almost guaranteed of success.

It has not happened because centralisation has prevented local authorities adopting their own priorities and has concentrated all the remaining purse strings of housing finance in the hands of government. Where councils such as Islington prioritised age and condition, government programmes have had other priorities. They targeted the high profile problems – the worst estates measured by social stigma and unpopularity. This meant that most of the improvement funding for multi-storey housing has been channelled into the large estates built during the 1960s and 1970s.

Estate Action has been by far the biggest government programme. By April 1995 Estate Action funding totalled £1,975 million covering 540,000 homes and over 1,000 individual schemes (DoE, 1996). Some of this was spent on cottage estates but the bulk was put into the improvement of multi-storey housing. By contrast the original HAT programme was estimated at £231 million covering about 25,000 homes (Burrows, 1989). The Challenge programmes have channelled further funding to housing alongside capital for more general urban regeneration. The government has spent large amounts of money on the estates it prioritised but serious questions remain over the efficacy of the investment. Research which the DoE itself commissioned into six early Estate Action schemes concluded that the schemes had been of limited effectiveness. Only one scheme represented clear value for money with the other five showing only 'possible' value for money (DoE, 1996, p 33ff). HATs seemed to be proving no more effective. In 1997, a report by the Audit Commission severely criticised Waltham Forest HAT for high unit costs and took the DoE to task for failing to set adequate fiscal restraints (*Inside Housing*, 1997).

At the same time there was evidence that some of the improvement schemes had completely failed. An early Estate Action improvement of a tower block in Dudley showed initial success but within three years it had deteriorated again with management problems as serious as ever. The failure was, apparently, due to a concentration on security problems while neglecting to provide adequate heating or insulation (Nevin, 1990). More spectacularly, during the 1980s, over £30 million was spent on improvements to the Chalkhill Estate – a system-built, deck access development of 1,200 flats near Wembley. Much of the money was spent on an elaborate, high-tech concierge security system. By the early 1990s, however, it was clear that the changes had not addressed the basic problems. The DoE commissioned a new 'option appraisal' and it was decided to demolish the entire estate (information provided by the Metropolitan Housing Trust, 1996).

Such instances may be exceptional – although they are highly costly – but they do serve to question the effectiveness of the programmes intended to ensure improvement. It may be that the regeneration process in these schemes was inadequate and could be improved with better procedures or the incorporation of more wide-ranging solutions. It may, equally, be that some multi-storey estates, particularly the larger, more recent developments, are impossible to improve and can only be cleared and rebuilt. These issues are central to the uncertainty over the future of multi-storey housing. To try to answer these critical questions a start can be made by examining in more detail the separate aspects of improvement which have become apparent since the mid-1980s.

SIX

Facets of regeneration

In the attempts to solve the problems of multi-storey housing several distinct strands of thinking have emerged – what might be called facets of regeneration. During the 1980s two quite different perspectives, each underpinned by a strong theoretical basis, generated considerable debate. The earliest was the Priority Estates Project (PEP) which centred on the presumption that changes in housing management was the main issue in seeking sustainable solutions. The other concentrated on the 'defensible space' concept and saw bad design as the key cause of failure. Physical changes might ameliorate the problems but, fundamentally, flats would always be inferior to houses. This defeatist line of thinking led to the most radical option – abandoning hope in multi-storey housing, clearing it away to be replaced by houses with gardens. More detailed examination and the benefit of experience suggests that demolition is not the trouble-free option it first appears. For the most part, ways will have to be found to redeem multi-storey housing for its continuous long-term use.

Efforts at redemption have revolved around several different approaches and these can be defined in four further facets. First is the view is that the failings of multi-storey housing are largely technical and that if these problems were solved dissatisfaction would evaporate. A second view sees the issue of insecure and uncontrolled access systems as the critical problem. In the attempt to solve this there has been increasing reliance on complex technology. A third, more radical, approach suggests that multi-storey blocks must be 're-formed' – either the occupants must be changed to suit the buildings or the buildings must be adapted to make them suitable for their occupants. Finally, there is a view that no amount of physical adaptation can compensate for the concentrations of poverty found on many estates; what is needed is a concerted effort to improve the economic prospects of their residents. Each of these seven approaches merits consideration in some detail.

The Priority Estates Project

The Priority Estates Project (PEP) was set up in response to growing concern over the problems of unpopular housing estates. In 1979 the Department of the Environment (DoE) appointed three women to act as consultants. Each was to take charge of a pilot project – a 'hard-to-let' estate on which attention would be focused to try to reverse its bad reputation. Anne Blaber was recruited from the Safe Neighbourhoods Unit (SNU), a group set up by the National Association for the Care and Resettlement of Offenders (NACRO). NACRO had concluded that certain estates had become breeding grounds for crime and, in 1976, had formed SNU to investigate this. Anne Blaber was asked to work on Wenlock Barn in Hackney – a multi-storey estate dating from the early 1950s. Lesley Andrews worked in the DoE. Her research had shown the alienation of tenants from centralised local authority management. She was asked to lead a pilot project on the Willows – a cottage estate in Bolton.

The third consultant was Anne Power who had worked with the North Islington Housing Rights Project. Under a review by the incoming Conservative government, the third pilot project was cut out. Instead, Anne Power was given a roving brief to liaise with local authorities throughout the country. One authority, the Greater London Council (GLC), cooperated by setting up a pilot project on the Tulse Hill Estate – an inter-war development of four-storey tenements in Lambeth where some of the findings of the wider monitoring could be tested in practice. The chief significance of the liaison role, as it developed, was that Anne Power focused on monitoring the efforts of various local authorities who had set up decentralised management in estate-based offices. These included Islington's early experience with 'Estate Action managers' working from estates scheduled for major improvement (DoE, 1980; DoE et al, 1993b).

Estate based management

High proportions of empty homes, high rent arrears, a large number of transfer requests, high rate of refusal of offers – these were the symptoms of unpopularity which characterised estates as 'hard-to-let'. Behind these symptoms lay a spiral of decline. High levels of vandalism led to accelerating disrepair. Abuse of the common areas made them dirty and litter-strewn, generating a breakdown of caretaking and cleaning services. As conditions deteriorated fewer and fewer tenants willingly moved to the estates. Those who could, moved away. The estates became concentrations of the most disadvantaged tenants and those with least choice. This, in turn, accelerated their decline.

These estates had deteriorated while under the care of the housing managers centralised in Town Halls which were quite often two or three miles away. The experiment of moving staff into offices which were actually on the estates offered three key advantages:

- *Local lettings:* allowing estate-based staff to manage lettings offered two main benefits. First, many authorities had restrictive rules. They might require that offers had to be made in strict priority order or that there must be an exact fit between household size and dwellings size. Where flats were hard-to-let, these rules were an encumbrance. A local letting policy might allow, for example, sons and daughters to be housed near their parents regardless of priority. It might allow some families to be offered flats somewhat larger than their strict entitlement. Secondly, a prospective tenant might refuse an offer on a 'hard-to-let' estate made at the Town Hall simply because of its reputation. But an offer made on the estate accompanied by a viewing often resulted in an immediate letting. Localising lettings was found to result in significant reductions in empty dwellings.

- *Local repairs and maintenance:* the difficulty of getting repairs done has been a constant complaint on council estates. Long delays often meant collateral damage – a leaking waste or overflow, if not repaired quickly, can easily cause mounting damage to other flats; a failed extract fan can result in extensive condensation damage. Several authorities experimented with locally based repair teams, although there were considerable organisational difficulties and it is still not clear that local teams have achieved their full potential. General maintenance and cleaning, however, was very often improved by local management. Estate managers could observe, first hand, any repairs required in the common areas as well as keeping a check on graffiti and the standards of cleaning.
- *Tenant involvement:* many of the problems of management and maintenance are likely to be improved because managers are accessible to reports and complaints from tenants. This is a two-way process. It puts pressure on managers but it also allows council staff to emphasise that problems are partly created by tenants. Cultivating a custodial atmosphere among tenants helped to reduce abuse on the estates. When it came to improvements, tenant involvement played a key role. Often, capital improvements had failed because decisions were made in central offices without residents being consulted. Local offices were able to provide a focus for organising participation so that tenants could be involved in discussing proposed improvements and, perhaps even more important, able to initiate improvements according to their own priorities.

Local offices are more expensive that centralised departments. But the apparent savings achieved through 'economies of scale' hid the costs endemic in remote management. Local offices were found to make savings to compensate for their extra cost. Reducing the numbers of empty dwellings, for a start, brought increased rent and tax revenue and savings in the costs of security. Having managers on the estate made it easier to combat and reduce rent arrears. More rapid maintenance and repair reduced the costs of neglect, while the general increases in tenant vigilance and reporting helped to reduce the costs of vandalism and abuse. In its first year, the local office on the Tulse Hill Estate was estimated to have produced a net saving for the GLC of at least £135,000 through extra income and savings on security and damage (DoE, 1981).

Monitoring 20 estates

A product of Anne Power's wide-ranging remit was the identification of 20 unpopular estates across the country. Progress on these estates was monitored through the 1980s and they were revisited in 1994 (Power, 1987; Power and Tunstall, 1995). Part of this monitoring looked at social changes on the estates, part looked at the changes brought about by locally based management. At the start of PEP the majority of estates had high indices of deprivation. In the most recent review the estates were even more deprived, with all 20 showing high levels of unemployment and concentrations of children and lone parents. This was partly due, no doubt, to general economic circumstances. Partly it was the result of increasing concentration of the most disadvantaged on the worst estates. This trend – known as 'residualisation' – was largely the result of the loss, through 'Right to Buy', of the most desirable housing in the public sector. Despite their increased deprivation, many of the indices which had characterised the unpopularity of the estates had improved. The reduction in abuse and the improvement in maintenance was particularly impressive. These improvements were accompanied by, and partly due to, much greater resident involvement in the management of the estates. Progress on reducing rent arrears was less impressive but this largely reflects the more disadvantaged social profile.

While these results seem encouraging they must be subject to two caveats. First, the 20 estates were a mixture of types – seven were 'cottage' estates; six were 'balcony' estates – walk-up tenement-type blocks; only seven were 'modern' estates, dating from the 1960s and 1970s – multi-storey estates with lifts and/or deck access systems. While this mix undoubtedly represents the range of 'hard-to-let' estates, the problems of each type and the nature of possible solutions is quite different. The second caveat is that most of the estates had had physical improvements *as well as* management changes. So it is difficult to be sure how much of the perceived improvement was due to local management and how much to other changes.

The problems of cottage estates are often due to location. Their resolution lies as much in economic improvements as in other changes. Where physical changes are necessary they are quite different from those required on multi-storey estates. It has now been shown conclusively that the form of the lower scale 'balcony' estates allows them to be successfully remodelled to make good housing. Nevertheless in the six 'balcony' estates in the survey only limited physical improvements had been made. It seems, for this type of estate, management can be critical. This is borne out by the more recent example of the Kingsmead Estate in Hackney where good order and tenant confidence has been restored by intensive management (Hugill, 1996). Despite the fact that virtually no physical improvements have been made since the estate was built and, in terms of housing quality, the flats remain substandard.

The big question mark hangs over the 'modern' estates. Of the seven such estates in the PEP 20, all had had substantial spending on security improvements. On five estates very significant capital improvements were planned. One was to be totally demolished and rebuilt. On the others far-reaching restructuring and block transformation were planned. The impact of these physical changes is unclear but what the PEP established was that estate-based management can make a significant difference and in some circumstances can be instrumental in restoring confidence in unpopular estates. In the drive to make multi-storey estates into good housing and, in particular, tackling the thorny problems of modern multi-storey estates, local management must be seen as a key part of any successful package of improvements rather than as a solution in itself.

The 'defensible space' controversy

The term 'defensible space' was coined by the American architect Oscar Newman. His influential book (Newman, 1972) was based on research on multi-storey public housing in New York. Drawing on historical examples from a wide range of cultural contexts, Newman showed that traditional housing commonly featured a 'stoop' at the entrance. This raised or semi-enclosed space was not part of the dwelling and nor was it part of the public street. It was, in effect, an area of transition – a buffer zone over which the householder felt a proprietorial right and which helped to protect the privacy of the dwelling from the public domain. Oscar Newman contended that this 'defensible space' had been designed out of multi-story housing and that this was the cause of much crime and abuse.

He investigated social housing which exhibited high crime rates and recorded a detailed study of two estates on adjacent sites in Brooklyn. Both suffered from crime and vandalism and were of a similar size and social profile. One –Van Dyke – comprised 14-storey blocks, each served by a single entrance giving access to between 112 and 136 households. The other estate – Brownsville – consisted of five-storey blocks each of which had three entrances serving six or 18 households. Despite the similarities of the two estates, Van Dyke had recorded crime levels more than 50% higher than Brownsville. Newman concluded that the critical difference lay in the number of families using each common entrance. Where this number was small the residents were much better able to 'defend' the common access space.

These conclusions seemed to provide compelling evidence that the economies in access systems introduced to lower the cost of multi-storey housing were the cause of serious social problems. Other observations in Oscar Newman's studies suggested that surveillance was a critical factor.

External balconies were less abused than internal corridors because they were overlooked by tenants' windows. Crime and assault in block entrances were less frequent where lift lobbies and waiting areas were close to public streets and overlooked by passers-by.

It has been suggested that Oscar Newman's findings are not directly applicable in Britain (Sim, 1993, p 112). This is partly because American cities provided a much lower level of social housing which serve only the most deprived; partly because crime levels in New York were, generally, very high. Certainly the sheer inventiveness of the American teenage vandal is unmatched:

> Youngsters not only commonly remove elevator doors entirely, but have found ways to anchor cables so that the elevator motors and pulleys tear the cabs from their railings – ripping apart the entire elevator shaft for the full height of the building. (Newman, 1972, p 189)

There must be reservations in applying lessons from the United States to a different cultural context. Nevertheless it is hard to argue with Oscar Newman's main conclusions that enclosing common entrances improves security; that access systems should be designed so that as few families as possible share a common entrance; that surveillance by residents and passers-by helps to deter crime and abuse; and that redefinition of external space helps residents to exert control over areas previously open to unrestricted public access. These principles have been absorbed by many estate improvement schemes.

Utopia on trial

In recent years Oscar Newman's work has been eclipsed and somewhat diminished by the link with that of Alice Coleman, Professor of Geography at Kings College, London (Coleman, 1985). Quoting extensively from Newman, and claiming continuity, Professor Coleman sought a 'scientific' approach to analysing and resolving the problems of housing design. Taking as their sample area the London Boroughs of Tower Hamlets and Southwark, the research team visited all 4,050 multi-storey blocks in these authorities.

As evidence of malaise they counted and recorded indices of abuse – litter, graffiti, vandal damage, urine and faeces. To these measures one social factor was added – figures for children in care provided by Southwark Council. These findings were then correlated to several, largely quantitative, features of the design. These included numbers of storeys and dwellings in the block, and the number served by each entrance; the types and position of entrances; the numbers of overhead walkways and their interconnection with vertical routes and horizontal exits; the numbers of blocks on the site, their spatial organisation and numbers of play areas. A close correlation was claimed between the numerical frequency of these features – for example, the number of dwellings served by each entrance – and the indices of abuse. From this analysis a 'disadvantagement score' ranging from 0 to 15 could be defined for any housing estate. The key to improvement of problem estates would be to introduce changes which reduced the disadvantagement score.

The publication of Alice Coleman's ideas prompted a storm of controversy. Architect Brian Anson challenged the view that design could induce anti-social behaviour and suggested this was more likely the result of poverty and deprivation (Anson, 1986, 1989). Local politician Bryndley Heaven posited that Coleman's proposals conflicted with residents' priorities. These would include safety measures; creation of jobs and training opportunities; and better social facilities (Heaven, 1986). These criticisms were easily deflected, stemming, as they did, from entirely different approaches to housing problems. One critic, however, attacked Alice Coleman on her own ground. Bill Hillier was a fellow academic – Reader at the Bartlett School of Architecture in London. He concluded that Coleman's claim to have established a 'scientific' connection between design features and social malaise was unfounded:

> To show this scientifically she has first to quantify design feature and malaise indicators, show that the two are correlated statistically (that one rises when the other does) and then make sure that the correlations between a design feature and a malaise indicator are not produced by a third factor. In this case the obvious third factors would be social.... Coleman has accomplished none of these. Her method of quantification of malaise is flawed, her correlations largely illusory and her attempt to test for social factors desultory. (Hillier, 1986, p 39)

He went on to suggest that many of the supposed correlations were simply a predictable relation between scale and frequency – for example, the more flats in a block the more litter is likely to be found. He also recalculated Alice Coleman's own figures to show that the supposed correlation between block size and children in care was, at best, questionable and, at worst, wholly fictitious.

Testing the theory

Despite the controversy it generated, *Utopia on trial* attracted the interest of the Conservative government. The DICE project (Design Improvement Controlled Experiment) was set up under Alice Coleman's direction and, in 1991, the DoE granted £50 million to improve seven selected estates (Coleman, 1992). The DICE approach was founded on a pilot estate improvement carried out on the Mozart Estate in Westminster. This was a multi-storey deck access development where a pattern of crime had become established. Various attempts at improvement had failed before Alice Coleman was asked to recommend modifications. She identified a key problem in the overhead walkways which connected 23 of the 29 blocks in a continuous pedestrian deck. The walkway and its vertical links of lifts and stairs offered a multitude of uncontrolled access points. Residents were unable to identify intruders and the system provided numerous escape routes for wrongdoers. Coleman's chief proposal was the removal of these walkways. She also proposed measures to give the blocks separate identity and security and to close off many of the through routes in the estate as a whole (Coleman, 1990, p 135ff).

From the start, the plans were resisted by some of the tenants and their misgivings were supported by a subsequent report from the SNU which found no significant reduction in crime. Burglaries, for instance, were found to be highest on smaller blocks and lower on long corridors where the perpetrators were more likely to be disturbed – the opposite of what might be inferred from Coleman's research (Brimacombe, 1989). More recently a comprehensive evaluation has been carried out by consultants Price Waterhouse on five estates on which DICE projects have been completed. The evaluation looked at both financial and qualitative issues and assessed the long-term durability of the changes. The results were mixed, showing no clear pattern of success or failure. Overall the consultants declared DICE projects to be no more or less effective than contemporary Estate Action schemes (Hill, 1997).

Some years on from the publication of *Utopia on trial* the heat of the original controversy has faded and the issues fallen into perspective. It is now clear how risky it is to try to apply science to housing. Scientific methods require precise definitions and comparisons with well defined controls and tests which can be repeatedly replicated. Such criteria are extremely difficult to apply to the complexities of multi-storey housing. Besides, it is not necessary to conduct an elaborate survey and analysis to come up with some common sense solutions. The failure to convincingly apply scientific evaluation, however, does not mean that design is of no importance. Oscar Newman established some important principles although he subsequently stressed that social changes are as important as physical design (Heck, 1987). Alice Coleman's particular contribution has been the idea of demolishing walkways and separating blocks in deck access estates. Design modifications undoubtedly have an important part to play in regenerating multi-storey housing but they are not an all-embracing panacea.

The dynamite option

The logic of Alice Coleman's analysis is the fewer storeys and the fewer entrances the better. It follows, and she explicitly states, that houses are better than flats. The logical consequence is to replace flats with houses. The case for demolition often rests on this very simple argument. Flats don't work for low-income families with children, therefore they must be replaced by family houses. Local authorities all over the country have acted on this conclusion, very often eschewing conventional demolition methods and adopting the quicker solution offered by dynamite. Many sound and adequate buildings have been demolished by controlled explosions. After dynamiting nine or more tower blocks (Flight and Xenakis, 1995), the London Borough of Hackney had become expert at this technique – or thought they had. One block proved so well built that when the charges blew it dropped 10 feet and then stood there, stubbornly stable.

Behind a demolition decision often lies a history of neglect. Halston Point and Thornhill Point were 22-storey tower blocks, part of the New Kingshold Estate in Hackney. The estate was built in the late 1960s by the GLC. In 1982 it was transferred to the borough council. Within a short time the support system the GLC had provided disappeared – resident caretakers were removed, gardeners no longer looked after the grounds, repairs didn't get done. By the early 1990s the blocks had deteriorated appallingly – disrepair and vandalism had wrecked the blocks; the lifts broke down repeatedly; flats were infested with cockroaches; and several had been burnt out by fires started deliberately. Unsurprisingly tenant pressure was intense and the blocks were dynamited in 1995 (Shaw, 1995; Faulkner, 1995).

If the decision to demolish is often taken for the wrong reasons it is also often taken too lightly. The belief is strong that it is an easy and incontrovertible option, that if bad housing is swept away, all the problems will disappear and will not recur in new family houses which are self-evidently problem-free. This approach ignores three key issues – that there are plenty of low-rise estates of houses which are very far from problem-free; that multi-storey housing, bad as it often is, contains valuable community networks and support systems; and that the sheer cost of redevelopment makes it prohibitive as a universal solution.

The false promise

Drawing on the experience of the mass of middle-class suburban housing built during the 1930s and after, many conclude that estates of houses are invariably trouble-free. This is simply not true. There are many cottage estates which have the most serious social problems. Seven such problem areas were among the 20 'hard-to-let' estates monitored by PEP, and there are many others. Some, such as Meadowell in North Shields, date from the 1930s and were stigmatised from the start by their association with slum clearance (Kelly, 1992). Others, like the Welland Estate in Peterborough, are much more modern (Peacock, 1995). The social problems tend to be the same as in multi-storey housing – high unemployment, large numbers of children and lone parents. But the physical manifestations are different – private gardens are neglected; the external environment is downgraded and litter strewn; and there are often large numbers of empty houses. At best these are boarded up, at worst they are burnt out or picked bare like skeletons by scavengers and vandals.

Such problems have often developed over a long period but it cannot be supposed that they can be avoided by building new family houses. David Page investigated new estates built by housing associations. Traditionally the role of housing associations has been specialised, generally catering for tenants whose needs were not provided for by public housing. Now that housing associations have been required to take over from local authorities as providers of new social housing, they are beginning to experience the same sort of problems:

> ... some newly built estates have begun to show significant signs of wear and tear after only two years; two of the estates [studied] had developed problems of vandalism, graffiti, incivilities and drug abuse so serious in only four years that a multi-agency approach was required to deal with them. The problems are not new, but the time-scale is: housing associations are getting there much quicker than local authorities. Run-down council estates are generally the result of two or three decades of decline: housing associations are now meeting similar problems in under 5 years. (Page, 1993, p 46)

Page identified three causes for this rapid decline. First, new estates are required to provide a high proportion of family housing resulting in unusually high child density. Second, there were concentrations of poverty. Many tenants were 'economically inactive' – perhaps unable to work through sickness or disability; there were abnormally high proportions of lone parents, more than half of whom were wholly dependent on state benefits; of those available for work, very high numbers were unemployed (64% at the time of the survey). This problem is exacerbated by a 'poverty trap' – if tenants get work they lose their Housing Benefit and cannot afford the high rents. Finally, many of the smaller dwellings were occupied by people released under the 'care in the community' programme and who were disadvantaged in various ways.

Destruction of communities

It sometimes seems that the lessons of history are never learned. One of the most regrettable aspects of the large-scale redevelopment of the 1960s was that the kinship networks, the surveillance and support systems, were swept away when the terraced streets were bulldozed. Protest at the destruction of communities was instrumental in bringing an end to clearance. Yet in the rush to clear away today's problem housing, the same thing is happening again. In the long suffering Gorbals, for instance, a vital community was destroyed and dispersed in the 1960s, when the tenements were demolished. In the early 1990s another community was destroyed when the multi-storey blocks were torn down, in their turn reducing acres of land to an empty sea of rubble.

Communities in multi-storey housing do not have the strength or longevity of those found in areas of older housing in the 1960s. But they should not be dismissed. Certainly many people are keen to leave unpopular estates and there is commonly a high turnover in tenancies. Kinship networks have often not developed because of strict prioritisation in rehousing policies. Often, however, there is a core of people committed to the estate. This is particularly true of older estates where a significant proportion of tenants may have lived there a long time and, in their mature years, become attached to their homes. Even in more recent estates a good many residents have considerable commitment. They may like the location. Some may know each other as friends and neighbours. Often people come together in playgroups, tenants' associations and community centres. These people are commonly the most active in trying to achieve change. Among them are the organisers of pressure for better management and physical improvements; and the stalwarts of community organisations. Community links on multi-storey estates may be weaker than in older areas of housing but they are valuable. They provide a strong focus which, properly cultivated and built upon, can become the starting point for successful improvement and regeneration.

The costs of redevelopment

Redevelopment is an expensive option. Even in the most elaborate refurbishment the foundations and superstructure are retained and these constitute 20-30% of the cost of a new building. Added to the higher cost of replacement buildings are the costs of demolition. In the case of multi-storey blocks, this might involve excavation of complex foundations. The costs do not end with construction. Housing is normally built using 60-year loans. Where relatively recent buildings are demolished there may be substantial debt charges outstanding which have to be written off. Added to this is the cost of rehousing the existing tenants. Housing must be provided before they can move and before any housing gain can be achieved through redevelopment. On top of this, tenants forced to move are entitled to compensation and the staff costs of organising their move must not be forgotten. Overall, the cost of redevelopment is likely to be at least 50% higher than the cost of a comprehensive improvement scheme.

By the mid–1990s, demolition was increasingly seen as a quick and simple solution to the problems of unpopular multi-storey estates which were often the focus of social problems and criminal activity. Aside from the lack of guaranteed success, redevelopment was highly disruptive, involved the loss of potentially valuable social housing, and was far and away the most expensive option. It should have become evident that demolition is far too costly – both fiscally and socially – to provide a universal solution to the problems of multi-storey housing. There are circumstances in which it may be necessary. Partial demolition may be a useful means to reduce density, increase amenity or make possible a more balanced housing mix Sometimes strong resident demands make demolition irresistible. There may be no alternative where buildings have comprehensively failed technically. But demolition should not be considered lightly for buildings that retain structural and constructional integrity. Before reaching for the detonator decision makers should seriously investigate alternative options of repair, remodelling or changing use and occupancy.

The major repairs approach

For some, the problems of multi-storey housing are technical. Dissatisfaction with blocks of flats is seen to stem from the discomfort or inconvenience caused by constructional defects or inadequate services. Older estates lack adequate heating or insulation, their gas, water and electrical services are worn out and well short of modern standards. In newer blocks of traditional construction the roofs might leak; the windows may have rotted causing draughts and water penetration; the flats might be cold and suffer condensation; the lifts might be of poor quality and repeatedly break down. The central issue, therefore, was seen as the need to address these technical shortcomings. In the early approaches to modernisation each problem might be addressed piecemeal – a new lift, new windows, more insulation.

It gradually emerged that there was often a syndrome of interrelated technical problems. This was particularly true of blocks built using industrialised building. A key survey by the Association of Metropolitan Authorities summarised the problems (AMA, 1984). Most such multi-storey blocks had been built using systems of interlocking precast concrete wall and floor panels. The most critical problem was 'progressive collapse' which had been highlighted by Ronan Point, where death and injury had been caused when part of the block collapsed like a pack of cards. As a result, most blocks of similar construction were subsequently surveyed and, where necessary, extra strengthening carried out to improve structural stability. During the surveys, however, a range of other problems came to light.

Very often panel joints had been improperly made. Differential expansion movement cased the outer joints to open up and expose the interior which was often not properly filled. The same thing happened around window openings. The result was that water penetration through joints was common. The presence of chlorides in the concrete and inadequate cover to steel reinforcement often caused pieces of concrete to spawl off, posing danger and exacerbating leaking joints. Most blocks had flat roofs which had a high failure rate. Leaks through roofs and parapets badly affected the upper floors. 'Cold bridges' though the structure were a common problem. Although multi-storey blocks were insulated to contemporary standards, heat loss was much greater at high levels due to colder air, wind chill and the turbulent microclimate created by high buildings. The problem of multiple leaks was exacerbated by condensation on external walls causing dampness and mould growth.

Overcladding

Once this complex of problems became apparent, experiments began in the early 1980s to find comprehensive solutions. Overcladding meant putting a new skin on the outside walls of the buildings to provide a weatherproof protection against water penetration. Generally new roofs complete the newly sealed outer face. Very often new windows form part of the additional external skin and balconies are sometimes enclosed to provide weatherproof conservatories. Overcladding allows high levels of insulation to be achieved, contributing significantly to energy conservation. Overcladding takes two main forms, which can be characterised as 'light' and 'heavy'.

The scope for adding additional loads to most buildings is limited. This is particularly true for blocks built from heavy panels where the constructional integrity is uncertain and the structural tolerances unpredictable. Lightweight overcladding avoids this problem (Figure 6.1). The new skin consists of a lightweight insulation protected against the weather. This protection might be a reinforced render or proprietary panels of resin-coated board or aluminium. These panels form a 'rainscreen' with a system of channels behind the joints which collect and discharge any water which gets through. The panels can be fixed from a motorised cradle which 'climbs' the building on 'masts'. This ingenious construction method avoids the costs of scaffolding which is usually required for rendered skins. Lightweight overcladding can be constructed relatively quickly and can be carried out without the need for tenants to be moved from their homes, although they have to endure considerable noise and vibration.

'Heavy' overcladding relies much more on traditional construction techniques (Figure 6.2). Generally this involves removing the outer skin of concrete panels. These are replaced with a new insulated skin of traditional brickwork tied back to the remaining structure with stainless steel angles.

The new skin is approximately the same load as the defective concrete skin removed. This approach is much more disruptive than adding a light external skin. Blocks often have to be emptied completely for it to be carried out although this offers the benefit that comprehensive improvements to the flats and the common areas can be made at the same time. 'Heavy' overcladding is much more expensive than lightweight systems – and it can be very expensive indeed.

Architects Hunt Thompson, having overclad several tower blocks, completed one of the most remarkable schemes in 1997. Winterton House in Tower Hamlets was one of only four tower blocks built by the GLC in the late 1960s using a lightweight construction system known as SFI. The system used plastic wall panels supported on a steel frame. Over time the cladding panels had deteriorated and the building was riddled with asbestos. The block was stripped to a skeleton comprising only the steel frame and the concrete lift shafts. A new brick exterior was built around the shell but, for structural reasons, this had to be entirely free-standing. At the top of the building the new brick skin and the original steel frame are braced together by a system of hydraulic jacks to prevent differential movement. It is claimed that the reconstruction was cheaper than providing the same amount of new housing on the ground. Even so, this 'refurbishment' was clearly close to the cost of rebuilding the block entirely (Evans, 1996).

Overcladding of tower blocks is illustrated in Exemplars 3 and 4 opposite and overleaf.

Figure 6.1: **Harvist Estate, Islington. (*above*) Panels fixed by a 'mast climber' create a new, lightweight external skin (*left*)**

Exemplar 3: Harvist Estate, Islington

Harvist Estate, built in the mid-1960s, was typical of the 'mixed development' approach to social housing established by the London County Council (LCC). Housing for large families was concentrated in four blocks of four-storey maisonettes with four 20-storey tower blocks providing one- and two-bedroom flats for small households. This pattern of accommodation ensured that few social problems developed on the estate. But there were technical shortcomings. The blocks were constructed using the 'heavy panel' system of industrialised building. In the tower blocks, poor insulation and deterioration of the fabric created a typical syndrome of water penetration and condensation problems.

In 1997 a scheme for 'lightweight overcladding' was commenced to improve the towers. The blocks were 'overclad' with a 'rainscreen'. This was a system of insulated resin-coated board fixed to aluminium channels. Open joints allow rain through, which then drains out at the bottom. The panels are fixed using a 'mastclimber' cradle, avoiding the need for scaffolding. The lightweight cladding is cheap to fix and can be carried out while tenants are in residence, although considerable noise, vibration and disruption is involved. The improved comfort and appearance provided by the overcladding was accompanied by new entrances with electronic intercom security and the construction of communal rooms at ground level.

Note: Improvement scheme by Islington Architects Department.

Figure 6.2: **Northwood Tower, Waltham Forest. Heavy overcladding with a new skin of traditional brickwork and replacement windows**

Exemplar 4: Northwood Tower, Waltham Forest

Northwood Tower was another system-built block dating from the 1960s. Again, its 20 storeys contained only flats for small households so there were few social problems. When the block was surveyed in the 1980s it was decided structural strengthening was needed to guard against 'progressive collapse'. Since tenants had to be moved out during the work it was decided to take the opportunity to overclad the block to address problems of water penetration and poor insulation.

The building had a hybrid construction with heavy precast concrete panels forming the main structure. Externally this was clad in brickwork and large timber infil panels. It was decided to remove the existing cladding and add a new insulated brick skin and new windows. This new external skin is tied back to the existing structure with a complex system of steel angles and brackets. The new cladding is about the same weight as the original so the integrity of the structure is not affected. To carry out the work five floors were emptied. The contractors worked on one floor at a time moving up the building with tenants being rehoused lower down as work was completed. The scheme included comprehensive improvements to the flat interiors; a new roof; and a new entrance hall with electronic intercom and CCTV monitored by a concierge (*The Architects' Journal*, 1992; Derbyshire, 1993).

Note: Improvement scheme by Hunt Thompson Associates.

The limits of technical refurbishment

Comprehensive technical improvement schemes often include internal modernisation and service renewal. Even so – and despite the enthusiasm of some architects – the major repairs approach has considerable uncertainties and clear limitations. Lightweight overcladding may seem a relatively quick and cheap solution which is likely to pay back its costs in energy saving quite quickly. In the main its use is limited to tower blocks where the cost advantages of repetition and rapid installation give economies of scale. Technically, however, it is relatively untested. The sorry tale of industrialised building itself should provide a clear warning about putting too much faith in systems unless they have proved effective over a long period. 'Heavy' overcladding is more technically reliable since it is based on tried and tested traditional materials and techniques. But it is relatively expensive and, most significantly, requires partial or total rehousing of the residents.

The major repairs approach has shown that the defects in multi-storey housing can probably be rectified. However, over-concentration on technical issues can leave too little attention focused on social shortcomings. Adding a lightweight skin may remedy dampness and condensation but it may ignore the problems created by high child density and offer nothing to tenants who are inappropriately housed. Heavy overcladding offers some rehousing opportunities but it may not address the problems created by an unsuitable mix of flat sizes. Comprehensive repair can resolve many technical shortcomings. At best, however, it provides only part of the solution for successful regeneration.

Estate security and surveillance

It is established that multi-storey housing estates are abnormally affected by crime. Petty crime involving vandal damage and abuse are the most visible, but more serious are the high incidence of burglaries, 'muggings' and personal assaults (DoE/SNU, 1993c). Both the social and physical environment are often conducive to drug dealing, which brings other associated crime in its wake. The opportunities for crime on estates are provided by the extensive common areas and access systems, uncontrolled, relatively little used and unsupervised by surrounding dwellings.

Some relatively simple solutions have proved effective. One is better lighting. More intense street lighting removes the dark corners where perpetrators might lurk and, more importantly, helps to remove the fear of crime. Better lighting can be particularly effective if coupled with a scheme for closing secondary routes and channelling most pedestrian movement along a few, more heavily used pathways. Similarly, closing off communal landscaped areas and restricting access provides a safer environment, particularly for young children to play. Such solutions have commonly been successful in reducing crime in external spaces but the most vexing problems have surrounded attempts to secure the communal access systems.

Until the mid-1980s, access security was based almost entirely on the electronic intercom or 'entryphone'. These devices worked well on large houses divided into a few flats. They generally succeeded on small blocks of flats, particularly 'staircase access' blocks where each stair served only six or eight flats. In Islington's programme of modernising tenement blocks, where the numbers of family flats were restricted on upper floors, entryphones worked reasonably well on entrances serving up to 20-25 flats. Where, however, electronic intercoms were installed on larger blocks, they almost universally failed. Within days of commissioning, systems were rendered inoperable and sometimes entire entrance doors smashed. Damage was apparently done by tenants, finding themselves locked out of their homes. Because of the relatively large numbers of flats the culprits could hardly ever be identified and the systems became impossible to manage.

The 'concierge'

It became apparent that such damage could only be prevented if common entrances were observed. A lead was taken from the 'concierges' who control the entrances to apartment blocks in France. One of the earliest experiments was introduced in 1984 at Gloucester House, a tower block on the Kilburn Estate in the London Borough of Brent. All secondary entrances were closed, a new entryphone system installed, and the common areas carpeted. A receptionist was stationed at the main entrance which was staffed from 8am to 11pm. Reduction in vandalism was dramatic and tenant confidence greatly increased (Ulleri, 1987). On blocks with a single entrance such schemes usually worked well. The receptionist often became a social asset – taking messages, taking charge of deliveries and generally providing a focus for the exchange of gossip and information which helped to generate a sense of community This, in turn, improved surveillance and bolstered the security system.

All this assumed that the perpetrators of crime and vandalism came from outside – something which is commonly claimed by tenants. Only in relatively few cases was this actually true. Where there were concentrations of children and teenagers or a few anti-social tenants, the presence of the 'concierge' was not sufficient to deter wrongdoers. More and more the receptionists began to be supported by video surveillance of the parts of the block which were out of sight. Increasingly security became dependent on high technology.

The 'high-tech' solution

Closed circuit television (CCTV) was first used in the early 1980s. Early systems were 'passive'. Video cameras were placed at strategic points, filming on a 'stop motion' mode – taking one frame every few seconds. If a crime occurred the film could be reviewed to identify the culprit (Smith, 1982). By the early 1990s CCTV had become much more sophisticated and interactive. As well as talking to visitors at the main entrance through intercoms, tenants can now view them through their own TV sets. They can also view the corridor outside or watch their children at play in the secured communal garden. Video cameras from various entrances can be linked back to a 'concierge office' where the receptionists can view them on multiple image screens. They can talk to visitors through intercoms and can monitor and control access to the blocks.

Cameras can be mounted in strategic positions on balconies, corridors, staircases and at critical points in the external areas. They can be fitted into lifts together with a public address system so that the vigilant concierge can instantly reprimand anyone caught in an act of anti-social behaviour. All this surveillance is backed by new high technology security. Tough steel doors now guard the common entrances. They are secured by electromagnetic locks which have no moving parts and are virtually impossible to force. The locks are controlled by electronic 'swipe' cards or key 'fobs' which can be programmed to restrict the range of access of the user. In the event of loss or theft the fobs can be remotely reprogrammed to prevent misuse.

The drawbacks of high security

With such flexibility and capability it might seem that such systems are 'fail safe'. A survey by SNU suggests that generally they do work well in tower blocks (DoE/SNU, 1994b). Partly this is because access can usually be limited to a single, easily controllable entrance. Partly because the concentrated vertical circulation is relatively cheap and easy to survey with cameras. On slab and deck access blocks there are often several entrances and the more extensive corridors are much more difficult to keep under surveillance. On this type of estate there have been spectacular failures, notably at Chalkhill Estate in Brent. There £10.5 million was spent on CCTV-controlled concierge systems which were, at best, only partly effective due to the large number of possible entry points (information provided by the Metropolitan Housing Trust, 1996).

There are two weaknesses in high technology security systems. One is that the cost of maintenance and monitoring of the system is high. It is questionable whether local authorities can organise or afford such high costs. Certainly the record of maintenance of public housing is poor. Yet unless there are maintenance systems that are outstanding, providing rapid response and repair, high-tech security will quickly break down. The other problem is human error. Successful concierges do more than just 'be there'. They need to be vigilant and skilful in operating the system, obdurate in pursuing wrongdoers and investigating incidents, and, on top, to be gregarious with ordinary tenants and courteous with visitors. This is a tough job description and such paragons are hard to find.

At root it is a dispiriting commentary on social conditions that housing estates should need to be turned into impregnable fortresses and that so many improvement schemes, under the strong sponsorship of the DoE Estate Action team, should have pitched for such solutions. They raise serious questions about civil liberties but even more serious concerns about urban conditions. There are large cities in Europe with much lower levels of urban crime. They have multi-storey housing estates which are completely unsecured and yet suffer negligible abuse. High-tech security addresses the symptoms of anti-social behaviour, the roots of which may well have more to do with general social policy. Even if these issues must be addressed solely within the housing sphere it might be better to seek solutions which are self-sustaining rather than relying on high levels of supervision and maintenance.

Re-forming multi-storey blocks

It has long been recognised that multi-storey blocks are unsuitable for families with children both because of the effects on family life and the impact of children and young people on the flats and common areas. From the early 1970s government began discussing with local authorities the possibilities of rehousing families in ground level dwellings (Adams and Conway, 1974). Many authorities followed this approach in one way or another. Some adopted a 'no child' policy for tenancies of multi-storey blocks. Some restricted families to lower floors only. Sometimes flats were 'underlet' to reduce child density – for example four-person flats let to three-person households. In other cases authorities recognised that management problems would be eased if flats in tall blocks were let only to people who expressed a genuine desire to live in them. Recognising that a key problem was that some types of household, particularly families with children, were allocated housing which was unsuitable, one line of approach was to transform multi-storey blocks in one of two ways. Either the population could be changed to suit the accommodation available, or the layout of the blocks could be changed so that it was made suitable for those already living there.

Re-dedicating high blocks

Multi-storey blocks have been successfully revitalised by dedicating them to specific types of occupants. If families can be rehoused in ground level accommodation whole blocks can be emptied and allocated to different target groups of tenants. Duncan Sim recorded an interesting experiment in the tower blocks at Red Road in Glasgow:

> In 1981 the Council rehabilitated one block with the result that floors 1-3 were then occupied by group and shared tenancies (ex-hospital patients and ex-offenders); floors 4-13 were let to mainstream tenants, floors 14-27 were let, furnished, to students and 28-30 were let as furnished executive flats. The 23rd floor was completely communal for the use of all residents. The initiative appears to have been successful and a second block was refurbished and let to the YMCA. (Sim, 1993, p 87)

In fact the YMCA block effectively functions as a student hostel. Student housing is a common use for multi-storey blocks. In the 1970s North London Polytechnic was allocated 'hard-to-let' flats in Islington as student accommodation. In the 1980s part of the massive Hyde Park complex in Sheffield was converted to student accommodation as a by-product of the World Student Games. More surprisingly, tower blocks have functioned as dedicated housing for young people with less advantages. In 1992 a specialist housing association took over an empty tower block in Wolverhampton. Refurbished with an energy efficient scheme and provided with a concierge controlled entrance, Phoenix Rise is now let to young single people, 80% of whom are on Housing Benefit (Thompson, 1995).

If young single people present few problems in multi-storey blocks, elderly people pose even fewer. Examples of tower blocks converted into sheltered housing can be found in Liverpool and Birkenhead (*Housing*, 1983d, 1987). Several are to be found in the West Midlands. Birmingham has led the field and has more than 50 blocks converted to sheltered housing (NHTPC, 1997). Even in the London Borough of Hackney, where the presumption to demolish was strong, tenants successfully campaigned for the retention of a tower block on the Holly Street Estate. Grange Court has been refurbished and reopened as the exclusive preserve of elderly tenants. A concierge system provides security and the basement of the block houses a lunch club, a resource centre and a health club (Thompson, 1995). Tower blocks are relatively easy to secure and, almost invariably, have space at ground level on which communal facilities can be developed. The cluster of community rooms around the base helps to reinforce the security by enclosing the entrance and providing extra surveillance.

Adapting multi-storey estates

There is plenty of evidence that tower blocks can be provided with successful security systems. When these are combined with sensitive lettings policies or schemes to dedicate them to more appropriate user groups, such blocks can provide good quality housing. Other types of modern multi-storey housing present more difficult problems. Attempts to introduce security systems in slab blocks have commonly failed. This is partly because such blocks often have a high proportion of large dwellings and high child density. The most serious difficulty is that there are commonly several entrances to each block. If a single entrance is breached the whole block may be open to abuse. This makes it difficult to devise security systems which can be successfully monitored and maintained. These problems become even more intractable where several slab blocks are linked together, as was common in schemes built in the late 1960s and 1970s.

These security problems are even more complex in the other common form of recent multi-storey housing – deck access estates. Continuous decks at high level were designed to provide pedestrian access, linking a large number of blocks together and sometimes several estates. Lifts and stairs serve the deck at various points leaving the walkways open to a wide range of crime and abuse. The configuration makes it extremely difficult to secure all the entrances. If the estate is broken down into secure zones it often becomes difficult to provide easy access to all the flats. On a few deck access estates improvement schemes have successfully modified the buildings to make them more secure.

The key to successful remodelling is to break down the access systems. A partial answer is to remove the high level walkways connecting the blocks as suggested by Alice Coleman. But effective solutions need to go further. Within each block the number of dwellings served by each entrance needs to be reduced to as small a number as possible. Access needs to be adapted so that as many flats as possible are reached directly from the ground. The high level pedestrian decks need to be closed off making them short cul-de-sacs rather than through routes. Where possible the walkways should be removed altogether. Parking areas, which are often the focus of misuse, need to be secured or converted to new uses (Figure 6.3).

An illustration of the transformation of a deck access estate is given in Exemplar 5 opposite.

Figure 6.3: **Angell Town Estate, Lambeth. Foreground, the modernised housing with ground level access. Beyond, the unimproved flats reached by a walkway with garages at ground level**

Exemplar 5: Angell Town Estate, Lambeth

Angell Town in the London Borough of Lambeth was one of the large low-rise high-density estates completed in the 1970s. The ground floor was entirely given over to car parking and the four storeys of flat above were all reached from a pedestrian walkway at second floor level. Even those with living rooms and patios at first floor level had to climb up to the second floor to reach them. Originally all the blocks were linked together by bridges. These were removed during the 1980s to reduce crime, although no other improvements were made. This left the blocks isolated and access to the flats even more difficult.

In the early 1990s a very radical improvement scheme was developed which made the estate similar to conventional terraced housing. This involved making separate entrances to all flats directly from the ground. Each vertical pair of maisonettes is provided with a new entrance and stair from the ground level which has been redesigned and newly landscaped. The former walkway space has been enclosed and turned into extra bedrooms. The ground floor parking has also been eliminated – some has been converted to an 'enterprise centre' which includes shops fronting on to the street. The rest has been converted to housing. Spaces which were the focus of abuse – the walkways, the underground parking – have disappeared entirely and with them have gone most of the security problems (*The Architects' Journal*, 1993).

Note: Improvement scheme by Burrrell Fowley Fisher.

Prospects for re-formation

The possibilities of re-forming multi-storey housing present a promising
alternative to demolition and a high degree of confidence that such housing
will be relatively free of management problems. Rededicating blocks does
mean, however, that they are lost to the stock of social housing suitable for
families. They may have to be transferred out of the local authority sector
altogether to organisations specialising in housing for alternative users. Where
slab blocks and deck access estates can be remodelled they remain suitable for
family housing, although it may be necessary to reduce the numbers of family
flats on upper floors and it is certainly desirable to reduce the density of
children on many such estates.

All this reduces the stock of family housing and may put intolerable pressure
on housing authorities. Such transformations may be relatively easy where
there is a surfeit of housing generally or where multi-storey housing is a low
proportion of the stock. In areas where multi-storey blocks predominate,
there are greater difficulties. Pointing to the high number of individual houses
lost through the 'Right to Buy' scheme, urban sociologist Richard Turkington
commented:

> ... the disproportionate scale of construction in such areas as the West
> Midlands, London and the North West means that their share of the
> high rise stock far exceed the national average ... reductions in the
> development of social housing will reduce even further the option of a
> conventional dwelling, and for more and more applicants high rise will
> be the only 'choice' available. The reality of this situation has been
> reluctantly acknowledged by a growing number of local authorities that
> have been obliged to reverse their 'no children in flats' policies.
> (Turkington, 1994, p 150)

This problem is particularly acute where the proportion of flats is high *and*
there is great pressure on authorities to rehouse the homeless and others in
need, as is the case in inner London. Re-use does provide a viable future for
multi-storey blocks but only if more social housing is provided to re-house
many of the families who are already living in them.

Economic regeneration

There is a view that social and economic issues lie at the root of the problems
of housing estates. It may be that physical changes can improve the quality of
multi-storey housing or reduce the impact of crime and anti-social behaviour
but they still fail to address the most critical issues. In 1995, under the Joseph

Rowntree Foundation's 'Action on Estates' initiative, Marilyn Taylor published an analysis of 33 separate research studies on urban regeneration and the problems of housing estates (Taylor, 1995). She concluded that there were three key ingredients of success. One was localised service delivery and management. The second concerned the participation of residents in management and development. These findings echoed the work of the PEP.

The third ingredient was the need to address economic deprivation. It had become apparent that problem estates contained concentrations of disadvantage. High proportions of people were unemployed. Large numbers were unable to work through sickness or disability. There were high numbers of lone parents, recognised as the social group with lowest incomes. Partly, no doubt, as a result of this, there was a syndrome of low attainment in schools linked with estates. This, in turn, meant that young people on estates were least able to compete in the job market. This social polarisation had worsened throughout the 1980s and early 1990s as the stock of social housing diminished and the most disadvantaged became concentrated in the worst estates. While this finding focused greater urgency on economic regeneration, the idea was not new. Measures to increase employment have been incorporated in estate improvement schemes for several years.

Stimulating employment

The link between urban deprivation and employment generation was a key component in community architecture. In the Black Road project in the early 1970s many of the residents had been unemployed. In improving their own homes they acquired building skills and experience in organisation. These skills then helped them to get permanent employment. Many of the community organisations which sprang up in the 1970s were concerned with skill training or community enterprise. Many more were focused on providing childcare to enable single parents to undertake training or employment (Towers, 1995, p 87). In 1987, Anne Power pointed out the importance of jobs based on estates: "... manual jobs are vital to the healthy operation of landlord services. Caretaking, local repairs and cleaning make the critical difference between a habitable estate and a veritable slum." These jobs could all be done, she suggested, by estate residents. Once local offices were established local people could also be employed in many of the administrative jobs involved in managing estates (Power, 1987, p 244).

These principles have been incorporated into quite a number of estate regeneration schemes. At Broadwater Farm in North London, following the notorious riots of 1985, the Youth Association set up a cooperative to train and employ young people on construction projects. It began by building public gardens on the estate but progressed to take on contracts for maintenance work. By 1993 it was able to undertake landscape subcontracts generated by Estate Action funding. Meanwhile government funding had provided 21 'enterprise workshops' on the estate to provide for new businesses and employment initiatives (Towers, 1995, p 220ff). Similar workshops have been provided on many estates by converting the extensive unused underground garages.

The Waltham Forest HAT has also placed a high priority on employment generation. A special sub-committee was established to develop childcare facilities. Two training workshops were set up – a construction skills centre, and a business skills training centre – where residents of the HAT estates could receive training free of charge. This was matched by creating local jobs. The construction contracts required builders to give priority to 'local procurement' with the result that, by 1996, 40 estate-based jobs had been created. Local residents were encouraged to set themselves up in self-employment so as to be able to take on estate maintenance work. In the locally based offices of the HAT, 25% of the jobs are filled by local residents. The HAT has set up a 'career advice and placement' service to advise people on routes into employment and supports 'capacity building', assisting local firms to bid for HAT contracts (WFHAT, 1996).

The downside of these initiatives is that many of them are short term. Many of the jobs depend on the government capital funding injected into estates to finance improvements or redevelopment. The permanent employment created in maintenance and administration will be relatively small. The skills acquired and the confidence gained through work experience should help some tenants at least into permanent employment. Some of the enterprises will succeed. One which has done spectacularly well is the WISE group in Glasgow. This started out providing draught proofing and insulation on housing estates and, by 1995, had mushroomed to employ 243 people and support 800 trainees mainly drawn from the long-term unemployed. It has remained a 'not-for-profit' organisation and has extended its activities to cities throughout Britain (JRF, 1997). Many people do not possess entrepreneurial skills, however, and the failure rate for community enterprise is high. At best employment initiatives can provide tenants in deprived estates with an introduction to employment. They rarely provide a permanent solution.

The urban dimension

There are some estates where employment and economic regeneration are the overriding issues. On some of the most problematic cottage estates there is some physical improvement needed but, basically, there is nothing wrong with the housing. The need to improve income and employment are the key issues. Often this is a product of isolation. Many such estates are on the urban periphery with no local employment and poor transport links. Sometimes the estates become stigmatised so that residents are refused mainstream employment just because of where they live.

Multi-storey housing estates in Britain, however, are almost exclusively in urban areas. Most are closely integrated with the urban economy as a whole. Most, too, are part of the deprived 'inner cities' where there is a general need for employment creation. Regeneration initiatives are often coordinated by local councils on an authority-wide basis. Community organisations operate more often on a neighbourhood or area basis rather than on particular estates. In this sense HATs have a rather particular remit which is outside the context of normal urban government and community activity. On local authority estates, employment projects have a part to play as a component of physical improvement programmes. But they play a supplementary role in the wider context of urban regeneration.

The case for plurality

Taken together, these seven facets characterise the range of approaches found in schemes for regenerating multi-storey estates sponsored by the government since the mid-1980s. Sometimes they are seen as exclusive panaceas. Demolition certainly is. So too is the single-minded approach to design changes promulgated by the DICE project. More often there is some diversity in any particular scheme. But still one facet tends to be seen as the critical or key issue. If there is a perception that security is the main problem an improvement scheme may concentrate on that. Some repairs might be included but the priority of such problems as poor insulation will be diminished. If the presumption is to address water penetration and heat loss it may be conceded that a security system is also necessary. Often, however, no consideration will be given to whether the social mix of the buildings is appropriate.

In the various approaches defined by the different facets there is a strong division between those who favour design/technical solutions and those who have managerial/social preoccupations. Each tends to underestimate the importance of the other. One stresses physical changes and improvements, the other sees the priority in local management, community development and economic regeneration. The result is that projects based purely on technical solutions often break down because of social misuse or managerial failure. Socially oriented solutions may solve these problems but seem to accept that people will continue to live in housing which is below contemporary standards of space, services and amenity.

Noting the debate between design-focused and management-centred approaches, David Page commented:

It seems to [me] that both of these arguments are probably valid, and do not materially contradict each other. Poor areas of housing are not caused exclusively by the property or the people who live in it but by the way in which particular groups of people react to, and interact with, their environment; so both management and development influences are important. (Page, 1993, p 9)

It now seems very clear that effective solutions can only be found in an appropriate combination of both physical and social changes. There has been some awareness of the need for an inclusive approach. In the DoE Estate Action programme, the 'option appraisal' system introduced in 1989 was supposed to ensure a comprehensive approach. In practice, however, it seems that projects have more often been driven by policy or funding priorities which create a presumption for a particular type of solution.

The realistic conclusion must be that all of the seven 'facets' are, or could be, significant. Yet because of the preconception or single-mindedness with which they have been applied each has, on its own, achieved only partial success. The challenge is to define an approach to regeneration that is pluralist – which ensures that all aspects are at least considered in developing improvement schemes. To do this the common threads must be drawn from the various approaches in an attempt to define a model for the regeneration process which is multi-faceted and for which success can be more confidently predicted.

SEVEN

Building a model framework

Analysis of the history revealed the shortcomings that were built into the multi-storey legacy. These inadequacies made the subsequent problems in use understandable, if not inevitable. Early attempts to remedy these problems were often inadequate, providing partial solutions or superficial upgrading. More recent approaches did focus on fundamental issues but, as the seven 'facets' identified in the previous chapter showed, they often revolved around a particular theoretical concept which weighted or distorted the solutions which emerged. Many of the resulting schemes achieved, at best, only limited success. In the theoretical concepts there was also a clear division between approaches that focused on 'design', stressing the importance of physical changes and technical innovations, and those that focused on 'management' issues, emphasising the needs of residents and the value of positively engaging them.

What emerged from the analysis of practice is that there are several distinct aspects to any improvement scheme, all of which may be important. In implementing the regeneration process there are three separate groups of people who have key roles to play if a scheme is to succeed. These are, first, the designers – architects and engineers who define and implement the physical and technical changes; second the managers – this includes not only the project managers and development officers but also the estate management and maintenance staff; third, the residents of the estate. Many problems might have been avoided if the potential residents had been consulted when the estates were built. It is now clear that their engagement is essential if successful solutions are to be found, implemented and sustained in the longer term.

Each of these groups has a different perspective on the regeneration process. In defining a model framework the aim is to draw together the essential components which have emerged from practice and to balance the interests and the respective roles of the three groups whose engagement is essential. The model has seven components:

A *Participation:* the demand for the participation of residents in design and development decisions first emerged from community action in the 1970s. It was absorbed, from the first, into the processes developed to regenerate multi-storey housing In the seven facets described in Chapter Six, participation is a common thread. Even in the most predetermined or technically oriented schemes the need to seek tenant agreement was recognised. In most approaches, however, there was a wish to go beyond merely seeking consent to genuinely involving residents in deciding the future of their estates. After many years' experience the techniques of participation are now well understood. But the record of practice shows that to make participation fully effective two other components are necessary to make the process truly open.

B *Opening options:* often, participation is criticised as a charade – a front erected for public consumption while the real decisions are made behind the scenes by development managers and designers. Too frequently the range of options is limited by preconceptions. Sometimes the process is constrained by policy priorities, sometimes by the negative attitudes of professionals. To counter these tendencies it is necessary to adopt a policy framework and procedures which ensure that basic options are genuinely open to public debate.

C *Open design process:* it is recognised, as a result of best practice, that effective participation informs the decision-making process, producing better solutions which are more likely to stand the test of time. The traditional attitudes of many designers – a closed and secretive approach to the problem-solving process – are a barrier to such effectiveness. Design needs to be stripped of its mystique and the decision-making process made transparent so that residents can be closely involved in defining the physical changes to be made.

D *Technical adequacy:* many technical shortcomings were built into multi-storey housing as a result of the economies made at the time of construction. Addressing these shortcomings became one of the key issues in regeneration, together with the need to improve buildings to contemporary technical standards. It is clear that housing blocks should provide acceptable standards of structural stability, weatherproofing and reliability of services. It is not always necessary, however, to pursue these standards to the highest level. The pursuit of technical excellence must be balanced against both value for money and ease of management and maintenance.

E *Social appropriateness:* it is apparent that, while multi-storey housing provided good standards of space and amenity within the dwellings, it was cheapened by economies in the access systems. Studies of multi-storey housing in use showed the impact of children on the common areas. This suggested that multi-storey flats do not make the most appropriate accommodation for families. In regeneration schemes the concentration on security and surveillance stemmed from abuse of the access systems. More durable solutions were sought through re-forming blocks. Achieving social appropriateness may mean adapting the buildings to make them more suitable for their residents; or offering residents the choice to move so that the housing they vacate can then be adapted and rededicated to occupants with more appropriate life-styles.

F *Local management and maintenance:* the importance of estate-based management was the key finding of the Priority Estates Project (PEP). It became an essential component of the government Estate Action programme. There is good evidence that allocations and transfers are more effectively dealt with by estate-based management. Local monitoring and control have also led to more rapid repairs, critical to maintaining an improvement scheme. In the design process the site-based architect was a key innovation of community architecture and participation through a local office became an essential element of estate regeneration. All these factors emphasise the key role of the estate-based office in both management and design.

G *Social and economic programmes:* omission of communal facilities was an 'economy' often made when estates were built. Many estates were disadvantaged from the start by lack of adequate social provision. More recently, research has drawn attention to the concentration of deprivation and social and economic under-achievement which characterises many multi-storey estates. Both these issues can be addressed by programmes which provide more social facilities but also link these with opportunities for skill training and personal development.

Figure 7.1: **A model framework: relationship between the three participant groups and the components of the model**

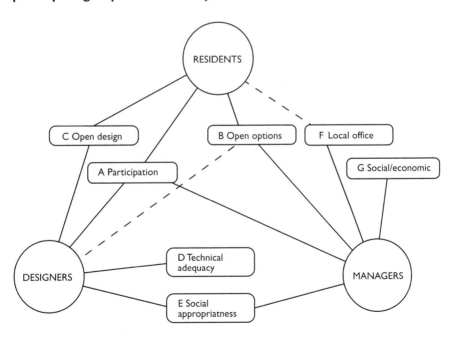

The record of past practice suggests that all seven components are interrelated and interdependent. They also interrelate with the three groups of participants. Components A, B and C focus on the involvement of residents. Components D and E are essentially the contribution of designers. The final two components, F and G, revolve around the role of managers. Most components, however, involve the interaction of more than one group. Figure 7.1 indicates this framework of relationships. No one component can be pursued as a priority or to the exclusion of others, nor can any group be allowed to dominate. The approach must be inclusive and is unlikely to succeed unless every element is strongly developed. So that the model can be more clearly defined, the implications of each of its components are examined in more detail.

Component A: Participation

In the community architecture that emerged in the 1970s, user participation in building design and development was the central tenet. Through trial and error, debate (and quite often considerable conflict) techniques were developed through which people with no previous knowledge of design or technical issues could be successfully involved in decision making. By the early 1980s – when estate modernisation began to get under way – participation was established as a principle and the techniques quite well understood. They have been applied, with increasing sophistication, to estate modernisation schemes ever since.

Participation techniques fall into three broad categories: *communication techniques* which aid the collection or dissemination of information; *decision-making processes* in which residents can take part; and *'hands on' approaches* which allow them a direct role in defining and resolving problems.

- *Communication techniques:* these are essentially 'one-way' channels either distributing or collecting information but allowing little opportunity for debate. Newsletters were a key factor in early community action. They could be cheaply produced and distributed house to house to give information about the progress of campaigns. They still have a useful role to play in regeneration schemes, particularly in stimulating interest at the start of an improvement process. The collection of information is commonly done through questionnaires, although the response rate is often poor. These can request data on family size, ages of children, car ownership and so on which can be helpful in assessing needs. Questionnaires are most useful in collecting factual information but they are also sometimes used to assess residents' attitudes and aspirations. As schemes develop, proposals can be exhibited at a local venue. Designers can be on hand to explain the details and comments can be collected. All these techniques can be useful channels for exchanging information but they do not provide opportunities for discussion and leave interpretation in the hands of the professionals.

- *Decision-making processes:* if estate residents are to be involved in decision making then discussion and debate is essential. This can only happen at meetings. Open meetings may be useful in conveying information or seeking general approval but, with relatively large numbers of people, they provide a poor forum for detailed discussion. Many people find them intimidating and they can easily be dominated by the most outspoken or articulate. Small meetings involving 10 to 15 people are more valuable, providing an environment in which everyone can contribute and decisions can be reached through constructive debate. Small groups may be representative – perhaps elected at a larger meeting – or they may be organised on a block basis or comprise a special interest group. On a detailed level there are many issues which affect residents individually – choice of finishes, layouts of kitchens or the detailed requirements of a disabled resident. Decisions on customising dwellings can be made at one-to-one meetings between designers and residents (Towers, 1995, p 166ff).

- *'Hands on' participation:* various game-like packages have been developed which allow participants to reach design decisions by using visual aids and following a set of rules. In Sweden, for instance, with its long tradition of design participation, a method has been developed where prospective residents use drawings and models to collectively generate alternative site layouts and house designs (Olivegren, 1984). In Britain the only 'hands on' technique in common use is 'Planning for Real', developed by the Neighbourhood Initiatives Foundation – sometimes called 'Design for Real' when used in estate regeneration projects. A large rough model of the estate is prepared and residents are given cards which represent problems or possible improvements. They are then asked to place these on the model in as many places as they think appropriate. Through discussion and evaluation key issues can be identified and options for improvement generated (Gibson, 1979, 1995).

Participation is often criticised by those in practice for being 'unrepresentative'. Sometimes this is simply a cover for the resentment some professionals feel at the supposed challenge to their authority. But there is a problem in ensuring that as many people as possible are effectively involved. No one technique will achieve this but a combination of techniques can help to ensure that a high proportion of those affected are reached by the process. On an estate modernisation project the following combination might be used effectively. A newsletter might inform residents about the onset of a project and call a public meeting. This might discuss general objectives and elect a committee of block representatives to meet with housing officers and designers. The committee would agree the format of a questionnaire and assist in its distribution and collection. A 'Design Day' might be organised with a 'Planning for Real' exercise. Using the information collected the design committee would formulate options and report these back to a public meeting or by a newsletter or an exhibition. The final design would also be approved by a public meeting. The committee would then oversee implementation and set the parameters for individual choice. Figure 7.2 illustrates the relative roles of individuals, small and large groups in such a combination of participation techniques.

Figure 7.2: **The participation of residents as individuals, small groups and large groups in a combination of techniques**

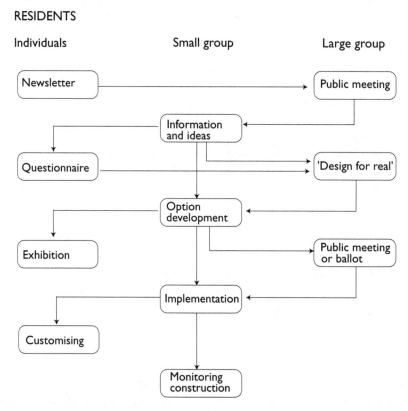

Similar combinations have been used to good effect on estate modernisation schemes since the early 1980s. Effective participation increases the confidence residents have in the future of their estate and contributes significantly to the long-term success of a scheme. Far from diminishing the role of professionals it enriches it by better informing the design and development process. This is likely to lead to more appropriate solutions which meet the real needs of the estate and stand a better chance of passing the test of time.

Component B: Opening options

Such benefits will not be realised if the participation process is constrained by policy preconceptions or procedural rigidity. Achieving successful solutions requires more than to go through the motions of a participation programme. It requires a willingness at the start of the process to open all options for debate rather than channelling discussion along a preconceived route. Early attempts at estate improvement were restricted both by a lack of money dedicated for the purpose and by the conception that the problems were essentially maintenance issues. In the 1970s most of the capital funding available for housing was dedicated to new construction. Work to existing estates had to be financed out of more limited revenue funds. Local authorities tended to divide these funds into rigid programmes – window replacement, lift replacement, entryphone security and so on. Estates would be placed in a programme without reference to the tenants.

Against this the more generalised approaches involved in Islington's Estate Action and Estate Improvement programmes were a considerable departure. Tenants were allowed a range of options for modernising their estates, although they were not allowed the ultimate choice of demolition. This more flexible approach was bolstered by the new funding regime introduced in the early 1980s. But a step back was taken when the government began to intervene directly in estate regeneration. Early schemes developed under the Department of the Environment's (DoE's) Estate Action programme had clear policy priorities. The emphasis was on physical changes – privatising common areas, separating blocks and introducing security systems. Major repairs to the blocks, improvements to the flats themselves or the provision of social facilities would generally not be funded. There seemed to be a preconception that security was the key issue. Participation was often limited to deciding how to achieve the best security scheme. This inflexible approach led to the introduction of a considerable number of concierge-based systems, quite a few of which proved largely ineffective.

The realisation that a more open discussion was needed led the DoE to introduce 'option appraisal'. On the face of it this was a considerable advance, but in many cases the options considered were extremely limited. In many projects only three options were appraised. A minimal works option was included largely to establish what the cost of ongoing maintenance and management would be if no changes were made. A single improvement scheme would be appraised, often based on the perceived priority of security. Demolition was the third and final option. But it was a condition of funding that any redevelopment must be carried out by a housing association or private developer. Many councils, under severe pressure of housing demand, were reluctant to lose their stock. Residents were often doubly anxious about losing their homes and their status and security as council tenants. As a result demolition was effectively precluded. No one seriously contemplated the idea of doing nothing. This left the improvement scheme as the only realistic 'option'. As option appraisal developed, it did become more flexible and offered a wider range of choice. At the point where it became a relatively open and useful procedure, Estate Action was abolished and replaced by the Single Regeneration Budget (SRB). Schemes developed under this funding regime had to be partnerships of local authorities, community organisations and the private sector. Because of the priorities of the private sector participants there was a presumption towards redevelopment – improvement seemed not to be an option.

The result of these policy priorities was that real choice was denied. Very rarely were tenants invited to participate in a debate about the future of their estates in which all the options were truly open. It need not have been so. There were, after all, no funding constraints. If money could be found for redevelopment – the most expensive option of all – then almost any improvement would be possible. A key part of a model framework for estate regeneration must be to open up basic options for genuine choice at the start of the process. These should include demolition, part demolition and change of use as well as various approaches to refurbishment. Only in this way is the most appropriate and successful solution likely to be found.

Component C: Open design process

Traditionally designs are prepared by architects in the secrecy of their offices and then presented to clients for approval. In large projects for institutions or local authorities the 'client' would be an official rather than the eventual user of the building. This 'closed' approach was essentially the one adopted in the housing boom when communication between architects and council officials was minimal and contact between architects and the future tenants non-existent. The lack of scrutiny and discussion in this approach was a major contribution to the shortcomings of multi-storey housing. Opening the design process to the participation of the residents is a big step towards better solutions and avoiding the errors of the past. But it requires of architects two critical changes of attitude, which their training and experience makes difficult for them to make. First they must 'demystify' the design process. Second they must engage in an open-ended debate rather than imposing their own ideas.

Demystifying design

It is extremely difficult for anyone to understand building designs. Architects themselves often have only an approximate idea how their schemes will look when they are built. How much more difficult, then, for those with no design training, to understand proposals put before them. Tenants in multi-storey estates often have little formal education of any sort. There is a wide gulf to be bridged. Designers need to develop new skills in communication. These can be achieved in three ways: simplifying language; producing images which are easily understood; and providing 'samples'.

Opaque language is often employed by professions to baffle the uninitiated and create an exaggerated prestige around their knowledge and skills. Architects often talk in florid terms about the poetry of space and light in an attempt to elevate design into an art. Even the more down-to-earth of the profession commonly lapse into terms such as 'massing', 'solid/void relationship' or 'horizontal emphasis' as a form of design shorthand. Such terms mean nothing to ordinary people and if the design process is to be opened up, the first step is to simplify the language. Professionals need to make a conscious and sustained effort to speak in terms which are in everyday use and commonly understood. This is important in any housing project but may be particularly significant when dealing with estates where significant numbers may be from ethnic minorities whose first language is not English. Interpreters and written translations are often necessary to bridge this gulf.

There is an increasing tendency for architects to treat their drawings as an end in themselves, making them works of art which fail to reveal their designs. Even if they are comprehensible, drawings are often of such high quality that they give the impression that their scheme is a *fait accompli*. Both approaches are antipathetic to an open design process. For good communication drawings need to be simple and bold. During discussion of designs the drawings need to be in a form that is easy to change so that alternatives can be explored. They need to be easily understood. Perspective sketches are often helpful. Plans can be more easily understood if they are placed alongside something which already exists – perhaps a plan of the tenant's own flat. Models can be helpful but, again, they must be in simple form which is easily adaptable rather than a beautifully made representation of the finished scheme. Computer imaging presents a lot of potential but may be most useful in simple exercises such as exploring alternative kitchen layouts rather than in generating comprehensive three dimensional representations.

Finally, it is always useful in a participation exercise to give residents real examples of what might be done. Photographs or slides of similar schemes may be shown at meetings. Coach trips could be organised to visit them. Illustrations can be prepared of alternative designs of particular elements – walls and fences, or paving patterns. At the most basic level real samples of components can be taken to meetings. These might be alternative types of window or kitchen units; they might be samples of finishing materials – wallpaper, tiles for walls and floors. Through simplification the design process can be made more transparent, its mechanism more easily understood by those without professional training.

Starting with a clean sheet

Opening the design process also means that designers must be prepared to enter an open discussion which involves the users, the management and development officers and the other members of the design team. The debate must start without preconceptions, genuinely exploring the relevant issues and examining alternatives before coming to an agreed solution. Sometimes a facilitator or tenants' 'friend' is appointed to act as an interpreter in this process.

In the Angell Town Estate regeneration scheme in Lambeth the Urban Regeneration Consultancy (URC) from Oxford Brookes University was appointed to work with the tenants' organisation, the Angell Town Community Project. They began by training a group of tenants to lead the process. Ian Bentley describes what happened:

> The process was to begin with a blank sheet of paper rather than with the URC making proposals to be discussed. We worked on the basis that the tenants had to educate us about the problems of the estate. Though they knew from experience what they were they could not necessarily identify their causes, so it was our job to help them articulate their knowledge. This we did through a lengthy series of meetings: asking questions rather than suggesting answers. Everyone said the biggest problem was dog excrement. Why? Because there are lots of dogs. Why? Because people feel unsafe without them. This led to a discussion of urban design issues – how few people you meet, how little surveillance there is – and culminated in a point at which we could begin to articulate the tenants' expertise.

This discussion led on to a second stage in which options were developed for the future. In a third stage decisions were made about which options to follow up with the working party preparing a questionnaire to involve all tenants on the estate. Bentley summed up URC's role:

> ... we have been acting as 'expert' clients helping to bring together two cultures of tenants and architects. This has involved reviewing the architects' drawings with the [tenants' organisation], to make sure that their implications are understood, and sometimes persuading architects to clear away cultural blocks which makes it difficult for [tenants] to do so. (*The Architects' Journal*, 1993, p 27)

It is a matter of concern that such facilitators should be necessary. It is a reflection of the prevailing attitudes of an architectural profession that pays far more attention to appearance and the pursuit of visual drama than it does to the needs of building users in general and the residents of housing estates in particular. It is also a result of the priorities of architectural education which largely fails to trains students in the techniques of design participation and the benefits of an open-ended problem-solving approach. Instead they are generally encouraged to 'conceptualise' solutions and develop their schemes as an expression of their own design ideas. Of course, some architects have overcome these handicaps and learned to communicate with tenants, engaging in a dialogue about their problems. But many have not. Tenant representatives and housing managers will need to maintain pressure on their designers if the design process in estate regeneration is to become truly open.

Component D: Technical adequacy

One area where architects and building engineers have not been found wanting is in providing technical solutions to the shortcomings of multi-storey housing. They have exercised considerable enthusiasm and ingenuity in analysing and solving technical problems. Too often, however, they have allowed the pursuit of these solutions to get out of hand. Architects have often been too anxious to try out the latest product or to explore the most advanced technical approach. In dealing with the recladding of multi-storey blocks, for instance, architects have sometimes specified lightweight overcladding systems which have a limited track record and where reliability over a long period is unproved. On occasion they have gone to extraordinary lengths to provide durability – building entirely new external walls or installing complex strengthening systems. On security schemes, electrical engineers have installed the latest 'state of the art' technology, apparently oblivious of the difficulties in operating and maintaining advanced computer systems.

Partly this is due to a fascination with the technical possibilities which has overtones of 'toys for boys'. Partly it is a desire to achieve dramatic transformations. But for the most part, it is the wish to achieve 100% solutions – comprehensive schemes which solve all the problems to the best standards that the latest technology can provide. To a degree, such an approach is defensive and is common to many professions. Designers wish to use their professional skills to the full. If they employ the most advanced technical solutions available they will not only ensure that they have done their best to solve the problems, they will protect themselves against future criticism should problems remain. Unfortunately this approach often leads to poor value for money and a reliance on unproved technology and systems. Quite often a more modest approach would be perfectly adequate.

The improvement of an Islington estate illustrates this principle. Tremlett Grove is a small estate built in the 1960s. It is constructed of precast concrete panels forming an open-faced crate-like structure. The façades are infilled with timber frames housing lightweight panels. Insulation was very poor and the flats suffered from serious condensation and mould growth. Early studies suggested that the only comprehensive solution would be overcladding, providing a new external skin and insulation. This was investigated in some detail but because of the configuration of the buildings the complicated cladding needed proved extremely expensive. An alternative scheme was developed involving replacement double-glazed windows and insulating the existing walls *internally* using inexpensive conventional insulation board. This solution did not entirely solve the problem of 'cold-bridging' at party walls but in every other respect was as good as the overcladding proposal. It proved very significantly cheaper – an effective scheme providing good value for money though not quite a 100% solution.

In most cases far-reaching technical solutions are probably not necessary. But it is necessary that multi-storey housing should be technically adequate. It should be structurally stable and it should not leak. It should not suffer unduly from condensation and to do this must attain an adequate level of insulation, heating and ventilation. In higher blocks the lifts must be good enough quality to be reasonably fast and mostly free from breakdowns. The aim must be to achieve these objectives without overkill; to provide technical solutions which are tried and tested; which are adequate for their purpose but still provide good value for money. It is also important that technical solutions address the question of sustainability. Ease of maintenance is a key issue, especially since social landlords have found efficient repair systems notoriously difficult to organise.

Component E: Social appropriateness

It is unquestionable that many of the problems in multi-storey housing are the result of the anti-social behaviour of some of the occupants. The design and physical form of much multi-storey housing make it inappropriate for certain social groups. Generally it has provided an unsuitable environment for families with young children. The absence of outdoor play space adjoining the home deprives the children and creates stress for their parents. At the same time the damage done to the communal areas by children and teenagers is one of the key causes of decline and stigmatisation. Research has shown that these problems are worse in estates where child density is high. Evidence suggests that the abuse is more serious on estates with extensive and uncontrolled common access systems. Multi-storey estates are also unsuitable for the small minority of tenants who have serious problems of social orientation – those who cause major noise nuisance or harass their neighbours.

While the drawbacks of flats as family housing have been widely accepted it is also evident that some groups adapt happily to multi-storey blocks. Flats do have inherent advantages over houses. Flat dwellers are relieved of the responsibility for organising external repair and maintenance or the necessity to tend a garden. Many feel more at ease at a high level where their security is protected by having only a single access and they are less easily disturbed by noise and traffic. On top of that there is uninterrupted sunlight and often spectacular views to enjoy. For many young people, single people, childless couples and for many elderly people, these are positive attractions.

Successful regeneration must attempt to achieve 'social appropriateness'. This means that either the population must be changed to suit the housing form or the housing itself must be adapted to make it more suitable for families and vulnerable tenants. Tower blocks often contain mostly small flats, particularly those that were built as part of mixed development schemes. Many can successfully be secured, upgraded and rededicated for use as student housing, sheltered housing for elderly people or simply let to those who choose to live there and whose life-styles are suited to living high.

Most multi-storey housing designed for family accommodation is, in fact, in relatively low blocks mostly not exceeding five or six storeys. Such blocks can generally be adapted. The key is to divide them up, modifying the access system to group a small number of dwellings around a secured entrance. Any anti-social behaviour can then be more easily monitored and controlled. If good play areas and open space can be provided close by, such blocks can be almost as suitable for children as housing reached directly from the ground.

The question is how this can be achieved. If tall blocks are to be rededicated, other housing must be provided to rehouse the families currently living in them. This is clearly a serious logistical problem especially given the pressures of demand and the fact that multi-storey housing is an increasing proportion of the stock of urban authorities. Policy and proprietorship may be a barrier. Dedicating blocks to housing elderly people might not be problematic – older tenants are commonly provided for in the social housing stock – but local authorities do not generally provide housing for students or single people, nor do most housing associations. Rededication for such occupants might involve complex negotiations with universities or with private developers.

Most lower-scale blocks can be adapted to make them more suitable for their residents. Even so, 'social appropriateness' can only be fully realised if people are not only housed in suitable accommodation, but accommodation in which they can happily settle. This is probably best achieved through a considerable degree of 'decanting'. Emptying flats as improvement work proceeds has several benefits. Residents are spared the noise and disruption of building work. The flats themselves can be comprehensively refurbished. Most important it offers choice and resolves imbalances. Tenants moved out can be offered a choice of new housing suitable to their needs. They can also be offered the choice of returning to their old flat. Overcrowding and under-occupancy can be resolved. There is also an opportunity to resolve conflicts and to reduce child density to a manageable level.

Component F: Local management and maintenance

The idea of decentralisation first emerged in the 1960s when the reform of local government established much larger authorities more remote from the communities they served. As a counterweight a well researched theory established that people living in cities identified strongly with small geographical areas. In the early 1970s a few experimental 'neighbourhood councils' were established (Towers, 1995, pp 138ff, 66ff). In 1980 the West Midlands Borough of Walsall decentralised its housing services into a network of 33 neighbourhood offices (Seabrook, 1984). In this they set a trend. Over the following few years quite a few urban authorities followed suit. Sometimes just housing services were decentralised. Sometimes other services were included (Hoggett and Hambleton, 1987). Almost always the local office had a neighbourhood basis which might include several estates as well as council-owned housing in converted older terraces.

The work of the PEP examined locally based offices. It established the value of local management in dealing more effectively with allocations, lettings and as a base to respond to problems creating conflict on estates. It also concluded that locally based systems helped to provide a more rapid and effective maintenance service. Most importantly, surveillance of the common areas was improved which helped to ensure that they were better cleaned and maintained in secure order and good repair. However, while there are many examples of decentralised offices, their organisation varies considerably. Catchment areas vary in size and the degree to which service delivery is decentralised also differs from one borough to another.

It is probably not critical that the office is actually on the estate, as the Estate Action programme insisted. After all, estates vary in size a great deal. What is important is that the office can be reached within easy walking distance and that it has a team dedicated to the estate. Experience suggests that the degree of local control *is* critical. In Islington, some housing services were decentralised but central departments kept a controlling role. Some cleaning and minor repairs were decentralised. Other cleaning services and more complex repairs remained centralised. The lack of clarity produced by this split responsibility created inefficiencies which ensured that poor maintenance and repair has remained a major bone of contention between tenants and the council.

The involvement of tenants through the local office is a key factor both in the development of improvement schemes and in long-term management and maintenance. In early community architecture schemes such as Byker and Black Road a key feature was that the architects' offices were based on site. Similarly, early neighbourhood councils were used as a vehicle for community participation in generating development proposals. For successful regeneration the local office can provide a base where the designers can meet tenants and carry out some of the work. Commonly, too, they are used as a permanent location for housing development and liaison officers to ensure effective communication with tenants in improvement schemes.

To make sure that the success of an improvement scheme is sustained in the long run it is important that tenants remain involved in the monitoring and supervision of service provision. Tenant participation through a representative structure is likely to ensure that management and maintenance problems are quickly brought to the attention of housing officials. The need for managers to report to a locally based committee is likely to maintain pressure to preserve and improve the quality of procedures and practice of the local office.

Component G: Social and economic programmes

Many multi-storey housing estates have become concentrations of multiple deprivation. This is partly a result of their stigmatisation. 'Hard-to-let' estates come to house increasing proportions of those with the least choice – those with the weakest social and economic skills. Such estates are characterised by high unemployment and low economic activity; by high proportions of single parents and large numbers of children; and by low levels of educational attainment (Power and Tunstall, 1995). Low attainment lead to low job and work search skills which, in turn, lead to unemployment and welfare dependency. It often means poor social skills which can lead people into debt, or to alcohol or drug abuse – all of which lie at the root of much personal conflict and many health problems. It often also means poor parenting skills which contribute to delinquency and youth crime – and lead in turn to poor educational attainment.

The long-term future of estates can only be assured if special attention is given to breaking this cycle. Part of the answer is to introduce programmes of employment generation and skill training. Localised job creation and training schemes can be included in improvement schemes, sometimes through requirements built into improvement contracts. However, these are inevitably small-scale. Much greater impact is likely to come from wider public policy initiatives, particularly the 'Welfare to Work' scheme announced in the 1997 Budget. This draws strength from substantial central funding but it may be possible to focus the benefits by working with localised community organisations. Even if successful, the generation of employment skills is not enough. Those with the lowest social skills are in the greatest need of the support provided by community facilities.

To improve this social support it is critical to make good the deficit evident in many estates from the start. Too many were simply stacked up housing units with bleak and empty outdoor spaces and a total lack of built spaces for social use. The residents of many estates need nurseries and creche facilities which give children a good start, and provide relief for their parents allowing them the opportunity to work or train for work. They need attractive and secure communal gardens where children can play out of doors in safety. They need community centres which might be crucial to the social life of many residents providing a focus for child and youth activities; recreational and sporting facilities for adults; and day centres for elderly people. Perhaps most of all there is a need for activities and facilities specifically targeted at young people. These can be highly significant in combating crime and improving social orientation among disaffected youths.

The critical challenge is to redress deprivation and generate social cohesion. This involves a realisation that social housing does not consist of shelter alone. It must include social and communal facilities and action must be taken to improve the skill levels and employment status of its residents. It does not follow, however, that all this is necessarily an integral part of an estate regeneration scheme. Multi-storey estates are part of the wider urban fabric and many of these facilities and opportunities might be available elsewhere. Training schemes might be provided by other agencies; social facilities might be available in other centres nearby. But a regeneration scheme cannot succeed unless it recognises these social and economic requirements, makes the necessary connections, and seeks to reintegrate the estate into the wider community.

Testing the model

The seven components of the model have all been drawn from the record of experience in regenerating multi-storey estates over a period of 15 years or more. The basis of the model is, therefore, soundly rooted in practice. It should have value as an operational tool which might be applied to new projects with some confidence of success. In order to substantiate its value a structured study was devised through which the model could be tested on five case studies in which improvement was substantially complete. The test revolved around applying the model to a focused sample of improvement projects then drawing conclusions about their success. To give a good level of comparability the selection criteria for the studies were set so that as many background factors as possible were common. The case studies were carried out on estates which had experienced problems in use and some degree of technical problems as well. They were schemes where refurbishment was the primary method of improvement rather than demolition. All the estates were in a similar location with comparable social structure and housing demand. All were improved under the same funding regime and by a similar organisational structure.

Information about the five case study estates was drawn from interviews with representatives of each of the three groups identified as key contributors – designers, managers and residents. The interviews were backed up with site inspections and material from documentary sources. Using the information collected, an assessment was made of the degree to which the improvement process on the estate under study matched the seven components of the model. A judgement was also made of the degree of success achieved by each scheme using seven separate 'measures of success'. These were:

- the extent of graffiti and vandal damage;
- the cleanliness and standard of maintenance of the common areas;
- changes in overall housing quality and 'manageability';
- changes in transfer requests, empty dwellings and refusal of offers;
- improvements in the comfort of the flats;
- improvements in the security of common areas;
- changes in quality of life on the estate.

Assessment of both the extent of conformity with the model and the degree of success achieved was made in qualitative and quantitative terms. Information was collected from a wide variety of sources which allowed balanced judgements to be made. For ease of comparison a score was also applied to each of the components of the model and each measure of success. Full details of the rational, methodology and the case study results are given in the Appendix.

The basis of the test was that if the model has value a good degree of correlation would be expected. In each case the degree to which the case study scheme conformed to the model would be expected to be similar to the level of success. A high degree of conformity to the model should be matched by a high degree of success – and vice versa. In four out of the five case studies there was just such a correlation:

- In case study A there was very little correlation with the components of the model. As might have been predicted the project had proved ineffective with very little of the improvement sustained for a significant period.
- Case study C showed a moderate degree of conformity with the model, with a score of about 50%. This was matched with a similarly moderate degree of success.

- In two of the studies – D and E – there was a close match with the components of the model with high scores achieved. Both schemes also scored highly on the measures of success, and had provided improvements sustained over a long period.

These four results suggest that there is a close correlation between the degree to which the model framework is followed and the level of success which is likely to be achieved.

The fifth scheme – case study B – was somewhat out of line. This study showed less close correlation than the others. While there was only moderate conformity to the model there was a higher degree of success than might have been anticipated. It can happen that one very strong factor can have a disproportionate impact – a strong design or a determined emphasis on improved management. In this case the mismatch probably derived from the strength of the design and specification of the security scheme and the fact that a special system, outside the normal management procedure, had been introduced to maintain it. While such distortions can produce considerable success in resolving some high profile problems, comprehensive improvement generally requires the application of all the components of the model. The most effective changes in management or security will not provide durable improvement if the flats remain substandard or the buildings technically inadequate.

The sample used in the test was small and the results are not conclusive. Further experiment would be useful in providing corroboration and refinement. With these limitations, the overall results of testing the model against the completed schemes suggests that it has considerable value as a procedural framework which should produce successful improvement schemes for the regeneration of multi-storey estates. It may be open to distortion by a very strong single factor but it seems to provide a convincing yardstick against which to evaluate the likely effectiveness of proposals in most circumstances.

EIGHT

Prospects for transformation

The lessons drawn from past practice made it possible to define a model framework for regeneration – one which requires a multi-faceted, holistic approach. The components of the model are a set of principles which could probably be successfully applied to the regeneration of any housing estate. Obviously, however, estates differ in their physical form. The contrast between low-rise 'cottage estates' and multi-storey housing is self-evident and many of the elements of successful regeneration schemes would need to take account of these physical differences. Within the sphere of multi-storey housing there are several different basic types, each of which presents different problems and opportunities for transformation.

The oldest types of multi-storey housing are the four- and five-storey walk-up blocks – 'tenement'-type estates. There is good evidence that such blocks can be successfully transformed to make good quality housing. Tower blocks are the most distinctive form of multi-storey housing. For these blocks, too, despite their poor reputation, there are many effective schemes which show they can be successfully adapted and improved. For other types of multi-storey housing the evidence is less clear. Deck access estates, where blocks are linked together by a network of pedestrian walkways, present seemingly intractable problems. Slab blocks are another area of uncertainty, particularly where they are linked together to form extensive chains of multi-storey housing. The issues surrounding the regeneration of such estates are complex. They need more detailed investigation and careful consideration.

Tenements and tower blocks

It is evident from Islington's Estate Action programme and other projects that 'tenement-type' estates can be successfully modernised (see Exemplars 1 and 2, pp 96-7). Most tenement blocks were built between the wars or in the late 1940s. Many have now become unpopular and regarded as poor housing, but this is largely due to low space standards, poor services and disrepair. With sufficient investment these shortcomings can be remedied relatively easily. More importantly, the form of the blocks mean they can readily be adapted. Ground and first floor flats can be combined vertically so that maisonettes can be provided for families with private gardens and their own separate entrances. The upper floors can be replanned to make small flats for households without children. Four-storey blocks generally have staircase access so that each entrance serves only a few flats and can easily be secured. Five-storey blocks with balcony access can be provided with lifts and access to the upper floors broken down into separate zones secured by electronic intercoms. The layout of estates often means that common areas can be divided into communal gardens private to each block. Such schemes have proved successful over more than 10 years.

The issues associated with tower blocks are also clear-cut. Sometimes these blocks are structurally unstable and this is particularly true of some built using non-traditional construction. In such cases demolition may be the only solution. If this is not necessary the technical problems can usually be solved by some form of overcladding and by renewing the services (see Exemplars 3 and 4, pp 123-4). Research has shown that security systems generally work well in tower blocks because all access can be concentrated on one entrance. A review of concierge schemes in tall buildings by the Safe Neighbourhoods Unit (SNU) suggest a high level of success (DoE/SNU 1994b). A post-completion survey of a CCTV security scheme in a tower block estate in Glasgow showed increased tenant confidence and a dramatic reduction in crime (Scottish Homes, 1999). The key area of uncertainty concerns the social structure of the population of such blocks. Where tower blocks are rededicated – to elderly people, to students or simply to those who choose to live there – they seem to provide successful housing. Continued occupation by families may cause problems but even this may be possible given sufficient investment, as Richard Turkington found in his research:

> What we have learnt is that futures can be built into tower blocks. It is an expensive business whose cost continues when refurbishment creates a commitment to higher levels of service. New uses can be found for blocks, but within limits. Not all the elderly want to be vertically sheltered; singles tend to become childless couples, and the couples with child. which ends that convenient cycle of designated allocations. Foyers, hostels, combined office space and starter flats, all can be accommodated within the tower blocks. But for all 368 blocks in Birmingham alone, the real challenge is refurbishment for family housing or general needs use....(Turkington, 1997, p 26)

Detailing the improvement which can be made to the exteriors and the common areas, he concluded:

> The tower block has confounded all the conventions. Surveys have, time and again, recorded satisfaction with Parker Morris space standards, but dissatisfaction with neighbour noise, poor heating systems and the

block. All can now be transformed with the value added of a safe and secure environment. The household of the 1990s has other priorities on its agenda than 30 years ago, and these can be met within the defensible tower block. We are at last in the position of being able to tame the tower block.... (Turkington, 1997, p 26)

A good example of such 'taming' is Trellick Tower, the 31-storey block in West London designed by prominent modernist Erno Goldfinger. The flats in the block provided generous space standards and good quality design. But the access system deteriorated rapidly after its completion in 1971. The lifts, stairs and corridors became badly abused – dirty and fouled, strewn with litter and refuse and defaced with graffiti. The flats were increasingly hard-to-let. In 1984 a new residents' association was formed and began to campaign for improvements. Within two years the council had changed its policy, agreeing to let flats only to people who wanted to live in a tall tower. A series of improvements followed, culminating in the introduction of a concierge system in 1994. Security staff now monitor the single common entrance on the ground floor and surveillance is backed up by CCTV throughout the building (Carroll, 1999). Decline was arrested and reversed. The building was listed in 1998 and "... is now particularly sought after as an upmarket address" (Brown, 1999).

Architectural journalist Robert Bevan, drawing on several examples of newly built and successfully refurbished tower blocks, underlined what can be achieved. Sensitively modernised, tower blocks can provide quality homes and remain a valuable resource in the social sector. They can even provide a model for developers building new housing for sale. But he drew this lesson from the controversies surrounding the design of various types of multi-storey housing:

> With the perspective of a few decades it has become clear that the real architectural villains were the endlessly-mundane slab blocks, built to accommodate crane runs more than people or ... warren-like ersatz communities.... (Bevan, 1997)

This conclusion neatly categorised the greatest area of uncertainty. The older types of multi-storey housing – the tenements of the 1930s and 1940s and the tower blocks of the 1950s and early 1960s – present relatively clear-cut problems and considerable opportunity for transformation and modernisation. The slab block and deck access estates – mostly constructed more recently – seem beset by greater problems and much more resistant to successful improvement.

The problem estates – five case studies

Five case studies of regeneration schemes on problem estates were carried out. The primary purpose of the studies was to test the model described in Chapter Seven and the feedback on the value of the model has already been described. It was important, however, that as stern a test as possible should be devised. There was little point in undertaking case studies on tenement estates or tower blocks. For both these types of housing there is a good deal of evidence about what approaches are likely to be successful. The case studies were therefore selected from the most difficult types of estate – slab blocks, linked slabs and deck access estates. They therefore offer important lessons on the likely success or failure of different approaches to regenerating such estates.

Five estates in inner London were selected as case studies. All were improved by local authorities using Department of the Environment (DoE) Estate Action funding. They are:

Case study A   Market Estate, Islington – *linked slab blocks*
Case study B   Packington Estate, Islington – *deck access*
Case study C   Gloucester Grove Estate, Southwark – *linked slab blocks*
Case study D   North Peckham Estate, Southwark – *deck access*
Case study E   Priory Court Estate, Waltham Forest – *slab blocks*

The characteristics of the five selected estates are shown in Table 8.1.

Table 8.1: **Key characteristics of the five case study estates**

	Market Estate	Packington Estate	Gloucester Grove Estate	North Peckham Estate	Priory Court Estate
Completion date	1968	Late 1960s	1972	1973	Early 1950s
Number of dwellings	277	538	1,210	1,444	507
Number of blocks	6	27	29	65	22
Type	Linked slabs	Deck access	Linked slabs	Deck access	Slab blocks
Height	Eight and four storeys	Six storeys	Four, six and eight storeys	Five storeys	Mainly six storeys
Construction	Traditional	Heavy panel system	Heavy panel brick clad	Traditional	Concrete frame, infil panels
Inception of improvement	1987	1988	1990	1990	1992

Figure 8.2: **Packington Estate, Islington. New estate office, entrance and lift shaft**

Case study B: Packington Estate, Islington

Packington was built in the late 1960s using a large concrete panel system of industrialised building. There are 538 dwellings – 60% of them large family flats. The buildings are six storeys high throughout – 27 blocks are arranged in a series of courtyards. All the buildings were linked together by pedestrian decks at ground and third floor levels, each deck serving flats on three levels and completely open to public access. This deck access system proved the key to the estate's decline. Within a few years the estate became notorious for its 'gang culture'. The open decks provided covered spaces for congregating and loitering and innumerable routes for escape in case of trouble.

In 1988 an estate working party began to plan improvements. Both the needs of the estate and the priorities of the DoE Estate Action funding pointed to a security scheme. The aim of the scheme was to break down the access system into secure zones. The overhead bridges were demolished and the walkways closed to through passage. Separate access was provided to upper and lower levels. On each deck metal screens were erected to restrict access from each entrance to a relatively small number of dwellings. These screens could be broken open in an emergency by a fireman's axe but could otherwise not be used for access. The aim was to allow a maximum of 25 dwellings reached from each entrance. As part of the scheme the courtyards were made private to specific groups of flats and provided with new landscape and play equipment. The DoE insisted on a new estate management office to operate the concierge system through camera surveillance and remote control of entry points.

In 1997, two years after completion of the final phase, the scheme seemed to be operating well. All the entryphone gates were secure and vandalism was very limited. The success seemed to depend on two factors. First the choice of materials for the entrances. These are metal gates set in metal grilles and secured by magnetic locks. Such a configuration in the most vulnerable part of the system is very hard to damage. The second factor is that the estate office has established a rapid response system so that breakdowns in the entryphone security are repaired very quickly. The landscaping and play areas have survived very well and have helped to lift the environmental quality of the estate.

New communal garden with secured and restricted access

Note: Improvement scheme by David Ford Associates and Islington Architects Department.

Figure 8.3: **Gloucester Grove Estate, Southwark. North façade showing new entrance enclosures**

Case study C: Gloucester Grove Estate, Southwark

Gloucester Grove, completed in 1972, comprises 29 linked slab blocks mostly six or eight storeys high. The estate had 1,210 dwellings – most of them family flats. Flats were reached by internal corridors on alternate floors accessed by 'drums' – circular structures containing stair and lift shaft – which linked two or three blocks together. The access system was continuous so that it was possible to walk the length of the estate at every level. The design made the public areas easy prey to abuse. Most stairs and corridors became layered in graffiti. Worse, rubbish was frequently dumped in them. Setting fires became a popular pastime for estate children and many staircases and corridors were blackened and fire-damaged. The pressure for more radical action peaked when someone died in a fire in a stairwell.

In 1991 the Neighbourhood Forum decided on an Estate Action bid and set up a 'project team' composed of tenants and officers. The scheme was based on radical changes in the access system. New lifts, stairs and refuse chutes were built – all sheathed in glass block enclosures. In the middle of the larger blocks, flats were demolished and new lift/stairs constructed. This reduced the number of dwellings per entrance although some still give access to up to 50 flats. All the main entrances were given electronic security and cameras.

On each of the upper levels a secured secondary entrance served a small group of up to eight flats. Fire escape doors were installed between each group which could be opened in an emergency. Originally there was a management office on the estate where security was to be monitored by a remote concierge.

The scheme has achieved critical success, winning an design award in 1995. But within two years there were reasons for concern. Security had failed on some main entrances and several secondary entrances. Some of the fire escape doors had been brought into use and this might open the blocks up again to unrestricted access. The intended concierge had never been appointed. Initially, 'reactive' monitoring of the camera tapes had been done but this had since declined. Despite these shortcomings the buildings remained in good condition and very clean. Some vandalism was apparent and a little low level graffiti. It was clear, however, that the situation was manageable and could be retrieved with more vigorous maintenance.

The stair/lift drums which originally linked the whole estate and were subject to intensive abuse

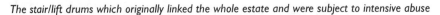

Note: Improvement scheme by Southwark Building Design Service.

Figure 8.5: **Priory Court Estate, Waltham Forest. Blocks improved with new roofs, windows and cladding**

Case study E: Priory Court Estate, Waltham Forest

Priory Court is the oldest estate of the five case studies, built in the earl 1950s. The 507 dwellings were mostly in six-storey slab blocks. Access to th blocks was straightforward, with a single stair/lift serving each group of 1. flats. When completed the estate was celebrated as a model of modern housing but time and rising expectations took their toll. The flats had no heating and were poorly insulated. The walls began to crack; the flat roofs began to leak. By the 1980s the estate had acquired a bad reputation which had more to dc with the deterioration of the housing and the concentration of low-income tenants than with crime or vandalism.

In 1991 an Estate Action bid was made and a wide range of options were considered. These were developed by a tenants' committee and put to a ballo of all residents. The selected scheme included the demolition of seven blocks and their replacement with family houses. The remaining 14 slab blocks were to be fully refurbished. This included central heating, new kitchens and bathrooms and full redecoration. New lifts were included and the stairwells secured. New windows and a proprietary overcladding provide better insulation and protect the walls from water penetration. The leaking roofs were countered by the addition of lightweight barrel vault roofs. These act as a 'rainscreen' to the old roofs and were cheaper than normal pitched roofs. Better use has been made of the ground. New flats have been developed at the base of the blocks. These provide dwellings suitable for disabled people and have their own private gardens. New secure communal gardens have been developed for each block which include play areas for children. A new community centre was planned. New workshops were proposed and European Union funding was obtained to train tenants in skills such as childcare, computer literacy, business and secretarial expertise.

In 1997 the blocks completed earliest still seemed in very good condition. The security on the blocks remained intact; no graffiti was in evidence; and the new external areas and communal gardens remained in good condition. Tenants expressed satisfaction with the scheme and housing officials were confident of a reduction in management problems, mainly because all tenants were being rehoused. Good management was also helped by an on-site office and the involvement of tenants in the supervision of the estate management contract. The scheme appeared highly successful, although it was still a long way from completion.

One of the unimproved blocks which had deterioated into poor condition

Note: Improvement scheme by Waltham Building Consultancy.

Lessons from the case studies

The impact of the five improvement schemes varied. One – Market Estate – almost entirely failed largely due to the limited consideration of the options available and their implications. Packington Estate provided a successful security scheme, despite limitations in the initiation procedure and consultation process. This was mainly due to the strength of the security design and the efforts made to maintain it. The scheme at Gloucester Grove Estate provides a dramatic visual improvement but the security system remains vulnerable. The North Peckham and Priory Court schemes were both very successful due to extensive consultation and the wide range of improvements carried out. Details of the research and the results for each case study are given in the Appendix.

The success or failure of estate regeneration schemes depends on a complex interaction of many factors. The model framework suggests that a positive outcome depends on the cooperative interaction of designers, managers and residents; open-ended review of problems and issues; design and technical innovation; and the introduction of facilities and procedures to ensure long-term success. Without detracting from the importance of the interaction certain lessons can be drawn from the case studies about some of the key factors involved in transforming the most problematic multi-storey estates. In many respects these lessons do not entirely support the presumptions which have shaped regeneration policies and improvement schemes.

Security

Unquestionably, the security of the common areas is one of the most critical problems of multi-storey housing. When it is inadequate it not only induces fear of crime but, through the resulting vandalism and abuse, diminishes residents' perceptions of the quality of their housing. Both these factors contribute significantly to the unpopularity of estates and lead to their becoming 'hard-to-let'. The key to generating security on the case study estates was to break them down into separate zones with each common entrance serving as few dwellings as possible. It is important that each zone is self-contained and not linked to other zones. If the security in any one zone does break down that becomes a clearly defined and manageable problem and the security of other zones remains unaffected. This conclusion fits with past research and confirms Oscar Newman's findings of the early 1970s.

The conventional wisdom about concierge systems, however, is not confirmed. These have, undoubtedly, worked in situations such as tower blocks where there is a single entrance and the security staff can establish a personal rapport with residents. The idea of 'remote' concierges monitoring multiple entrances through CCTV and electronic intercom systems was promoted by the government during the late 1980s as a solution to slab and deck access estates. It has not proved effective. Such a system was adopted at Chalkhill Estate in Brent and deemed a failure. Three of the case study estates were supposed to have such remote concierge systems. None of them was ever implemented. Central budgets, under increasing strain, could not provide funding and tenants could not afford the considerable addition to their rents which would have been required to raise the money from the estates. The scheme at Market Estate was dependent on the effective operation of a concierge system. That it was not set up was a key reason for the failure of the scheme. Both at Packington and Gloucester Grove Estates, remote concierges were intended although they were never brought into operation. In these estates, however, the critical improvement was to break down the blocks into small zones which helps to maintain security without surveillance. On both estates the CCTV system has been used to a degree for reactive monitoring – using the tapes to identify and deal with wrongdoers after an incident has occurred. It is recognised that retrospective monitoring needs to be strengthened but may be the best solution – much cheaper than continuous monitoring and almost as effective. Retrospective monitoring has subsequently been introduced at Market Estate.

One other lesson can be drawn from these salutary experiences. It has been clear from the earliest attempts to install security systems that careful commissioning is critical. It is fatal to start the system in operation until it has been fully tested, every tenant has been provided with keys and fully briefed on how to operate the system. Failure to do this has led to tenants being forced to break into, or sometimes out of, their blocks. Effective commissioning requires careful and methodical organisation. Shortcuts almost certainly lead to disaster. Poor implementation has caused the failure of many security schemes and was one of the key factors in the breakdown of the system at Market Estate.

Technical adequacy

Generally, the case studies showed that designers had provided an adequate technical response to the problems on the estates. On Market Estate, the design of the entrances could have had a better specification which might have prevented them being wrecked, although this probably was not the key factor leading to the breakdown of the scheme. The entrance design at Packington Estate, on the other hand, proved particularly appropriate – secure and easily maintained without invoking a fortress image. On the other estates, design and specification of new work showed the competence which it is reasonable to expect from architects for whom technical expertise should be a stock in trade.

The verdict was less clear on the 'high-tech' security installed at Market Estate, Packington and Gloucester Grove Estates. These included a multitude of surveillance cameras linked to systems which were designed to provide remote monitoring from a central point. This was to be done using computer-controlled multiple-screen monitors and electronic intercom with all entrances and with tenants' flats. To a considerable degree this technology had broken down. Either there were problems at commissioning stage or the system was difficult to maintain in effective operation. Nowhere was the technology being used to its full effect. This was partly because neither landlords nor tenants could afford the substantial staff costs needed to make it fully operational; and partly because the systems were so complex that few would have the skill to exploit their full potential. The security schemes that succeeded relied primarily on physical barriers and easily maintained entrance controls. It is highly questionable whether the technology justified its high capital cost and whether a more simple system might have been just as effective.

One factor that should be emphasised is that it is not simply a question of solving technical problems. The way they were solved had a major impact on some schemes. The new roofs and overcladding at Priory Court Estate transformed the appearance of the blocks. The new entrances and, particularly, the landscaping at Packington Estate introduced new variety and softness to an environment which had been harsh and monotonous. The visual quality of the improvements to Gloucester Grove Estate was rewarded with an award for good design form the Royal Institute of British Architects. Good design can play a significant part in transforming tenant confidence in their home environment. This can be particularly telling if residents are closely involved in the decision-making process. The improvements at North Peckham Estate are not of outstanding visual quality but they did change radically the appearance of the estate, largely as a result of choices made by the tenants themselves.

Decentralised management

All the five estates had some form of decentralised management. The evidence suggests, however, that the greater the degree of decentralisation and the more involvement by the tenants, the greater the success in maintaining the integrity of the scheme after completion of the technical work. In this, the case studies support the conclusions of the Priority Estates Project (PEP). Packington Estate, with its own dedicated on-site office, was more successful than Market Estate where the on-site office was also responsible for several other estates. This relative success was achieved despite the fact that both were working within the same cleaning and maintenance regime which was over-centralised, slow in response and ineffectively organised. In neither of the Islington estates were tenants involved in the management of the estate and this marks out the difference from Priory Court Estate. There, as at Market, the on-site office served several estates but tenants were involved in supervising the maintenance contracts and this seemed to have clear benefits on the ground.

The best systems were in the two Southwark estates. Both had on-site offices dedicated just to the estate. The borough has introduced delegated budgets so that each office has its own defined funding for repairs, cleaning and grounds maintenance. On North Peckham the Council has gone further and delegated day-to-day management to an Estate Management Committee controlled by tenant representatives. The result of these changes was evident in a high standard of cleaning and maintenance. Partly, such strongly localised management was possible because of the sheer size of the estates – both in excess of 1,200 dwellings. The more recent decision to demolish large parts of both estates has made necessary a reorganisation which will merge estate offices. This will make management less local and may have a deleterious effect on its quality.

Social appropriateness

Past theory and practice suggest that reducing child density in general and, in particular, housing families on the ground, are key factors in successful regeneration. The case studies carefully considered the degree of social appropriateness but the findings do not wholly support the preconceptions. On all the case study estates, families continued to be housed on the upper floors. Given the shrinkage of housing in the public sector – and particularly the great reduction in houses with gardens – this is inevitable. On Market Estate this was clearly one of the key problems with children and teenagers continuing to cause extensive damage and disruption. On Packington Estate, on North Peckham Estate and on Priory Court Estate the housing of families off the ground seemed to create fewer problems. This was partly a result of the security system which meant that only a small number of flats shared each common entrance. This seemed to ensure that any abuse by children was quickly and easily brought under control. While dwellings with private gardens may still be the best family accommodation – particularly for those with small children – a flat in a block which is not too high with a well designed communal garden at ground level may provide an appropriate alternative.

On the other hand there was evidence that non-family flats on upper floors were not trouble free. The London Borough of Southwark had a policy of 'underletting' in an attempt to reduce density. This meant that one-bedroom flats were only let to single people rather than couples or single parents. A large proportion of these single people were teenagers who were homeless or who had been in care – groups towards which the authority had a statutory obligation. On Gloucester Grove Estate two blocks had a high concentration of one-bedroom flats, most of which were occupied by single youngsters. These blocks had serious management problems with a high incidence of parties, noise nuisance, drug problems and higher levels of vandalism than on other parts of the estate. It is probable that such young people are more appropriately housed in 'special needs' centres such as the growing numbers of 'foyers' which provide support and training in life skills (Ward, 1997). While non-family upper floor flats are generally trouble free, in the context of lack of housing investment and a shortage of appropriate housing they can be the focus of unexpected problems.

One measure of social appropriateness is the degree of choice offered to tenants. It has become evident that multi-storey housing is more likely to be successful if those who live in flats do so by choice. On one level it can be argued that if tenants opt for refurbishment rather than redevelopment they have chosen to live in flats. Clearly, however, choice is most positively offered if tenants have the chance to move. In some of the case studies this choice was not offered. On Gloucester Grove Estate, even after improvement, some families continued to occupy flats far smaller than they needed. This caused concentrations of children which placed the improvement scheme under greater strain. On two estates a high degree of rehousing – 'decanting' – was carried out. On Priory Court Estate all tenants were rehoused. Most were offered permanent moves although all had the option of a temporary move, returning to their old flats after the completion of the work. This meant that any household in inappropriate accommodation could move to a suitable flat or to a house. On North Peckham Estate there was also a high level of rehousing. Generally, the higher the number of flats emptied during the refurbishment, the more likely it is that a scheme will offer real choice to tenants and ensure that all are appropriately housed.

Social stability

The root causes of some of the problems of multi-storey housing lie in their history. When the estates were developed the flats were offered to those with highest priority on the 'waiting list'. Often these were families with young children. This produced a concentration of children all of a similar age. As they grew up together they became the cause of abuse and vandalism and eventually of the gang culture which characterised Packington Estate. Over time, this pattern tends to change. Children grow up and move away. Their parents are left in flats with room to spare. Overcrowding and child density are reduced. The profile of the estate population comes closer to the social structure of the local community. This pattern seems to characterise Priory Court Estate where the population had stabilised over a long period. It is also partly true of Packington Estate where stabilisation had probably begun before the improvement scheme took effect.

On some estates, however, this stabilisation never happens. Vandalism, abuse and anti-social behaviour are so bad that those who can exercise choice leave the estate – either through rehousing themselves or persistently pressing for transfers. Left behind are those with the lowest incomes and the poorest social skills. The places of people who leave are taken by those who, quite often, have no other choice. Commonly these are households in greatest need with the most serious social problems. This is the process by which an estate becomes 'hard-to-let' and often leads to allegations – as at North Peckham Estate – that the estate is used as a 'dumping ground'. On that estate the cycle seems to have been broken partly by offering many tenants the choice of new homes; partly by ensuring that remaining tenants were fully involved in decisions about their estate and the modernisation of their own homes. On Market Estate no such options were offered and the cycle of decline was not broken. Choice and genuine participation seem to be key to creating and maintaining social stability.

An open and stable policy framework

In generating real choice and open-ended participation the policy framework has a crucial influence. All the case studies were improved under the government's Estate Action programme. Over the period of the studies, however, the requirements of the programme changed quite considerably. When the earliest schemes – Market and Packington – were started, the Estate Action programme was quite prescriptive. There was a presumption of the need for a local management office, regardless of the way its services were organised and monitored. There was concentration on the external areas and a preconception that the introduction of concierge systems was the optimum solution. There was no consideration of alterations to the flats themselves or of social and economic issues. All this constrained choice and severely limited the effects of participation.

Two years on, when the Gloucester Grove and North Peckham schemes were started, there was more flexibility. Some internal improvements could be considered; some social facilities could be included. 'Option appraisal' had been introduced although the range of choice was severely limited. At Gloucester Grove Estate four options were considered. First, a 'do nothing' option was included purely to provide a cost yardstick. Second, was an option to carry out limited security works – these had already been tried on the estate without success. Total demolition was included but few residents took this seriously since the DoE rules would have required that they cease to be council tenants – something they had already decisively rejected in the ballot on the proposed Housing Action Trust. This left a major security scheme as the only realistic option.

Option appraisal and a more open policy had introduced greater choice but there were still serious restrictions. Two years on again, when the Priory Court scheme was conceived, the Estate Action programme had advanced to its most sophisticated form. A full range of options could be considered including internal improvements to the flats, the provision of social facilities and the development of employment and training schemes. Demolition was a realistic option and, although it was still the rule that new housing be provided by an alternative landlord, this requirement was flexibly applied. The greater openness and choice offered by the advanced form of Estate Action was a critical factor in the success of the scheme.

Sustained success, however, requires not only that the policy framework makes possible open choices but also that it produces a stable framework and a consistent funding regime. Of the five case study modernisation schemes only one – Packington – was completed as planned. The first phase of Market Estate was inadequately funded and the DoE refused to fund the second phase at all, leaving the cost to fall on the council's limited resources. At Gloucester Grove Estate two phases of major improvement were funded by the DoE Estate Action. When this programme was abolished, all funds for improvement were withdrawn and the rest of the estate scheduled for demolition. The same thing happened at North Peckham Estate. At Priory Court Estate funding was approved for the whole estate but no allowance was made for building cost inflation. The result is that lack of adequate finance to complete all phases as planned threatens the success of the scheme.

The regeneration of large estates must, inevitably, take place in phases over a long time period. It cannot be successfully completed on the shifting sands of changing ground rules and abrupt policy changes. The uncertainty which is introduced seriously damages the confidence of tenants and imperils the success of the scheme. It is a serious barrier to achieving social stability and solutions which are sustainable in the long term. If modernisation is to be effective it requires a policy framework which is consistent and a funding regime which is flexible enough to ensure its success.

Completing the picture

Three conclusions emerge about the future of multi-storey housing and the prospects for physically transforming estates. The first is that demolition should never be a first choice solution although, properly considered, it must remain an option. Second, that there is now good evidence that most types of multi-storey estate can be successfully transformed to make good housing. These include older estates, tower blocks and also the derided deck access estates.

Third, that the most difficult type of housing to deal with is the slab block and especially linked slab blocks. Even here though, principles have emerged which suggest that they could be successfully improved.

Rehabilitation versus redevelopment

The failure to break the cycle of decline on multi-storey estates commonly leads to despair. Such despair often lies at the root of decisions to demolish blocks of flats. The decision whether to redevelop is not always taken on a rational basis but proper consideration would take into account the considerable costs involved. Partly these are social costs – the costs of requiring people to leave their homes; the disruption of community networks and social organisation. These costs are largely non-monetary. They are difficult to quantify but should not be underestimated.

The fiscal costs are easier to estimate. Two of the case studies included costed option appraisals contrasting rehabilitation with rebuilding. These are shown in Figure 8.6. In both the schemes – North Peckham Estate and Priory Court Estate – the refurbishment proposals costed were extensive and comprehensive. Nevertheless redevelopment is shown to exceed the refurbishment cost by 55% in the case of North Peckham and by more than 70% at Priory Court. These figures are probably typical of most schemes and in resolving the debate the much higher cost of redevelopment must always be a consideration. But cost is not the only issue. It is significant that, despite the higher costs, substantial redevelopment was carried out on both these estates.

Figure 8.6: **Comparison of redevelopment and rehabilitation costs on two estates**

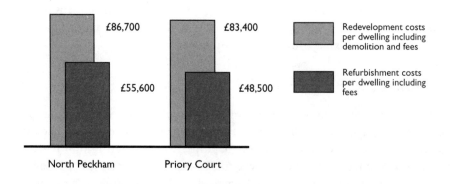

£86,700   £83,400   Redevelopment costs per dwelling including demolition and fees

£55,600   £48,500   Refurbishment costs per dwelling including fees

North Peckham   Priory Court

At North Peckham, and at Gloucester Grove, the decision to demolish came about, not as a rational choice, but because of an abrupt change in the funding regime. With the introduction of the SRB in 1994, Estate Action funding was cut off except to schemes where it was already committed. Further funding for these estates could only be obtained under SRB and for this the government was intent on introducing private finance. This meant redevelopment. Despite good evidence of the success of the comprehensive improvement schemes and despite the very much higher costs, large parts of both estates were scheduled for demolition. The decision was arbitrary and so was its implementation. Selective redevelopment might have been justified by social and environmental objectives. What was actually done was simply to demolish a swathe of housing blocks – the dividing line between new and old cut straight through the middle of each estate.

At Priory Court Estate the process was quite different. Demolition – both partial and total – was considered alongside a range of options. These were open to discussion with tenants and, in the end, were the subject of a ballot. The chosen option included partial redevelopment – the demolition of some of the slab blocks and their replacement with family houses. The redevelopment was carefully planned and integrated with the remaining part of the estate. This partial rebuilding served to offer a choice of housing type and to ensure that most tenants could be appropriately housed. It was probably a significant factor in sustaining and reinforcing the social stability of the estate. It is a good illustration of the proper consideration and implementation of the redevelopment option.

Estates which can be transformed

It had been established that tenement estates could be successfully regenerated. There was also plenty of evidence that tower blocks could be made into good housing partly by adapting them for population groups whose life-styles are well suited to multi-storey living. For these types of building the picture was clear but the future of slab blocks and deck access estates was less perceptible. The case studies were specifically selected to illuminate these questions – to test whether successful improvement schemes could be devised for these types of estate. The conclusions are somewhat surprising. The deck access estates are often considered the most problematic. The concentration that Alice Coleman placed on this type of estate is evidence of this concern. Findings of the case studies suggest that deck access estates can be successfully adapted and that the most severe problems are in dealing with slab blocks.

The key to solving the problems of deck access estates is, as Professor Coleman suggested, closing and removing the overhead walkways. From that common starting point at least three different solutions seem to offer success.

At Packington Estate the decks were broken down into zones each reached by a common entrance serving a small number of flats. This involved dividing and segregating the access system rather than physical changes to the blocks. At North Peckham Estate, the blocks were physically separated and adapted so that all entrances were brought down to ground level. Half the flats are entered directly through their own gardens. The others are grouped around what is left of the walkway, each small group served by a secured common entrance at ground level. At Angell Town (see Exemplar 5, p 131) the entrances to all the flats are brought down to the ground separately or in a pair and the walkways eliminated entirely. The ground level car parking deck has been converted to provide community facilities or housing. It seems that each of these schemes achieved a high degree of success and that variations on these approaches could be used to modify most deck access estates.

Figure 8.7 illustrates diagrammatically how blocks can be transformed. The principles of the schemes for the deck access estates at North Peckham and Angell Town are illustrated. These are compared with the way in which tenement blocks can be modified so that family accommodation is concentrated on the ground with smaller flats above. This principle is the key to transforming low-scale blocks of multi-storey flats.

Figure 8.7: **Transforming multi-storey blocks**

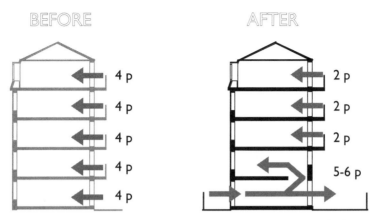

Islington Estate Action: Inter-war tenement block converted to concentrate family accommodation in ground-level masionettes entered through their own gardens. Upper floors converted to small flats for households without children.

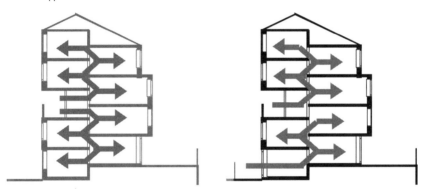

North Peckham Estate, Southwark: Deck access estate. Bridges removed to separate blocks. New entrances provided to lower level dwellings entered through their own gardens. New common entrances each serve a small number of upper level dwellings.

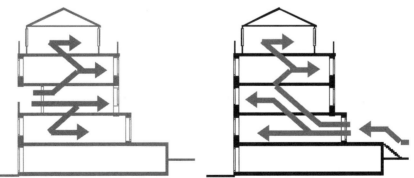

Angell Town Estate, Lambeth: Deck access estate with parking at ground level. Walkways removed entirely and space converted to bedrooms. New entrances provided to all dwellings – each pair of masionettes given separate entrance accessible from ground level. parking converted to workshops and community facilities.

Slab blocks – an area of uncertainty

The evidence of the case studies is that no sure solutions offer themselves for slab blocks. The scheme for Market Estate had a similar starting point to the deck access schemes – severing the links between blocks. But separating the blocks was not enough; the access system within each block was not successfully broken up. At Gloucester Grove Estate, improvement also hinged on severing the grim continuous corridors. The access system was separated into small zones but these remain linked by the fire escape doors and several zones are served by each common entrance. The scheme seems fragile and at risk of breaking down so that the blocks are again open to abuse. Access at Priory Court Estate was divided up with each entrance serving only 10 upper floor flats. This, however, was not the result of the improvement scheme. It was the way the original slab blocks were designed. Basically they were 'staircase access' blocks with one lift and stairs serving two or three flats per floor.

Staircase access was very much the preferred system in the 1940s and early 1950s when this estate was built. Another contemporary scheme to use this principle were the eight-storey blocks at Woodbury Down in Hackney (see Figure 3.1). These blocks were built with one family flat and one one-bedroom flat per floor – a total of 16 flats per entrance. When visited in 1997, almost 50 years after it was built, some of the entrances had entryphone security. But on many entrances this had, apparently, not proved necessary. These were totally unsecured with glazed doors left unlocked and open to public access Despite this there seemed to be few problems. The stairs and lift were in need of decoration, modernisation and better cleaning but were unaffected by vandalism or graffiti. The success of the security scheme at Priory Court Estate, and the remarkable longevity of Woodbury Down, suggests staircase access may provide a model for improving other slab blocks.

The option of inserting new stairs/lift access shafts was briefly considered at Market Estate, though not pursued. At Gloucester Grove Estate a few new stair/lift shafts were introduced, although their success may be limited and the durability of the scheme is uncertain. For a scheme on such an estate to fully succeed it may be necessary to insert even more new access shafts, reducing the number of flats served to two or three per floor. To maintain security the groups of flats around each access shaft must be entirely separated from each other (see Figure 8.8). To make this work two objections have to be overcome. One is that having only one lift can cause elderly or infirm people to be isolated in case of a breakdown. Access systems from the 1950s onwards were usually designed on the principle that each flat was served by more than one lift. However, breakdowns were mostly caused because the lifts were over used. Woodbury Down has only 12 flats using each lift above first floor level. With this small usage, lift breakdowns are likely to be very infrequent. The second objection is fire escape. There are no firm rules and fire officers have considerable discretion. The most serious problem, however, is to provide escape from flats at the higher levels – above the height that can be reached from a turntable ladder. Woodbury Down has linking balconies from the fifth floor upwards so that occupants can escape to another flat in case of fire. This device has been commonly used in multi-storey blocks and could be a key to the transformation of slab blocks.

Figure 8.8: **Adding additional lifts/stairs to slab blocks to restrict the numbers of dwellings served by each entrance**

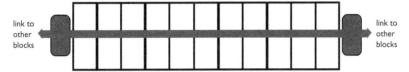

Unimproved linked slab block: Diagrammatic plan of eight-storey block on Gloucester Grove Estate, Southwark. 88 Dwellings with unrestricted access within and between blocks. Common areas suffered extensive vandalism and abuse.

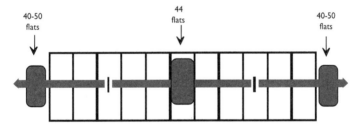

Improved block: Diagrammatic plan of block improved by insertion of new lift/stair complex. Each main entrance now serves a relatively small number of dwellings. Corridors are severed and secured secondary entrances are provided at each level serving five or six flats. The system is complex to operate and maintain and vulnerable to break down.

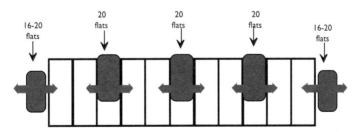

Full staircase access: Introduction of additional lifts and stairs would convert the block to traditional staircase access. Each main entrance would serve only a small number of flats and corridors would be eliminated entirely. The risk of the access system breaking down would be minimised and management and maintenance problems greatly reduced.

Such an approach, involving the insertion of several new lift/stair towers, seems not to have been applied to the modernisation of slab block estates. It would be expensive, although less so than redevelopment and less wasteful than the loss of investment caused by the breakdown of an inadequate improvement scheme. Should such remodelling prove successful then the last frontier would have been crossed. It would make all types of multi-storey housing capable of successful modernisation.

The ingredients of success

The evidence suggests that refurbishment of multi-storey housing can always be a serious alternative to redevelopment. The counsel of despair which dismisses all such problem estates as irredeemable can be countered. Only in the case of serious technical failure should demolition be the only option. Nevertheless, the record of regeneration projects is not good. Too many have failed or have achieved only partial or short-term success. This patchy performance has resulted partly from the disruption created by too frequent changes in policy and in the funding regime which shapes improvement schemes. The critical problems, however, have been an over-prescriptive approach to solutions and an inflexibility in evaluating the lesson of practice.

The early regeneration programmes developed by central government were heavily directed from the centre and strongly focused on preconceptions. There was concentration on improvements to exteriors regardless of conditions within the flats. There was insistence on provision of on-site management offices with too little consideration of how these operated. There was a presumption in favour of concierge-controlled security schemes regardless of the physical form and layout of the buildings. All this limited options and prevented an open-ended discussion of problems and possible solutions. Worse still, it created a reliance on technical solutions and complex computerised control mechanisms.

Partly as a result of centralised control and monitoring there was a slowness in recognising the shortcomings of many attempted solutions. There was insufficient flexibility to observe that an approach which worked on one type of estate might not necessarily work on another; that successful solutions needed to be worked out locally by the people most directly affected. There was also tardiness in recognising certain key components of success. It is now clear that social appropriateness is important and that achieving it means offering a high degree of choice to tenants. Housing quality is important too – the flats very often need improvements as much as the exteriors and the common areas. Providing social facilities and employment training are also key issues in addressing disadvantage. All these things were eventually incorporated into the most effective schemes but these have been too infrequent and successful combinations have not always been recognised.

The early emphasis on physical solutions and systems has now been replaced with a focus on economic deprivation and urban management. While these factors are important there is a danger of their being overemphasised. A focus on management can diminish the importance of housing quality or the need for physical re-formation. The evidence is now strong that successful regeneration requires a balanced consideration of managerial issues, physical changes and social concerns. A multi-faceted framework is required in which all these factors are given consideration and appropriate weight.

NINE

Ending the estate syndrome

It has become apparent that all types of multi-storey housing can probably be successfully transformed. The older, smaller estates can be modernised and converted to provide a mix of family housing and smaller flats in a form which mirrors traditional Victorian street patterns. Tower blocks can be technically improved and successfully secured to provide good housing for smaller households and a range of specialised uses. The much maligned deck access estates can be adapted and broken down to provide successful multi-storey dwellings. Slab blocks turn out to be the most problematic housing type but, even here, there are solutions which can be attempted. None of these solutions is cheap. Properly done, the effective transformation of multi-storey blocks is an expensive exercise. But never so expensive as the more apocalyptic option. Wholesale clearance is the most expensive solution both in fiscal and social terms. It is now clear that regeneration is, almost always, an alternative to demolition. In any comprehensive strategy, however, demolition and part demolition must remain an option. It may be necessary in order to create a better housing mix or to meet strong resident demands.

Nothing can be achieved without adequate funding, but the way in which funding is applied is of critical importance. It is evident that the funding regime has been a key determinant of the shape and form of multi-storey housing. If the problems of urban housing estates are to be effectively resolved, the funding system must embody two key characteristics. First it must allow local communities to establish their own priorities and encourage residents to play an active role in the future of their housing. Second it must be flexible enough to support and encourage a wide range of alternative solutions. Given such flexibility, radical changes can be made to urban estates making them better suited to their residents and more manageable. But physical changes are not enough – social changes are needed too.

Urban estates should not be the preserve of the poorest, the most deprived and the least capable. Such concentrations of disadvantage are self-sustaining. If coupled with a supply of new social housing, the ghetto status which commonly afflicts urban multi-storey estates can be ended. Many families with children and many single residents with special needs are not well housed in multi-storey estates. If the most needy can be rehoused in more suitable new developments then large parts of the estates can be adapted and rededicated. The aim must be to make urban estates more mixed communities; to reintegrate them into the urban social environment; to make sure that those who live in them do so by choice and have housing that is appropriate to their needs.

Form follows funding

Le Corbusier's famous dictum 'form follows function' became a motto for the Modern Movement. It was always questionable how far Modernists allowed the needs of building users to override their artistic preoccupations. But as far as housing was concerned it is clear that the prevailing funding regime was a more potent determinant of form than were functional requirements. From the early days of slum clearance the legislative and administrative framework exerted a powerful influence on the shape and form of multi-storey housing.

The requirements of successive Acts of Parliament which governed clearance served to ensure that redevelopment took the form of high-density flats. At the same time there was constant pressure for new housing to be built at the lowest reasonable cost. Progressive improvements were made in the standards of the flats but that meant that economies had to be found in the form of the buildings. The most cost-effective type – the five-storey tenement block with balcony access – became the most common solution. In the post-war period, new standards were laid down. The war-time Dudley Committee set minimum space standards and required that every flat should have a private balcony. It also recommended that flats over three storeys should be served by lifts. The familiar five-storey walk-up blocks were no longer acceptable. Once lifts were introduced it was evident that more economic use would be made of them by building higher than four or five storeys. Blocks of eight to 11 storeys became increasingly common. The height subsidy, introduced in 1956, was an incentive to go even higher. Blocks of 15, 20, 30 storeys were introduced and became an increasingly large proportion of new social housing. In the 1960s increased space standards were introduced and the funding system was changed. The Housing Cost Yardstick no longer favoured high buildings but it did support high density and was instrumental in spawning the high-density low-rise estates of the late 1960s and early 1970s.

Throughout this period the need for economy persisted. 'Low-cost' housing was essential to realising the massive programme of slum clearance. Minimum space standards were strictly applied, so any further savings had to be found elsewhere. Access systems were made to serve more and more dwellings with increasingly utilitarian design and finish. Industrialised building methods were introduced to try to reduce construction costs. Common amenities and social facilities, long since considered desirable, were omitted to save money. By the 1970s it was becoming increasingly evident that these very factors were causing mounting problems. It should have been obvious that rigid rules produce bad solutions and that good quality housing cannot be produced on the cheap.

In addressing the multi-storey legacy a more flexible approach was initially adopted. The Project Control system introduced in 1981 monitored only the financial viability of improvement schemes making possible a wide range of approaches. This allowed local authorities to determine their own priorities and gave the opportunity for tenants to have considerable choice in the improvement of their estates. Under this system, over time, higher and higher budgets were allowed making possible the generous funding needed to transform estates into housing of high quality. But from the mid to late 1980s increasing rigidity crept into the framework for estate regeneration.

Progressive and substantial reductions in housing capital allocation meant that local authorities no longer had scope for implementing their own strategies. They could no longer build new housing. They could not carry out major modernisation schemes from their general credit allocation. Many had difficulty in funding the maintenance of the multi-storey stock. Large-scale and generous funding was still available but only for schemes selected and vetted by central government itself. Once again increasingly rigid rules were introduced which largely determined which estates received investment and which were a critical influence on what was done to them.

Under the government's Estate Action programme the schemes selected for funding were mostly those with the highest public profile and those that were perceived to have the greatest social problems. Generally this meant that funding was only allocated to large estates even though some of the most run-down multi-storey housing is in isolated blocks or small estates of 100 or so flats. In any local authority area one or two big estates could receive generous funding for modernisation while a large quantity of housing in equal or greater need got nothing at all. Even for those estates allocated funding the scope of improvements was generally tightly defined by central policy priorities. The policy on diversity of tenure and the requirement that new development should be carried out by housing associations has been a particular constraint. This was a disincentive to considering redevelopment and relatively few schemes funded under Estate Action involved demolition.

On the other hand, Housing Action Trusts almost invariably involved the demolition of multi-storey blocks. This was partly because estates had already been transferred to new landlords and tenants did not suffer a loss of security through opting for redevelopment. Partly, too, it was a reflection of the very generous funding allocated to the trusts. The partnership funds – City Challenge and Single Regeneration Budget (SRB) – seemed to positively encourage redevelopment. This may reflect the priorities of tenants but more likely it was because development companies and large building contractors were often key partners. Their priority was to maximise the amount of new building for the benefit of their own organisations.

The record shows that, in the past, the financial regime has been instrumental in determining housing form and quality. The rules attached to funding together with the continuing priority of providing 'low-cost' housing for the working classes was instrumental in creating many of the problems of multi-storey housing. In addressing these problems it was often recognised that improvement cannot be done on the cheap and that funding must allow for good quality schemes and adequate levels of management. Indeed it can be argued that funding was often indiscriminately lavish, producing poor value for money. Apart from the relatively brief operation of the Project Control system, however, the lesson has not been learned that regimes need to be more flexible. The rigid rules applied to funding from the mid-1980s onwards meant that local communities were not able to establish their own priorities in housing regeneration, and the tenants of run-down estates did not have an open choice in determining the future of their housing.

New Labour policies

The efforts to address the problems of multi-storey housing have almost entirely taken place under the long period of Conservative government. During their 18 successive years in office Conservative policies had had a major impact on social housing. First they had dramatically cut housing investment. Over a 20-year period capital investment had been reduced by more that than 75% to less than £3 billion per annum (Perry, 1998a). Completion of new homes in the social sector in England had fallen from 91,000 to just over 20,000 each year (DETR, 1999a). Second, there had been a relentless centralisation with more and more of the diminishing capital funding absorbed into programmes managed and directed by central government. This greatly restricted the options of local authorities and allowed government objectives to override local priorities. Third, the Conservatives seemed to regard privatisation as the answer to everything – a one-step solution to any problem. In housing this not only affected tenure and ownership; the means of procurement and management were also extensively privatised.

In May 1997 the Conservatives were replaced by a Labour administration. In opposition, the Labour Party had recognised the problems created for local authorities and had pledged increased investment in public housing. As a first step they promised to release the £6 billion of capital receipts which had accumulated in local authorities' bank accounts from the sale of council housing (Spitties, 1995). Labour had also criticised the way the competitive approach of the various 'challenge' funds was creating winners and losers rather than prioritising needs. They proposed a system where bids for funds would be assessed against rational criteria and allocated on the basis of need (Hirst, 1996). Many housing professionals looked to the new government to reverse the priorities of their political opponents; to adopt a more positive approach to the management, development and improvement of social housing.

The policy framework

In government, Labour's first act was to combine the Environment and Transport Departments and incorporate responsibility for regional policy under the title Department of the Environment, Transport and the Regions (DETR). The new Department quickly introduced two initiatives which had a significant impact on housing. First there was a pledge to end compulsory competitive tendering (CCT), which had had a major influence on both housing management and the professional services required to develop housing capital schemes. CCT was to be replaced by a duty to achieve 'Best Value'. Instead of total reliance on competition the performance of services and policies would be reviewed by applying tests known as the 'four Cs' – *challenge* the way existing arrangements work; *compare* with best practice in other authorities and social providers; *consult* with the users of services and the local community; *compete* – look at other organisations which might help deliver services perhaps through partnership. This last maintained the option of putting services to tender where this might have qualitative benefits (DETR, 1999b).

A key part of the achievement of 'Best Value' in housing was a renewed emphasis on tenant consultation. The aim was make all councils implement policies to empower tenants and to ensure their participation in decision making. There would be a requirement that all authorities negotiate a local agreement – a 'Tenant Participation Compact'. These would operate both on a council-wide basis and at neighbourhood level. The compacts would be developed through discussion with tenant representatives and tailored to local needs but would share common objectives. They would involve tenants in decisions about all aspects of housing policy and strategy; in the management of housing services; and in the development and implementation of regeneration programmes and improvement schemes (DETR, 1999c).

The second initiative was to boost investment in housing. Capital receipts were released – £174 million in the first year, £610 million in 1998/99 and the promise of more to come. The money was not released simply on the basis of allowing councils to spend the money they held. Instead, a supplementary capital allocation was given to each authority. One third of this allocation was based on the receipts already held. Two thirds was based on indices of housing need included in the government's 'General Needs Index'. The money was to be spent on improving the existing housing stock including repair and renovation; energy efficiency; environmental improvements; and security measures. If new housing was to be provided then it was to be done in partnership with housing associations (DETR, 1997a). More funding was made available in the Comprehensive Spending Review of 1998. Over the three years 1999-2002 an extra £5 billion was to be allocated to housing and regeneration. This included the release of further capital receipts (DETR, 1998a). Despite these telephone number figures the overall rise in housing capital has been modest – by 1999/2000 a net increase of less than 5% since the General Election (DETR, 1998b). Nevertheless, it represented a decisive reversal after years of decline.

Regeneration programmes

The new general capital allocation increased the housing funding available to local authorities, which had shrunk to minimal levels. This gave them new flexibility in the repair and modernisation of their estates. The new government also inherited three specific centralised programmes from which housing estates could benefit. These were placed under review:

- *Single Regeneration Budget (SRB)*: the programme was kept in place and bids were invited in the autumn of 1997 on the same basis as previously. Subsequently procedure was revised with a view not to abolish competitive bidding but to control it within a clear framework. Bids were to be assessed on the basis of clear published criteria. At the same time the programme was to be focused on the worst problems – the bulk of the money (80%) would be channelled to large projects in the most deprived areas. Schemes involving housing regeneration could still be funded but only where they included training, employment and economic development as well (DETR, 1998c).
- *Estates Renewal Challenge Fund (ERCF)*: this was initially retained on a modified basis although Labour ministers were keen to see it as an option in housing strategy rather than as a vehicle for divesting local authorities of their estates. A third round of bids were invited in the spring of 1998 after which the programme was abolished (DETR, 1997b).
- *Capital Challenge*: this programme, covering all local authority capital spending, was set up on a pilot basis in 1996. At that time projects were awarded funding for a three-year period. No new bids were invited in 1997 and the programme was discontinued.

In initiating a review of regeneration programmes the new government clearly expressed its commitment to resolve the problems of estate housing. Barely a month after taking over, Tony Blair made a high profile visit to the Aylesbury Estate in Southwark – a massive development of linked slab blocks with a multitude of problems. The new Prime Minister focused on the social stresses on such estates – the high levels of unemployment, the large numbers of single parents, the problems of drug abuse, the lack of basic skills and poor educational performance (Bevins, 1997). This concern led to the setting up of the Social Exclusion Unit (SEU), with a brief to coordinate policy across government departments. Research by the new Unit identified 44 local authority districts, all in urban areas, which suffered concentrations of deprivation. On measures such as unemployment and low attainment, concentrations of single parents and high child density, as well as on poor quality and run-down housing, these districts had much more serious problems than the rest of England. From the work of the SEU a new regeneration programme emerged.

- *The New Deal for Communities:* 17 of the 44 authorities were invited to become 'pathfinder' areas. Each was invited to identify a small deprived residential neighbourhood and to prepare a scheme for its regeneration starting in 1999. The schemes were required to develop a multi-agency approach to regeneration. They were expected to concentrate on social and economic initiatives and changes in urban management rather than on physical improvement. A total of £800 million was earmarked to fund the first three years of the 17 projects. Following evaluation of the pathfinder schemes, other areas would be invited to bid. Each scheme is expected to take 10 to 20 years to come to fruition (SEU, 1998).

After the review there remained just two central government regeneration programmes. The SRB was refocused to address large parts of run-down inner urban areas with limited money available for housing. The New Deal was directed to housing regeneration. It grew out of concern over the worst estates although it was tailored to improve the residential environment in all respects rather than to treat the problems as housing renewal in the traditional sense.

The impact of policy

The new policies have changed the framework for the regeneration of multi-storey estates but it is not clear what their impact will be. More money has been made available for housing investment. But the overall increase is small, and much of it will be needed to make good the backlog of repairs. The impact of the central regeneration programmes is likely to be limited. The SRB will concentrate on the general revitalisation of urban areas with limited funding available for housing. The New Deal concentrates on deprived residential areas although these will not necessarily include multi-storey estates. Even if they do it is not clear that sufficient funding will be available to meet the cost of comprehensive physical transformation. In any case the programme will initially fund a relatively small number of projects. Local authorities will still need to find additional large-scale funding if multi-storey housing is to get the investment it needs.

It has been a central theme of New Labour policies to bring private finance into public projects. Although it has since been abolished, the ERCF showed how such funding could be brought into housing capital investment. A key attraction of ERCF was that it avoided the restrictions of Treasury rules. If a local authority borrows money to improve its estates, the loan is guaranteed by the government and becomes part of the national debt. If a housing company borrows money for the same purpose it is regarded as a private loan, much like a normal mortgage. The Housing Company would use its buildings as collateral, the only limit to borrowing being the value of its estates. Public subsidy is only necessary to cover the shortfall between rents and loan repayments (Rowlat, 1997). It is possible that this principle could be taken further. Supported by the Chartered Institute of Housing several local authorities have been examining whether they could restructure their whole housing operation using private finance but without having to transfer their estates to another landlord (Jenks and Fairclough, 1997). Meanwhile in Scotland several large cities including Edinburgh and Glasgow have been contemplating transferring all their housing to non-profit companies or trusts where improvements would be financed by banks and building societies (Perry, 1998b). The possible advantages of large-scale stock transfer stimulated the growing interest of central government.

Even if new money is made available, it remains to be seen whether the Labour government will recognise the importance of a stable and flexible funding regime. From the late 1980s onwards housing regeneration was greatly hampered by over-centralisation, rigid funding rules and constant changes of policy. Decentralisation is necessary to allow local communities to establish their own priorities. Flexibility is important so that a range of options can be opened for genuine choice. Stability is essential to ensure that regeneration schemes can reach fruition over the long period necessary for design and phased development. The early signs are promising. The introduction of Tenant Participation Compacts should ensure more attention to local priorities but only if user groups are allowed to discuss fundamental options. In the spending of capital receipts councils have been relatively free to develop their own priorities. Schemes are not subject to detailed controls and authorities are only required to report on the make-up of their work programme as a whole. In the New Deal there seems to be a commitment to maintain funding in the long term. In many ways the tenor of the new policies strikes the right notes. It contrasts sharply with the directive and prescriptive approach of regeneration programmes that went before.

An alternative strategy for regeneration

It is the proper and necessary role of central government to coordinate the resolution of problems. This includes collecting comparable information and analysing this to identify the key issues. It includes defining common criteria which can be used in comparative evaluation so that relative priorities can be established between one local area and another. The job of government includes identifying and channelling resources and monitoring performance in the application of funding at local level. Its role includes monitoring and disseminating best practice. But it should not be part of the function of government to decide on priorities within a local community, still less to become closely involved in the details of any one project. It can be argued that government's increasing involvement in these detailed issues during the late 1980s and early 1990s stemmed mainly from a desire to circumvent the housing function of local authorities. It may well be that this 'hands on' approach seriously distracted central administration from its proper strategic role.

At best such an approach can be justified as 'targeting'. This involves identifying the most critical problem areas and focusing attention and funding to solving those problems. Targeting is based on the view that some areas are the focus of a plethora of problems which make them atypical, deserving of special treatment. Thus it was that generous and often lavish funding was focused on a relatively small number of high profile multi-storey estates. Quite often money was wasted by pouring it into schemes which proved ineffective. Very often these high profile projects were allowed high unit costs which represented poor value for money. Meanwhile, older and smaller estates got nothing. Cynics could argue that the money went to estates which drew attention to themselves – where there was high profile campaigning, civil disorder or persistent youth crime which focused public attention. The national publicity given to such estates as Hulme in Manchester, Broadwater Farm in North London or Meadowell in North Shields certainly did not harm their efforts to attract funding.

An alternative view is that the targeted estates are not atypical. That they are simply the tip of an iceberg and that many others have similar problems if less extreme. One alternative strategy would be 'blanketing' – spreading available resources thinly so that all deprived areas could benefit. This was often the approach in early estate improvement projects and it too often led to piecemeal solutions which might solve one key problem but leave others untouched. For instance, a repair programme might replace the windows in a block, improving thermal performance, but leave the common parts unsecured allowing them to continue being disfigured by abuse. The basis of a successful strategy might be drawn from Islington Council's approach during the 1980s.

There was blanketing of sufficient resources to keep the estate stock in reasonable condition. At the same time more generous funding was targeted, not at the most high profile problems, but at the oldest estates which provided the worst housing conditions. The modernisation carried out to the tenement estates and the smaller post-war blocks proved highly successful.

One approach to resolving multi-faceted problems – such as a complex design issue – is to start with the least difficult aspects. Often these are areas where the answers have already been tried and tested and can be confidently reapplied. If decisions are made about the easiest choices it serves to isolate the most problematic elements. The most difficult part of the problem can then be analysed more clearly. This is an approach which might be summarised as 'start with what is already known'. It is now known that older tenement estates can be turned into good housing. Similarly the smaller lower-scale estates of the 1950s and the isolated blocks which stand alone in terraced streets can be very successfully modernised. Making these a first priority would create a pool of good quality social housing providing good value for money. Alongside this, in many areas, more new social housing is needed. This could be newly built or acquired by buying existing housing. Using this pool, pressure could be relieved on the large problem estates, offering rehousing to some tenants, reducing overcrowding and the concentrations of children. This, in turn, would allow parts of the large estates to be rededicated to other uses or demolished and redeveloped. Far from targeting the large problem estates as a top priority, attention could be given to gradually relieving the pressure so that, in the end, their problems would be easier to solve.

No effective strategy can be adopted, however, either by central or local government, until the nature of the problem is better understood. It does not seem that there is sufficient reliable up-to-date information about the extent of multi-storey housing and the nature of its problems. Urban authorities could be asked to undertake a series of rapid surveys of all their estates. These would draw upon the expertise of housing managers, local architects or surveyors and the tenants of the estates. Each survey would aim to establish an 'estate profile'. This would identify the mature of the estate – size, form, age and so on; and its problems – both physical inadequacies and social stresses. By consulting their representatives the profile could also outline residents' priorities for the estate. Clearly the initial surveys would concentrate on the unimproved estates and those perceived as the most inadequate. A picture could then be quickly assembled of the most serious problem areas.

This information could be used to establish local strategies. The exercise would be particularly important if there were various sources of funding. If, as seems likely, private finance is to become increasingly significant, then certain types of estate are more likely to prove suitable for this form of reinvestment. An estate where there was likely to be substantial demolition – whether through low demand, pressure from tenants or for technical reasons – would make poor collateral for private loans. On the other hand, an estate where successful modernisation could be confidently predicted might make an ideal candidate for transfer to an alternative landlord. Defining a successful strategy will depend both on collecting more accurate information and engaging in an open debate about basic options before any irrevocable decisions are made.

Towards the mixed community

Given adequate funding, it should be possible to define a strategy which will result in the physical regeneration of multi-storey estates – one which would turn them into good housing. Beyond the basic physical objectives, however, must be the aim to ensure that there is greater choice – that everyone can have access to housing which is suited to their own needs. Deeper still there must be an aspiration to create social stability and to integrate the estates into the wider community.

The mixed community has long been an objective of housing policy. It was a key objective of the Garden City movement and was influential in early developments such as Hampstead Garden suburb and Letchworth (Davey, 1980). Aneurin Bevan, the first post-war housing minister, believed strongly that housing should not just be of high quality but should provide for mixed communities combining all social classes and all age groups (Foot, 1973, p 77). Within the housing standards promoted by the Labour government in the late 1940s was the objective that social housing should provide for elderly people, for single workers, for students and apprentices and for those who performed essential social services such as nurse and midwives. Not least important was a suggestion that local authorities should provide, on housing estates, some housing for higher income groups to create mixed communities. Higher space standards could be provided to attract professionals such as doctors who might live and work on the estates (MoHLG, 1951).

In the event, no significant effort was made to realise such objectives. Some social housing was provided for elderly people but rarely for any category of single person and for the professional classes hardly ever. The focus was on those in greatest need. This meant families and particularly low-income families. Estates became concentrations of working-class families with children, their social composition very far from representing the community at large. During the 1980s this distinctiveness was compounded. As the most desirable housing was lost to the public sector through the 'Right to Buy', many estates became still more the preserve of the poorest households, those least capable of improving their lot through their own efforts. There was concern that such concentrations of disadvantage were creating an 'underclass' characterised by high levels of illegitimacy, crime and unemployment. Such phenomena, it was suggested, were stimulated by a poor attitude to educational attainment and a negative work ethic (Murray, 1990). There was plenty of evidence that the social character of urban estates was generating gang cultures often associated with drug dealing, crime and anti-social behaviour. On more outlying estates unemployment, low attainment and gang culture resulted in widespread eruptions of social disorder (Power and Tunstall, 1997).

It was such concerns which led to the resurrection of the idea of mixed communities in government policies. The Conservative government had been driven by the idea that most housing should be provided by, and be part of, the private sector. A central plank of its policy had been the 'Right to Buy' for council tenants. This was accompanied by less successful attempts to sell off blocks of flats to private developers. By the late 1980s it was becoming clear that these policies were having no impact on large multi-storey estates. Few, if any, estate tenants had exercised the 'Right to Buy' while, because of sales elsewhere, the estates became increasingly indispensable as rented social housing. Selling off blocks became logistically impractical. Instead many were demolished and new housing developed by housing associations or other social landlords. This was designed to create 'diversity of tenure'. While it had certain advantages – giving tenants a choice of landlord, encouraging innovation in management – it did not create mixed communities. The social profile of the occupants of the newly built housing was identical to that on the estates, particularly where there were significant nomination rights. The determination to create genuine diversity led to increasingly draconian measures. In City Challenge, and the SRB that followed it, the inclusion of new housing for sale became a requirement of any housing proposal. Large parts of problematic estates were scheduled for clearance and replacement by owner-occupation.

This whole policy framework could be described as obsessive privatisation and it was applied universally and without flexibility. It was highly controversial because the 'Right to Buy' and redevelopment for sale caused an overall loss of social housing in areas of greatest need. Quite often the most desirable housing was sold off which created considerable pressure on that remaining. The controversy generated was regrettable because it served to obscure the very real benefits that diversity of tenure might have in resolving the problems of multi-storey estates. First, there must be significant benefits in reducing child density and breaking up concentrations of disadvantage where a culture of underachievement becomes self-sustaining. Second, opening access to housing through diversity of tenure means that families and friends can find housing near to each other and help to recreate kinship networks which were a feature of old urban communities. It also means that people who are more skilled or educated can move in. Often they will be those who provide a vital social function in the community such as nurses or teachers. Some of them will be those who are most likely to lead community social and political activities, campaigning for and organising improvements. Finally, those who own their own homes do have a stake in their community and a vested interest in protecting it against deterioration.

If it is accepted that housing cannot be totally privatised, that a significant proportion of housing must be provided through not-for-profit organisations, then a viable future can be found for multi-storey estates though diversity. It must be recognised that housing for families is best provided on the ground. An additional stock of family houses or maisonettes with gardens is essential to relieve the pressure in multi-storey housing. Given that, the way would be open to remodel and revitalise urban estates. Many multi-storey blocks can best be converted to mixed use. Tenement blocks are best used to provide family housing on the ground with smaller flats above. Slab and deck access blocks can be converted to a similar mix. Tower blocks are best suited for use as small dwellings perhaps for the general needs of single and childless households, perhaps for special needs.

There are many successful examples of multi-storey blocks reused as sheltered housing for elderly people or as student housing. These might seem negative or defensive projects – using up cheaply an unwanted resource, making the best of a bad job. Multi-storey housing has had a bad press, after all. A good deal has already been demolished. Critics such as Alice Coleman have declared that houses are always better than flats and that the design of multi-storey blocks positively induces anti-social behaviour (Coleman, 1990). More colourfully, in his novel *High rise*, the science fiction write J.G. Ballard suggests that multi-storey housing prompts even the most wealthy and privileged to degenerate into primitive tribalism and the most depraved forms of barbarism (Ballard, 1975). In the circumstances it may seem surprising that, in some quarters, multi-storey housing has a positive image and that new developments are still being built.

In the Gorbals in Glasgow many of the multi-storey blocks built in the 1960s have been demolished. In their place are being built four-storey terraces of flats, largely for owner-occupation. The wheel has come full circle – in form the new housing is almost identical to the tenements demolished 30 years ago (Crewe, 1994). In Birmingham in 1997, Aston University unveiled a scheme to build 650 student rooms in two densely developed blocks ranging from eight to 15 storeys (Rattenbury, 1997). Perhaps most remarkable was this advertisement:

Montevetro: Taylor Woodrow announce that work has started on this new landmark residential development designed by Richard Rogers Partnership.

Rising 20 floors at the highest point and sitting on the banks of the Thames at Battersea, opposite Chelsea's Cheyne Walk, Montevetro will offer the most striking apartments anywhere on the river.

- 24-hour security
- underground car parking
- leisure centre with tennis court
- 999 year leases
- private landscaped gardens

Spacious 2-, 3- and 4-bedroom apartments with large balconies, river views and west facing aspects from £330,000 to £1.7 million. (Advert in *The Guardian Space*, 31 October 1997)

Lest this be thought an aberration providing *pieds à terre* for the super rich, a similar but more modest development was completed in North London in 1995. The Beaux Arts Building, a 10-storey neo-classical office block built in the 1930s for the Post Office, was converted to housing for sale. The development provided more than 160 flats ranging from one-person studios to three-bedroom family flats and including rooftop penthouses. The development included a gym, a sauna and three communal gardens – two on the ground and one at roof level. The whole complex is policed by security guards backed up by CCTV.

What does seem ironic is that such new developments are taking place at the very same time as multi-storey housing in the public sector is being demolished. Given appropriate policy and organisation and relieved of the pressing need to provide housing for families, multi-storey blocks of urban estates could easily be rededicated to new uses. Transferred to universities they could be adapted as housing for students; or to health authorities as hostels for trainees and young staff. Transferred to developers they could be modernised at modest cost to provide housing for rent on the open market or for sale to first-time buyers. Properly managed, such housing could prove attractive to single people or as starter homes for young couples wanting to stay close to their parents.

It is clear that there is a way to end the syndrome of the urban multi-storey estate as stigmatised concentrations of the disadvantaged. Large estates can be broken down into identifiable and manageable zones. Some blocks can be converted to provide a mix of housing. Other blocks can be rededicated to new uses – for elderly people, for students, for young workers. The interests of developers and owner-occupiers can be allowed into parts of the estates. In this way the population can be diversified, the social structure can be stabilised. Over time, tenants will develop confidence in their estates, more will exercise the 'Right to Buy'. The regeneration process will be entrenched and the estates reintegrated into the wider community.

The place of social housing

Modernising the urban estates in this way can be amply justified as an end in itself. But there is a broader reason why it should happen – housing investment is a key to more comprehensive urban regeneration. In the 1960s many areas of inner London were concentrations of poor rented housing both in multiple occupied terraces and old estates. Islington was deemed the most seriously deprived area (Milner Holland, 1965). During the 1970s and 1980s large-scale public investment took place in the Borough's housing – selective renewal with small new estates, municipalisation and rehabilitation of old street housing, and not least the modernisation of the older estates. All this served not just to make good housing, it improved the urban environment as a whole making it attractive to owner-occupiers to move in and make their own investment. In 1995, almost 47% of Islington's housing was still privately owned despite the loss of several thousand through the 'Right to Buy' scheme. Another 20% was owned by housing associations. Only one third was privately owned (Islington Housing Department, 1996). Despite this, Islington was one of the most high profile and high value residential areas in the country. The minority of relatively wealthy homeowners had stimulated new businesses, new shops and a plethora of restaurants. This not only provided a wide range of services to the community but generated significant new employment.

It could be argued that this would have happened anyway; that the operation of the property market alone would have ensured regeneration especially given Islington's proximity to central London. But in neighbouring Hackney there has been only limited regeneration. In Tower Hamlets and Southwark it is more limited still. In these inner London boroughs there are acres of unimproved tenements as well as more recent estates with serious problems. Some of the poorest communities in Britain lie cheek by jowl with the wealthy City of London. The evidence is strong that public investment in social housing is a key to stimulating private investment and more general economic regeneration. There will need to be considerable investment in housing over the coming years but the focus of that investment has become a matter of considerable controversy.

Much debate has been generated by government estimates, of 1995, that 4.4 million new homes will be needed by the year 2016 to accommodate a rapid growth in the number of households. This estimate was subsequently revised downward to 3.8 million by 2021. This still represented very substantial new growth of more than 180,000 dwellings each year. The New Labour government appointed an Urban Task Force to investigate how such expansion could be accommodated (DETR, 1999d). Within this overall demand it was estimated that there was a shortfall in social housing which could only be rectified by the construction of about 100,000 new homes each year over a 20-year period in England and Wales alone. This was based on the realistic presumption that, within the expansion of overall demand, there is a practical limit on the potential growth of owner-occupation (JRF, 1995, 1996). At the end of the 1990s output of new homes in the social rented sector was a long way short of what most experts consider necessary. The public pressure to invest more in social housing was supported by a wide range of concerned institutions including the housing charity Shelter, the Royal Institute of British Architects and the Parliamentary Select Committee on the Environment.

These blanket projections of demand have been criticised on two grounds. Environmentalists object that a strategy based on 'predict and provide' is flawed. The numbers of new households will not necessarily translate into new houses (Smith et al, 1998, p 214; Birch, 1998). Given appropriate policies there could be more emphasis on sharing homes and on adapting existing buildings to make more intensive use of them. Even if large numbers of new homes were required there is considerable scepticism as to whether 40-50% of them would need to be in the conventional social rented sector. Alternative forms of housing and housing tenure may provide more appropriately for part of this demand.

The second ground of criticism is the growing evidence that demand is very uneven. In many parts of Britain and particularly in the South East the private housing market is very buoyant. In London the demand for social housing is still high. In 1996 there were almost 180,000 households on council waiting lists. Homelessness in the capital remained in excess of 26,000 households (LRC, 1997). At the same time there were severe problems of overcrowding in social housing with a serious shortfall in the numbers of three-, four- and five-bedroom units. This partly reflects the disproportionate loss of such accommodation under 'Right to Buy' and the increasing concentration of families in the smaller dwellings on multi-storey estates (LRC, 1994).

In other parts of the country the picture is very different. Housing demand is patchy and, in some areas, very low indeed. Recent research suggests that large parts of some inner city areas have suffered from a collapse of confidence which has led to many houses, and sometimes whole areas, being abandoned. This phenomenon has been evident for quite a long time in some council estates in the North of England. It now appears to be more widespread affecting cities such as Newcastle, Leeds, Manchester and even parts of the

Midlands. It is also not confined to council housing. Housing association stock, some of it newly built or refurbished, is also proving hard-to-let. Some areas of privately owned and owner-occupied housing has suffered from abandonment (Cooke, 1998; JRF, 1999a, 1999b; DETR, 1999e).

However, Richard Best, Director of the Joseph Rowntree Foundation, has warned against drawing sweeping conclusions from the new prominence given to low demand. Drawing on his organisation's extensive record of housing research he points out that the overall rise in empty social housing is statistically very small. Furthermore, low housing demand does not affect whole regions; it is restricted to certain urban neighbourhoods or particular estates. Nor are 'hard-to-let' estates a new phenomenon and have been evident for a long time in even the most prosperous areas of the country. What is needed is investment in these problem neighbourhoods (Best, 1998). As well as the housing being in poor condition, evidence shows that weak management and inadequate facilities were often key issues in areas of low demand. Regeneration requires a broad brush approach. Investigating initiatives in one of the worst affected cities, researcher Sheila Spencer found that Newcastle City Council was:

> ... putting in resources to fill gaps they identify in services and facilities, across the whole range from employment to play and child care. A task force approach which consults people about perceptions and experiences, and aims to work corporately and in a multi-agency way, is seen as the only alternative to major demolition. (Spencer, 1998)

All of which reinforces the view that housing investment is a key to urban regeneration and for this to be done successfully it requires the active participation and contribution of people living in declining and deprived areas.

The investment needed covers a broad range of issues including education, employment and various aspects of urban management. But as part of this investment there is a significant need for new social housing, particularly in areas where multi-storey housing predominates. This is needed to make up for years of shrinking investment. Much of the need is for new family houses for rent, partly to make good the loss of this type of housing to the social sector. As the exercise of the 'Right to Buy' continues, more new housing will be needed simply to replace additional losses. In part, new houses are needed to relieve homelessness and to provide for families bottled up in unsuitable multi-storey flats. As these flats are vacated, a proportion of them could be made available to house the growing numbers of single people who make up a significant proportion of the increasing demand for housing. A large majority of the growing number of new households will be single people

– younger people; the divorced and separated; and an ever larger proportion of elderly people (DETR, 1999d, p 35). For this group, the flats would provide suitable accommodation in desirable locations close to city centres. This process could make a significant contribution to adapting estate housing, reusing substantial parts of it for appropriate purposes which would prove sustainable.

Transferring a proportion of family accommodation would not only reduce child density but allow those who were least suited to living in flats to be rehoused. To make multi-storey housing work there are other groups who should also be housed elsewhere. Social housing has always been an unhappy combination of housing as a social right and housing as a social service. Most of the social sector provides for those who can only afford modest housing costs. Their key distinguishing characteristic is low income. In every other respect they lead normal lives and behave with respect for their neighbours and their environment. These people are those who are entitled to social housing by right. There are other groups who need various levels of special support. Those who benefit from housing as a social service include:

- *Elderly people:* commonly elderly people live in general needs housing but there is an increasing tendency to provide them with sheltered accommodation. This allows them to have their own homes but to enjoy the benefit of communal rooms and the support of a resident warden.
- *Sick and disabled people:* disabled people commonly need adaptations, both inside and outside their homes, to make them accessible. General needs housing is often difficult to adapt. Purpose-built housing is often needed and the more seriously handicapped need to be in managed residential homes.
- *The mentally ill:* care in the community has meant the release of non-violent hospital patients to live in their own homes. Very often they are allocated general needs social housing. Though peripatetic support is provided, this is often sporadic and inadequate. The erratic behaviour of some patients can cause problems for their neighbours. They might be better housed in a form of sheltered accommodation.
- *Addicts:* those addicted to drugs or alcohol can also cause problems for those who live around them through various types of anti-social behaviour. They can often be accommodated in detoxification centres and other forms of hostel accommodation which provide a supervised environment.
- *Young single homeless:* young people moving from care or homelessness are often allocated general needs housing. Many lack social orientation causing serious problems for their neighbours. The growing 'foyer' movement provides a supervised environment which offers training in basic education and life skills (Ward, 1997).
- *Problem families:* many families with difficulties need social services support but otherwise cause few problems. It is widely recognised, however, that

there is a small minority who make life extremely difficult for their neighbours through noisy, abusive or violent behaviour. One such household living on a multi-storey estate can cause severe disturbance to dozens of others. The common solution is to isolate such families, but at least one experiment, in Dundee, has forced several problem families to live together in a secured and supervised special unit (Arlidge, 1996).

There is an increasing tendency, then, for 'social services' housing to be recognised as a special need requiring separate and more intensively managed accommodation. Some of this could be in multi-storey blocks on urban estates. Sheltered housing for elderly or sick people certainly could. Foyers probably could, too. Other types of supported housing would be better provided in residential homes or small-scale self-contained developments. If more new social housing is to be built, perhaps a good proportion of it should be for specific groups of vulnerable people. Many such people are currently housed on multi-storey estates where their behavioural problems or the neglect of their needs is the cause of considerable resident disenchantment and management difficulty. New opportunities could be offered for those with special needs and new choice given to families with children through the provision of more social housing.

If the lessons of the past are to be learned, large estates will not again be built which are monolithic in form, in social composition and in tenure. Still less will multi-storey housing be allocated to precisely those who are least suited to live in it. New social housing, whether it be for families or for special purposes, should be in small developments integrated into the urban fabric. This, in any case, has been the pattern since the late 1970s when large-scale urban slum clearance ceased. Nevertheless, much of the required new social housing should be in the inner cities. Many of those in greatest need of rehousing live there and most would choose to stay near friends and families. There are extensive development opportunities in the cities. There are still many derelict 'brownfield' sites formerly used by industry or public utilities. There are also many small unused parcels of land suitable for infill schemes. Such new development could be used to relieve the existing multi-storey estates and allow them to be adapted for residents well suited to them.

If such a programme is put in hand then the early years of the 21st century could see the resolution of the last manifestation of the housing problems which have troubled Britain's cities since the Victorian era. These were first evident in the overcrowded and crumbling slums which distressed social reformers for so long. But the problems did not disappear when the slums were cleared. To a large extent these have been distilled into the legacy of multi-storey housing estates. The means exist for these estates to be transformed both physically and socially. Given the will, the estate syndrome can finally be ended.

TEN

On broader horizons ...

Multi-storey housing in Britain has followed a tortuous path through history. A long slow build up when it was seen as an humane solution to the dense and unhealthy industrial city. A short period of high-minded idealism culminating in large conglomerations of cheap substandard mass housing. A rapid decline followed by intensifying efforts to put right the results of false economies and to reverse mistaken policies. The lessons from the record of improvement programmes show that given adequate investment and appropriate allocation policies, all such housing has the potential for redemption. A model framework for regeneration has been defined; a strategy has been set out through which reinvestment can be prioritised. Using these approaches, multi-storey estates can come to take a positive place in the diversity of cities. These lessons need to be applied in contemporary Britain but they may also have value in wider spheres.

On the geographical horizon there is much multi-storey housing beyond Britain's shores. Forms of multi-storey living are common throughout the world's cities. Often, cultural differences and varying policy framework make comparisons difficult. But in many parts of Europe there are strong parallels. There was often a similar history of urban industrialisation which commonly led to a developing commitment to social housing. In the post-war period large multi-storey estates were developed in and around many European cities. In recent years many of these have been beset with technical and social problems similar to those on British estates. Their continuing decline has created a widespread need for regeneration. With many of the problems sharing similarities, it may be that some of the lessons can be successfully reapplied.

On the temporal horizon lies the future shape of our cities and the pattern of the urban life-style. Continuing dispersal into low-density suburbs and satellite towns has created serious environmental concerns. The high cost of servicing such development and the huge demands generated for transport create massive energy consumption and increasing levels of pollution. Sustainability requires more compact, higher density cities. This goal can best be achieved by drawing on the traditions of urban living and making the best of the stock of buildings that already exist. The legacy of multi-storey housing – renovated through investment, repopulated with more suitable occupants and integrated into the wider community – can make a major contribution to cities which have a better quality of life and more sustainable systems.

The main findings

British multi-storey housing has its origins in slums. It was built to replace the substandard mass housing produced in the rapid urbanisation of the 19th century. Much of that housing was poorly built and provided insanitary living conditions. Most often it was overcrowded, which exacerbated health problems. Multi-storey flats were designed to solve these problems and, in the short term, seemed to provide great improvements. Now many are revealed to have constructional problems or technical defects such as poor insulation and water penetration, which generate new health hazards. Many, too, despite high space standards, have become badly overcrowded. The environment of multi-storey estates is often degraded and poor quality. In many ways the wheel has come full circle. The new housing that was to replace the slums has, very often, come to house the poorest households in the worst conditions.

For a long time the ready solution to bad housing was to demolish it. The massive slum clearance programme was the culmination of this approach. But redevelopment has very often continued to be seen as a sure-fire solution. The Gorbals in Glasgow, for instance, has been redeveloped three times in the last 150 years. First, the chaotic jumble of old buildings was replaced by orderly tenements for the middle classes. When these deteriorated into overpopulated slums they were replaced with high-rise flats. Now these, too, have been torn down and replaced. Each time there was a high capital cost; each time a community was destroyed. Still, the results of redevelopment remain uncertain. Recent research on the deterioration of new estates makes this abundantly clear.

It is now apparent that housing problems cannot be solved simply by replacing the buildings. This study has focused on regenerating multi-storey housing without substantial demolition. It has concentrated on the adaptation, rehabilitation and reuse of multi-storey blocks. In this examination six key issues have emerged:

- *Many of the problems of multi-storey estates derive from economies made when they were built.* The concentration in inner urban high-density redevelopment and the relatively high cost of multi-storey housing led to a continuous search for savings. Economies made in construction led to technical failures, a poor environment and frequent breakdown of essential services such as lifts. Key social facilities were commonly omitted to save money. Above all, economies in the design of access systems left them prey to crime and abuse (Chapter Three). The problems in use caused by these economies quickly became apparent (Chapter Four).

- *Many attempted solutions have been partial or governed by single-minded preconceptions.* Early improvement schemes were based on a maintenance approach and often addressed particular technical shortcomings without considering social issues or management problems. More recent programmes, such as the government's Estate Action, were commonly distorted by undue concentration on particular issues such as security systems or on the achievement of diversity through privatisation. Such preoccupations denied choice to estate residents and compromised the success of regeneration (Chapter Five).

- *To achieve successful regeneration an holistic approach is required.* Differing perspectives on the nature of the problems led to a series of divergent approaches to regeneration, each of which focused, sometimes exclusively, on a single key issue (Chapter Six). In fact, all of these 'facets' can be important. To bring them together an overarching model framework for regeneration has been defined. This concentrates on effective resident participation in the decision-making process – opening options for improvement and democratising the design process. The model also stresses the need to ensure technical adequacy and social appropriateness in the buildings; the development of estate-based management; and the implementation of programmes to address social and economic disadvantage (Chapter Seven).

- *All types of multi-storey housing have the potential for successful transformation.* It has been established for several years that older tenement-type blocks can be adapted and modernised to make good housing. Successful schemes have also been developed, in recent years, to secure and improve tower blocks. Some successful – although expensive – approaches have been developed to remodel deck access blocks. Linked slab blocks emerge as the most problematic type. For these, no transformation scheme has yet proved wholly successful although principles have emerged which might be further developed with good effect (Chapter Eight).

- *A successful strategy might not concentrate directly on the worst estates.* Recent strategy for major improvement programmes has been to target investment on estates with the most high profile problems. This has sometimes led to high profile failure and is frequently poor value for money. A more successful approach might be to direct funding first to the development of new social housing and the improvement of older estates. Pressure on the worst estates, and many of the social problems, could then be relieved by offering new homes to those in greatest need, particularly families with children (Chapter Nine).

- *There is a need for a diversified approach which reintegrates estates into the wider community.* Most multi-storey estates are in dense urban areas but are physically distinct from their surroundings, almost exclusively rented to low-income households, and have many residents who are inappropriately housed. New initiatives should try to blur these distinctions. Through new housing provision some families and those with special needs could be rehoused nearby. Estates could then be diversified by rededicating blocks to groups such as elderly people, students, or key professionals in healthcare and education. Some could be converted and sold as starter homes. The interaction of more diverse interests would help to regenerate and reintegrate the estates into the surrounding communities (Chapter Nine).

The stock of multi-storey housing is large. In Britain alone there are about 1.8 million flats. A high proportion of these have technical or social problems. Even if it were desirable, the demolition and replacement of such problem housing would be prohibitively expensive. But there is a clear and extensive need to invest in the regeneration of multi-storey estates. By drawing on the experience of the past, and following the conclusions set out above, permanent and successful solutions can be found to long-standing and seemingly intractable problems. Beyond Britain there are similarly extensive concentrations of multi-storey estates. Many are experiencing or developing social or technical problems. There are many parallels and the British experience might have lessons to offer in the search for solutions.

Europe's problem estates

There are fundamental similarities between housing in Britain and that in Europe. Most European countries have had a strong commitment to social housing and this came to form a substantial proportion of the housing stock. Most social housing has been developed in and around cities and, to a large degree, multi-storey developments have been the predominant form. Both in the extent and form of social housing Britain has more in common with Europe than with other developed regions of the world. Within this broad correlation, however, there are key differences.

First, the ownership of social housing varies widely. Unlike in Britain, the state often did not play a direct role in housing development. In most Western European countries social housing was built and owned by independent organisations. For the most part these were similar to British housing associations but in many countries housing cooperatives have played a significant part. Sometimes, private developers have been encouraged to provide social housing. In Eastern Europe, in the post-war period, the state has been the main owner and provider of urban social housing. But even in the Soviet bloc housing cooperatives had a substantial role. These were large organisations, more like housing associations than their small-scale Western counterparts.

A great deal of Europe's social housing has taken the form of multi-storey flats. However, in the location of this new development, there is a second critical contrast with British cities. Although urban housing was poor quality and densely populated there was little slum clearance in most European cities. Most new social housing was built in the urban periphery and there were three key reasons as to why. First, it was a matter of public policy to relieve overcrowding in the old urban areas and to facilitate renewal. Second, land on the urban periphery was cheap and readily available. Third, there was a desire to clear chaotic marginal land and to redevelop the squatter communities which had commonly accumulated on the urban fringe. In most European cities, multi-storey living was the traditional pattern and it was natural that these peripheral estates should comprise blocks of high-rise flats. This was the pattern of development through much of Europe – East and West – in the post-war period.

While most European countries have their share of multi-storey estates, such housing is by no means universally problematic. The Mediterranean countries have largely escaped the stresses of industrialisation. Urban migration and growth has been limited and so has the demand for new housing development. Tower block estates can be seen on the fringes of some cities but there is no evidence of serious or widespread problem housing. Nor are such problems evident in Scandinavia. There is a good deal of multi-storey housing. The planning and design of many forms of flat building were pioneered in the Nordic countries, as were the industrialised methods of construction. But there has been a continuous and strong commitment to investment in social housing. This has pre-empted many of the problems that have arisen elsewhere and has ensured that any deterioration is quickly remedied (Elander, 1999; Hansen and Andersen, 1999). It is in the central belt of the European mainland that the mass of multi-storey housing is concentrated and where, in a variety of ways, it has created a continuing challenge for urban management.

The West

Although there were dense concentrations of tenements in many of the Western European industrial cities, there was little of the philanthropic intervention which helped to ameliorate conditions in Britain. In the inter-war period there were innovations in social housing and a few model schemes were developed but there were no large-scale or decisive interventions. After the Second World War there followed a long period of economic growth in the course of which there was housing development on a large scale. In each country events took a different course although with broadly similar results. France was slow to initiate housing development but increasing housing stress in the cities led to the introduction of a large-scale programme of peripheral multi-storey estates. West Germany was initially preoccupied with urban reconstruction and regeneration but there, too, housing pressures eventually led to a large-scale programme of multi-storey housing.

Urban growth in France created mounting pressures and there was little action to deal with the problems until the mid-1950s. When it came, however, the response was on a massive scale. Under central direction a programme of development was commenced in 1958. A total of 140 *zones à urbanisations prioritaires* (ZUPs) were announced, all around major cities and many on the outskirts of Paris. On these *ZUPs* massive estates of multi-storey housing were built, known as *grandes ensembles*. These were developed by the French equivalent of housing associations and managed as rented housing for low-income households. To minimise costs the housing was built with concrete panel industrialised systems. Such systems are most cost-effective when used on a large scale. So the estates were huge, often as many as 5,000 dwellings, sometimes more; and the blocks within them were often massive – commonly eight storeys, often higher and each might contain hundreds of flats. Between 1960 and 1980, 2.5 million flats were built using these methods (Power, 1993, pp 40-53).

The new Federal German state was initially preoccupied with war damage and the need for urban reconstruction. To cope with this crisis a complex housing system was introduced which involved not only owner-occupation but rented housing for all income groups. Higher income rented housing was provided by private landlords. Low-income housing could be provided by housing associations, cooperatives or private organisations. All forms of renting were regulated and all forms of housing were state-subsidised to a greater of lesser degree (Dorn, 1997). Under this system six million dwellings were built by 1960, half of which were various forms of low-income rented housing. Despite these achievements urban housing demand was maintained through economic growth and migration. In the late 1960s and early 1970s an ambitious programme was implemented to meet these needs. A total of 250 multi-storey estates were built on the periphery of large cities. Many were built around old industrial cities such as Cologne, Dusseldorf and Frankfurt. Like their French counterparts these estates were large – two thirds of them had over 2,000 flats. Many were built using industrialised methods – between 1965 and 1980 more than 600,000 flats were built using concrete panel systems (Power, 1993, pp 108-31).

Many of the multi-storey estates in Western Europe quickly began to suffer serious problems. The pattern of degeneration was much the same as on similar British estates – breakdown of services, abuse of common areas, unpopularity leading to concentrations of disadvantaged tenants. In some ways the problems were worse because the estates were generally larger and their peripheral location gave more limited access to employment and services. The high public profile created by such degeneration stimulated action. In most countries programmes were set up to tackle areas of problem housing. These programmes usually involved a combination of physical improvements to the buildings and managerial changes.

Studies of such schemes (Blair, 1992; Power, 1997; Fribourg, 1999) suggest that the progress of estate improvement in Western Europe has been similar to that in Britain. Early approaches had serious shortcomings. In later schemes both the process and the measures taken had become more effective, but the results were variable. There were some successes but many schemes remained vulnerable to abuse or breakdown in the management systems.

The East

Developments in Eastern Europe have followed the pattern set in the Soviet Union. During the Second World War Russia suffered loss of life and destruction on a massive scale. This created an immense housing crisis with 25 million homeless. Initially efforts concentrated on repair and rehabilitation but this soon led on to large-scale new construction. In 1954 a massive programme of prefabricated construction was introduced. Under a series of five-year plans the amount of urban housing was quadrupled in a period of 20 years. Thousands of multi-storey flats were built in and around major cities. The whole programme was state funded and centrally directed. Standard designs were produced by a Central Institute in Moscow working under the direction of a State Committee. Zonal Institutes adapted the standards to suit regional climatic and geographical conditions. The actual construction was carried out by local administrative organisations under a system of central approval and inspection (Zhukov and Fyodorov, 1974).

In the post-war settlement several Eastern European countries, along with the Baltic States, came under the dominance of the Soviet Union. All these countries adopted policies of industrialisation and urbanisation. The details of policy and implementation varied from one country to another but the results on the ground are very similar. All major cities in the former communist countries now have a large stock of multi-storey housing mostly built using industrialised systems of large precast concrete panels. System-built flats in Eastern Europe were the predominant form of urban housing built during the post-war period, generally built in large estates housing 2,500 to 10,000 people and more. They now comprise a substantial proportion of the housing stock estimated at over 70% in some regions and cities (EAUE, 1998), but their residents were not confined to the most needy families. Social housing in Eastern Europe was intended for all occupational groups and household sizes.

After the fall of communism in 1989, governments in all Eastern European states set about reform of their housing systems. The aim of these reforms was to terminate the role of the state in housing provision and management. The production of new state housing was greatly reduced and, in many areas, largely ceased. Everywhere programmes of privatisation were introduced. Tenants were able to buy their flats with the help of generous discounts. In some areas ownership was transferred to tenants without charge. The result is that privatisation has been substantial but, in most places, well short of 100%. In most blocks of flats there is now a mix of ownership, with social landlords retaining control of a substantial proportion.

The new owners and managers of there blocks have inherited a range of daunting problems. Standards in housing had declined steadily from the 1960s, reaching a nadir in the 1980s. Space standards in the newer dwellings were low and so was the quality of construction. Problems included water penetration, deterioration of concrete panels and failure of drainage systems (Turkington, 1994). Added to this there were serious problems with energy efficiency both in the shortage of insulation and the inefficiency of district heating systems. These most severely affected the colder northern countries, particularly the Baltic States and Poland (EHEN, 1997). All these shortcomings were compounded by lack of maintenance, largely because it was generally the responsibility of residents to manage and repair their blocks. More recently it has become apparent that the polarisation that characterises housing in the West is also developing in the East. With greater choice and new opportunities to move, some estates are becoming unpopular and housing increasing concentrations of disadvantaged residents (Egedy and Kovacs, 1999; Kutarba, 1999).

Many Eastern European estates have a complex of social and technical problems. Privatisation, on its own, has done nothing to solve these problems. The new flat owners can do little to implement the comprehensive changes needed to their blocks. Both organisation and finance are needed. In many estates 'apartment associations' are being formed. These could provide the basis for the collective organisation of regeneration. But they can do nothing until, somehow, large-scale capital funding is provided for long-term housing investment.

Reflections of the British experience

In many ways, the development of multi-storey housing in Europe has followed a familiar pattern. As in Britain, many of the estates were built at the lowest possible cost. Throughout Europe, the search for economies led to the adoption of prefabricated construction using large concrete panels. The technical shortcomings of these are now well known and are repeated almost everywhere. They are particularly severe in the colder climates of the countries of North Eastern Europe. Similarly, there has been a general tendency to use the cheapest materials and equipment in mass multi-storey housing, leading to poor environmental standards and breakdown in services. Despite these similarities there are considerable variations in design. Some Western European estates were designed with economies in the access systems similar to those in Britain. This does not seem to have happened in Eastern Europe although major savings were made in the standards inside the dwellings.

The record of improvement schemes in Western Europe also seems to parallel that in Britain. Following her studies of such schemes, Anne Power suggests, there was a similar failure to consider strategic options:

> The main characteristic of the programmes was their piecemeal, incremental nature. There was never enough money to do everything required.... Each programme on each estate evolved somewhat jerkily and individually. Programmes were pieced together from many fragments of activity and ideas within each estate. (Power, 1997, p 119)

Anne-Marie Fribourg, commenting on the French improvement programme, noted that procedures had improved but the success achieved, even the most recent schemes, had limitations:

> The almost exclusively technical approach of the early years has now expanded to take social considerations into account. Nevertheless, the general view is that the results are fragile. The effect of investment in buildings is often short term – in some areas, having to be redone five years later. Local officials are still not sufficiently involved to make meaningful contributions to solving problems of peripheral estates. (Fribourg, 1999, p 173)

Such comments suggest that even in the developed West, there is a long way to go before regeneration programmes reach a form which is likely to ensure comprehensive success. In the East such programmes have hardly started. Renovation schemes are relatively rare and mostly concentrate on small-scale technical improvements. Such shortcomings in Britain led to the conclusion that an holistic approach was required which was defined by the model framework. Such an holistic approach may provide the most fully effective approach to improving European estates. The implications of such an approach might be divided into three broad categories: the impact of user participation in development and design; the need for physical changes on estates; and the organisational implications.

Participation

It is a characteristic of multi-storey housing throughout Europe, East and West, that at the time it was built neither the end users nor local communities were involved in its planning and design. Had they been the results might have been different. In Britain this lack of involvement led directly to the 'community action' movement. There were similar protest movements in other countries such as Denmark, where residents opposed slum clearance and demanded a role in decision making (Hansen and Andersen, 1999). Later, when dealing with the problems of the estates, social landlords came to accept that actively engaging the residents in decisions was not only good politics, it also led to better solutions. In any case, regeneration programmes were rarely initiated solely by the authorities. Often they resulted from action by the residents either in the form of positive campaigns but sometime more negatively in various manifestations of social unrest.

For all these reasons 'resident participation' came to play a role in estate regeneration programmes in most of Western Europe. Despite intentions which were generally good on the part of those involved, it is unclear how effective these processes were. In Britain, there was a long learning curve and a great deal of experiment with techniques before formats emerged which could be considered effective. Much the same is probably true of most improvement schemes in Western Europe and 'participation' probably ranges from a public relations façade to a complex of techniques in which residents views are genuinely sought and acted upon. In this it is likely that the Scandinavian countries are the most advanced. Participation in Scandinavia is much more deeply rooted and tenant involvement, both in management and development decisions, is now institutionalised.

In Eastern Europe little action has yet been taken to address the problems of multi-storey estates and the issue of resident participation is at an embryonic stage. The effect of widespread privatisation creates new imperatives. If far-reaching improvement schemes are to be carried out then, given the large number of individual flat owners, they cannot be done without widespread agreement. The 'apartment associations' or similar bodies must evolve into agencies for organising and implementing collective decision making. It has long been accepted that there is a hierarchy of participation in which residents are able to exercise greater and greater power. At the top of this hierarchy is 'citizen control'. Experience suggests, however, that where community organisations are able to exercise such control their scope for action is severely limited by lack of resources (Towers, 1995, pp 157-61). The new flat owners in Eastern European blocks are in a similar position. Despite having nominal control their options are severely restricted by an almost total lack of funding. If funding does become available, whether provided by private organisations or the state, it will certainly have strings. Funders will have their own priorities in protecting and maximising their investment. The best that can emerge is a productive 'partnership' between residents and funding agencies.

The final yardstick for participation is an open design process. This depends partly on the goodwill and awareness of designers; partly on the openness of the decision-making process; and partly on the degree of control exercised by users. It is unclear how well this has operated in Western European improvement programmes. In Eastern Europe the potential for design participation is good. Residents' organisations should be in a position to select and appoint their own architects and to monitor and supervise the progress of design work.

Physical changes

The physical changes needed to estates can be divided between the improvements necessary to make them technically adequate and physical adaptations to provide a good living environment. In both East and West Europe a large number of blocks of flats were built using prefabricated concrete construction which have serious technical shortcomings. Systems of overcladding have been developed which seem to provide comprehensive answers to most of the problems of concrete failure, water penetration and poor insulation but these are expensive and require large scale funding. In Eastern Europe this is not available and, in the meantime, technical improvements have been modest and applied incrementally.

While the technical problems are similar throughout Europe there is considerable variation in the changes needed to ensure multi-storey housing is appropriate for its social purpose and provides a good environment. The design of modern estates differs considerably between East and West Europe. Many estates in Western cities have design problems similar to those in Britain. There is often an unbalanced mix with a high proportion of flats designed for families and too few for smaller households. Many estates also have interlinked corridors or deck access systems which serve very large number of dwellings creating extensive uncontrolled areas open to abuse. There seems considerable scope for block transformation to break up access systems to concentrate family accommodation on the ground and to improve the size mix of dwellings. The large estates could be divided up to channel movement and focus blocks around secured communal areas.

In contrast, multi-storey housing in Eastern Europe was designed for all social groups and commonly has a much better range of flat sizes. Social changes may take place but, because of their more balanced dwelling mix, Eastern estates are less likely to come to house concentrations of large families. Similarly, access systems are, generally, much more straightforward. Soviet standard type plans provide for four flats per floor grouped around each stair/ lift (Zhukov and Fyodorov, 1974). 'Staircase access' seems to be the common system in Eastern multi-storey blocks and it is now clear that this form presents the least problems, being the easiest to secure and supervise. In many estates, the stairs and lifts need to be upgraded. Better use could be made of the public areas which were often poorly designed, left incomplete and seriously neglected (EAUE, 1998). Overall, however, the adaptations needed to the layout of Eastern blocks are modest. The more critical problem is defining a suitable social mix of residents which will prove sustainable in the long term.

Organisation

Good management is critical to the success of multi-storey housing. Even in the most upmarket private blocks there are key tasks that need to be addressed. The external fabric and common services must be maintained in good order; the access systems must be kept clean and secured against intruders; someone must be available to deal with allocations and resolve disputes between residents. The private block might employ several management, maintenance and security staff for this purpose. In mass multi-storey housing these services are often inadequate or missing. The housing was built at low cost and it has been managed at low cost.

In Western European social housing this often resulted in a failure to adequately carry out repairs and cleaning and an arm's-length approach to tenant management. In Britain these problems have been addressed by decentralising many of these functions to on-site offices. On continental improvement schemes there also seems to have been a recognition of the need for more concentrated management. This has often been realised by breaking down ownership on large estates and providing more intensive and proactive caretaking and supervision. Because many estates are polarised with high concentrations of ethnic minorities, regeneration programmes have also included measures to improve the social mix. These have often been coupled with targeted projects to improve social organisation and employment skills (Power, 1997).

On Eastern European estates management has often been virtually non-existent. This has led to a neglect of many buildings and high levels of disrepair. At the same time these estates seem to have suffered little from the social problems evident in the West. Following privatisation new management organisations are being developed, although there is a long way to go. Many have modelled themselves on management systems used in private apartments in America. In the short term they do need to develop the services provided in private blocks of flats. In the longer term they need to acquire the necessary organisation and skills to implement comprehensive improvements. They also need to be aware of the polarisation which has caused so many problems in multi-storey housing in the West and to try to develop management policies to prevent such negative social change.

The positive prospects

It emerges from experience in Britain that all types of multi-storey housing have the potential for successful regeneration. A commitment to an holistic approach is required as is an awareness of the physical and organisational changes necessary. British experience also suggests that a careful strategy is required which relieves some of the worst problems before attempting comprehensive improvements. On the most difficult multi-storey estates the pressures for decline are strong causing confidence to break down. These can be relieved by relocating some of the most inappropriately housed residents. If this is done, multi-storey estates can be reintegrated in the wider community. To do this successfully a perspective is needed of a positive urban future – a vision in which European urban culture can play a central part.

The sustainable city

European urban tradition is, to a large degree, quite different from that in Britain. A strong attachment to multi-storey living has developed over several centuries and has been self-sustaining. The preference for living in flats made much higher densities possible and this had a positive impact on both urban quality and life-style. Concentrations of buildings, coupled with enlightened urban design, created high quality architecture and townscape. Concentrations of people stimulated a wide variety of cultural and recreational facilities. These characteristics made cities pleasant to live in and reinforced the tradition of living in flats for all classes of society. These positive qualities characterise both the great cities such as Paris or Berlin and the smaller ones such as Amsterdam or Prague. The attractions of Europe's cities has made them widely admired and many have become magnets for tourism. In Western Europe the need to respect and build on the urban heritage is recognised in public policy. An influential Green Paper from the European Union has highlighted the need to conserve the distinctive character of cities and in new development to avoid sprawl, waste and social segregation (EC, 1990).

In Britain, outside London and the larger Scottish cities, there has been little attachment to flat living. In any case the potential attractions of urban living were largely obliterated by the negative impact of rapid industrialisation. The preference for houses coupled with the rejection of the industrial city has led to continuous decentralisation for most of the past century. Stimulated by the ideals of the Garden City movement people have moved from the old cities to low-density suburbs and satellite towns. These trends could be intensified by the growing demand for new housing. The Urban Task Force, under the chairmanship of leading architect Richard Rogers, had been set up in 1997 to consider urban futures. Their report lamented the fragmentation created by sprawling residential development of the recent past. But it found in some older British cities such as Bath, Edinburgh, Harrogate, Oxford and Brighton 'models of urban excellence'. It also found the beginnings of an urban renaissance:

> After decades of decline, some of the central and inner London Boroughs
> are now showing increases in population. Intense urban regeneration
> activity has also served to create renewed market confidence in certain
> areas ... Leeds, Newcastle, Manchester and Glasgow, as well as, a number
> of other cities are, as a result, enjoying an influx of new residents into
> their centres. (DETR, 1999d, p 35)

In the developed world the pressures on land and scarce resources is enormous. New urban development must aim to be in balance with the environment. The attractions of European urban culture and the positive aspects of Britain's heritage are models that must be built upon if the sustainable city is to become reality. Part of the attraction of these models lies in their aesthetic qualities. These need to be protected, reinforced and developed. Partly, too, it is the cultural diversity which stems from the national and international migration which has focused on the major cities. But the key factors which create sustainability are the inherent benefits of high densities and the potential such cities have to reduce energy consumption.

The benefits of high density

Urban densities vary widely. In overall terms the population density of Paris is twice that of London. In the inner areas the ratio is even higher, with central Paris housing almost three times as many people in the same land area (Sherlock, 1991, p 216). Barcelona is a city widely admired for its heritage and its recent achievements in regeneration. Its population density is more than double that of even the most heavily populated part of inner London, such as Islington. And even these densities are rarely matched in Britain. Most urban areas have densities which are much lower than inner London.

Drawing attention to this the Urban Task Force focused on a critical dilemma. Charged with defining the means of satisfying the demand for new housing, the report concluded:

If we were to build 3.8 million new dwellings at prevailing average density levels for new development, they would cover an area of land larger than the size of greater London. If we did only develop ... 45% of dwellings on greenfield land at prevailing average densities..., they alone would cover an area of countryside bigger than the size of Exmoor. (DETR, 1999d, p 46)

A key aspect of sustainability, then, is economy in the use of land. The profligacy in developing land at low densities is simply not affordable, particularly in densely populated countries where open country is at a premium. Research has repeatedly shown that even a modest increase in development densities would yield significant savings in land take.

Achieving higher densities must be accepted as a necessity but there are also positive benefits. One reason why European cities are so admired is that their higher density creates more vitality, more diversity. Bigger concentrations of people stimulate and support the provision of more services and facilities, making possible a wider choice of restaurants, theatres, cinemas and other recreational opportunities. They support specialist centres and services for minorities which are not possible where such minorities are dispersed in low-density sprawl. All this stimulates interdependent economic development which creates new employment opportunities and greater choice of employment. Above all, in higher density urban areas, all this diversity is within easy reach of where most people live. Ease of access is a key factor which will have critical implications for a sustainable approach to energy use.

Energy considerations

As development density increases the per capita cost of providing such services such as water, gas, electricity and waste disposal reduces. The cost of transporting materials and goods also declines. As the costs reduce so does the consumption of energy. Of most significance is the cost of personal transport which diminishes rapidly as density increases. At low densities people are dependent on private cars for personal transport. As density increases public transport becomes increasingly necessary and viable. At high densities fast, frequent and reliable public transport systems become fully effective with dramatic reductions in energy costs. More and more trips can also be made on foot or by bicycle, eliminating fuel consumption and pollution altogether.

Two Australian environmental scientists, Peter Newman and Jeffrey Kenworthy, have carried out wide-ranging studies of the relationship between transport and urban form. They suggest that there is a threshold density above which diverse, less motor car-based personal transport systems become viable. This threshold coincides with the density of a group of European cities such as Paris, Stockholm, Hamburg, Frankfurt and Amsterdam, all of which provide a high quality urban environment coupled with diverse and effective transport systems. These cities proved to have personal transport costs (measured in fuel consumption) which were less than one third of those in low density North American cities (Newman and Kenworthy, 1989, p 127ff).

In the debate about global warming and the imperative to reduce energy consumption the implications of urban form are sometimes ignored. It is argued, for instance, that petrol consumption is higher on congested urban roads than in low-density areas where cars are able to travel at constant speeds. In reality, any such advantage is more than outweighed by the fact that people in low-density areas travel more than twice as far each week as people in more compact cities, not to mention the greater efficiency to be gained by making more journeys by public transport. Similarly, there is strong emphasis on improving insulation to reduce energy consumption in heating. This is sometimes pursued without consideration of wider implications. Research in the USA has shown that a family living in a very energy efficient house may, if it is in a low-density location, be highly dependent on car transport. Their overall energy consumption may be greater than a similar family living in a wholly uninsulated house in the inner city (Smith et al, 1998, p 41).

Energy efficiency is a necessary goal but the sustainable city can be most effectively achieved by increasing densities. Energy savings can certainly be made by better insulation and fuel economies in buildings. In the high-density city these savings are reinforced by the effective use of mass transport and by the greater concentration of activities which reduces transport needs altogether. European cities proved models which are not only efficient but they are also attractive and enjoyable places to live. In achieving the aims of more sustainable development, multi-storey housing has a central part to play.

The future for multi-storey housing

If the aim were simply to maximise urban densities then there are compelling models outside Europe. In the Far East, high profile cities such as Singapore, Hong Kong and Tokyo have densities much higher than those found in Europe. While much of North America is notorious for its low-density urban sprawl, the centres of some large cities such as Toronto or New York are also exemplars of the attractions of high density. Manhattan is, perhaps, one of the most appealing models of vitality, drawing to it many of the world's rich and famous – the very people who have the maximum choice about the location of their homes.

The glamour of such cities generates the most powerful popular images of high-density living. At the same time the drawbacks are also well known – the oppression of concentrations of tall buildings; the stresses of congestion;

the health risks of high pressure urban life-styles; the threat of violence and crime. Above all, perhaps, the inequalities. While the rich live well in New York or Hong Kong the poor are crammed into run-down, overcrowded and highly priced apartments. It is rare in such cities to find good quality social housing which helps to redress the disparities of wealth and income.

In the lower urban densities found in Europe a better balance is struck between the highs and lows; the attractions and the disbenefits. In the period of optimistic reconstruction following the Second World War, such a balance is to be found in the ideals of those who helped to generate the legacy of multi-storey social housing. This was supposed to provide communities which were mixed both socially and physically. Working-class households would live alongside the middle classes. There would be individual houses for families, mixed with flats for smaller households. Everyone would be entitled to a home which had high standards and was well constructed. This vision was lost in the creation of estates of cheap multi-storey flats for low-income families. But the opportunity now exists to transform this legacy and to recreate the original ideals.

There must be a clear aim of achieving higher densities but this is not necessarily attained by the building of large blocks of multi-storey housing. Blocks of flats can certainly be built at high densities. But high density is not necessarily high rise. Some of the highest densities in Britain were achieved in slum clearance developments of five-storey tenements in the late 19th century. In contrast, many more recent multi-storey estates were built at densities which were relatively low with tower or slab blocks surrounded by large areas of relatively useless open space. Studies have shown that that many urban estates were at densities similar to, or lower than, the typical London street of three- or four-storey terraced houses. Such houses have, typically, been converted to provide family maisonettes with gardens and flats for smaller households above (Sherlock, 1991, p 217ff).

It is now clear that the key to transforming lower-scale blocks of flats lies in just such conversions and that this can create a more appropriate and sustainable mix of accommodation. For taller blocks, their most positive future lies in a different direction. Many cannot function as good accommodation for families. Their redemption lies in the creation of new family houses on the ground. Such development is possible because of the relatively low density of many high-rise estates. Opportunities for adjoining development present themselves whether these estates are in the inner cities of Britain or the urban fringes as in Europe. With the pressure of family accommodation relieved, tower blocks can be recommissioned to provide good housing to help meet the demand from small households and single people of all ages. Such people are very suited to multi-storey living and are well placed to take advantage of and enjoy the benefits of the high-density urban environment.

The renaissance in urban life-styles is evident in the continuing popularity and enrichment of European cities and in the trend in Britain to repopulate the urban centres. In the light of this trend the legacy of multi-storey housing estates need no longer be seen as a liability. They do not need to continue to deteriorate physically and socially. They do not need to be cleared away at great expense and replaced with new buildings of uncertain prospects. Given appropriate policies they can be adapted to more suitable uses. Given adequate reinvestment they can be regenerated as good quality housing. They can be reconnected to the urban fabric helping to generate physical diversity and social equity. They can make a positive contribution to the recreation of vital urban communities.

Bibliography

Adams, B. and Conway, J. (1974) *The social effects of living off the ground*, DoE Housing Development Directorate Occasional Papers, London: HMSO.

Allen, J. (1992) *Berthold Lubetkin: Architecture and the tradition of progress*, London: RIBA Publications.

AMA (Association of Metropolitan Authorities) (1983) *Defects in housing Part 1: 'Non-traditional' dwellings of the 1940s and 1950s*, London: AMA.

AMA (1984) *Defects in housing Part 2: Industrialised and system built dwellings of the 1960s and 1970s*, London: AMA.

Andersen, H.S. and Leather, P. (eds) (1999) *Housing renewal in Europe*, Bristol: The Policy Press.

Anson, B. (1981) *I'll fight you for it! Behind the struggle for Covent Garden*, London: Jonathon Cape.

Anson, B. (1986) 'Don't shoot the graffiti man', *The Architects' Journal*, 2 July, p 16.

Anson, B. (1989) 'Bending the facts to fit', *The Architects' Journal*, 13 December, p 81.

Arlidge, J. (1996) 'Ghetto from hell sparks estate fury', *The Observer*, 27 October.

Ballard, J.G. (1975) *High rise*, London: Jonathan Cape.

Barnes, W. (1973) *A century of Camden housing*, London: London Borough of Camden.

Beattie, S. (1980) *A revolution in London housing: LCC architects and their work 1893-1914*, London: GLC/The Architectural Press.

Best, R. (1998) 'Don't panic! Just learn the lessons of the past', *Roof*, July/August, p 10.

Bevan, R. (1997) 'No fear of heights', *Building Design*, 11 July.

Bevins, A. (1997) 'Blair's pledge to the dark estates', *The Independent*, 3 June.

Birch, J. (1998) 'Builders beware!', *Roof*, March/April, p 21.

Blair, T. (1992) 'Bijlmermeer: designing the future of urban renewal', *The Architects' Journal*, 2 December, pp 17-19.

Bowley, M. (1945) *Housing and the state 1919-1944*, London: George Allen & Unwin Ltd.

Branson, N. and Heinneman, M. (1971) *Britain in the nineteen thirties*, London: Wiedenfeld & Nicolson.

Brimacombe, M. (1989) 'Beyond design', *Housing*, September, p 11.

Brimacombe, M. (1991) 'Taking stock of Estate Action', *Housing*, February, p 25.

Brown, P. (1999) 'Electronic eyes turn seedy flats into des res', *The Guardian*, 6 January.

Building Design (1993) 'Tenants expected to opt for HAT status "success"', 16 April, p 3.

Bulos, M. and Walker, S.R. (1982a) 'Here to stay! High rise housing in the '80s: Part one: The legacy of high rise', *Housing*, May, p 9.

Bulos, M. and Walker, S.R. (1982b) 'Here to stay! High rise housing in the '80s: Part two: Possible alternatives', *Housing*, June, p 12.

Burnett, J. (1986) *A social history of housing 1815-1985* (1st edn published 1978), London: Routledge (2nd edn).

Burrows, L. (1989) *The Housing Act 1988*, London: Shelter.

Carroll, R. (1999) 'How did this become the height of fashion?', *The Guardian*, 11 March.

Chadwick, E. (1842) *Report on the sanitary conditions of the labouring population of Gt Britain*, (first published 1842), Edinburgh: Edinburgh University Press (1965 edn).

Christenson, T. (1979) *Neighbourhood survival*, Dorchester: Prism Press.

Coates, K. and Silburn, R. (1970) *Poverty: The forgotten Englishman*, London: Penguin.

Coleman, A. (1985) *Utopia on trial: Vision and reality in planned housing*, London: Hilary Shipman.

Coleman, A. (1990) *Utopia on trial: Vision and reality in planned housing* (revised edn), London: Hilary Shipman.

Coleman, A. (1992) 'The Dice Project', in 'High rise housing', special issue of *Housing and Town Planning Review*, London: National Housing and Town Planning Council, June.

Community Action (1972) 'Birmingham; against the encroachment of "slumdom"', no 1, February.

Community Action (1972/73a) Reports in *Community Action*, no 1, February 1972; no 2, April-May 1972; no 3 July-August 1972; no 6, January-February 1973; no 8, May-June 1973.

Community Action (1972/73b) Reports in *Community Action*, no 4, September-October 1972; no 5, November-December 1972; no 8, May-June 1973.

Community Action (1972/73c) Reports in *Community Action*, no 1, February 1972; no 11, November-December 1973.

Community Action (1972/74) Reports in *Community Action*, no 3, July-August 1972; no 16, October-November 1974.

Community Action (1973) Reports in *Community Action*, no 6, January-February; no 8, May-June.

Community Action (1973/75) Reports in *Community Action*, no 9, July-August 1973; no 21, August-September 1975.

Cooke, M. (1998) 'No easy answers for low demand northern estates', *Housing Today*, 23 July.

Cooney, E.W. (1974) 'High flats in local authority housing in England and Wales since 1945', in A. Sutcliffe (ed) *Multi-storey living*, London: Croom Helm.

Crewe, C. (1994) 'Rebirth of the Gorbals spirit', *The Guardian*, 20 December.

Cullingworth, J.B. (1976) *Town and country planning in Britain* (6th edn), London: George Allen & Unwin.

Cullingworth, J.B. (1979) *Essays on housing policy: The British scene*, London: George Allen & Unwin.

Daunton, M.J. (ed) (1984) *Councillors and tenants: Local authority housing in English cities 1919-39*, Leicester: Leicester University Press.

Davey, P. (1980) *Architecture of the Arts and Crafts movement: The search for earthly paradise*, London: The Architectural Press.

Denby, E. (1938) *Europe rehoused*, London: George Allen & Unwin.

Derbyshire, B. (1993) 'The high rise can be redeemed', *The Architects' Journal*, 10 February, p 26.

DETR (Department of the Environment, Transport and the Regions) (1997a) *Capital receipts initiative: Guidance to local authorities*, October.

DETR (1997b) *Estates Renewal Challenge Fund: Round 3 bidding guidance 1998/ 99*, July.

DETR (1998a) Press Release 611, 22 July.

DETR (1998b) Press Release 1094, 17 December.

DETR (1998c) Press Release on 'Single Regeneration Budget Bidding Guidance: A guide for partnerships', 10 September.

DETR (1999a) *Housing key figures*, updated 23 February.

DETR (1999b) *Best Value in housing*, Framework Consultation Paper, 22 January.

DETR (1999c) *Tenant participation compacts*, Consultation Paper, 25 January.

DETR (1999d) *Towards an urban renaissance: Final report of the Urban Task Force chaired by Lord Rogers of Riverside*, London: HMSO/E & F Spon.

DETR (1999e) *National strategy for neighbourhood renewal. Report of policy action team 7: Unpopular housing*, London: HMSO.

DoE (Department of the Environment) Housing Development Directorate (1980) *Priority Estates Project: Upgrading problem council estates*, London: HMSO.

DoE (1981) *Priority Estates Project 1981: Improving problem council estates*, London: HMSO.

DoE Estate Action (1989a) *New life for local authority estates: Guidelines for local authorities on Estate Action and Housing Action Trusts and links with related programmes*, London: HMSO.

DoE Estate Action (1989b) *Handbook of estate improvement: volume 1: Appraising Options; volume 2: External areas; volume 3: Dwellings*, London: HMSO.

DoE Estate Action (1991) *New life for local authority estates* (revised edn), London: HMSO.

DoE (1993a) 'Stock analysis of 1992/93 HRA subsidy data: type of dwelling by age', London: DoE.

DoE/Howard Glennerster and Tessa Turner (1993b) *Estate based housing management: An evaluation*, London: HMSO.

DoE/Safe Neighbourhoods Unit (1993c) *Crime prevention on council estates*, London: HMSO.

DoE Information leaflet (1994a) *You have the initiative: The Single Regeneration Budget*, London: DoE, May.

DoE/(SNU) Safe Neighbourhoods Unit (1994b) *High expectations: A guide to the development of concierge schemes and controlled access in high rise social housing*, London: HMSO.

DoE (1996) *An evaluation of six early Estate Action schemes*, London: HMSO.

Dorn, V. (1997) 'Changes in the social rented sector in Germany', *Housing Studies*, vol 12, no 4, pp 463-75.

Dunleavy, P. (1981) *The politics of mass housing in Britain 1945-75: A study of corporate power and professional influence in the welfare state*, Oxford: Clarendon Press.

Dwelly, T. (1990) 'More than bricks and mortar', *Roof*, July/August, p 24.

EAUE (European Academy of the Urban Environment) (1998) *A future for large housing estates: European strategies for prefabricated housing estates in central and Eastern Europe*, Berlin: EAUE.

EC (European Commission) (1990) Commission of the European Communities *Green Paper on the urban environment*, Brussels, EUR 12902 EN.

Egedy, T. and Kovacs, Z. (1999) 'Social exclusion and the future of high rise housing estates: The case of Budapest', Paper presented to Congress of the Association of European Schools of Planning (AESOP), Bergen, Norway.

EHEN (European Housing Ecological Network) (1997) *Newsletter no 1*, May; *Newsletter no 2*, December.

Elander, I. (1999) 'National strategies for urban renewal and housing rehabilitation: the case of Sweden', in H.S. Andersen and P. Leather (eds) *Housing renewal in Europe*, Bristol: The Policy Press.

Engels, F. (1844) *The condition of the working class in England* (first published 1844; translated and edited by W.D. Henderson and W.H. Chaloner), Oxford: Basil Blackwell (1958 edn).

Erskine, R. (1984) 'Designing between client and users', in R. Hatch (ed) *The scope of social architecture*, New York and London: Van Norstrand Reinhold.

Evans, B. (1996) 'Multi-storey masonry', *The Architects' Journal*, 7 November, p 46.

Faulkner, J. (Director) (1995) Film 'The estate revisited', London Weekend Television, broadcast on 10 November.

Finnigan, R. (1984) 'Council housing in Leeds 1919-39: social policy and urban change', in M.J. Daunton (ed) *Councillors and tenants*, Leicester: Leicester University Press.

Flight, J. and Xenakis, N. (1995) 'Is there a future for tower blocks?', Paper presented to conference, London: Housing Centre Trust, 7 November.

Foot, M. (1973) *Aneurin Bevan: A biography. Volume two 1945-1960*, London: Davis-Poynter.

Frew, R. (1990) 'A HAT's last stand', *Roof*, November–December, p 12.

Fribourg, A.-M. (1999) 'Strategies for urban renewal and housing rehabilitation in France', in H.S. Andersen and P. Leather (eds) *Housing renewal in Europe*, Bristol: The Policy Press.

Garland, D. (1981) 'Housing finance', *Housing*, November, p 14.

Gaskell, S.M. (1986) *Model housing: From the Great Exhibition to the Festival of Britain*, London: Mansell.

Gauldie, E. (1974) *Cruel habitations: A history of working class housing 1780-1918*, London: George Allen & Unwin.

Gibson, T. (1979) *People power: Community work groups in action*, Harmondsworth: Penguin.

Gibson, T. (1995) 'The real planning for real', *Town and Country Planning*, July, p 187.

Gittus, E. (1976) *Flats, families and the under-fives*, London: Routledge & Kegan Paul.

GLC (Greater London Council) (1976) *Home Sweet Home: Housing designed by the London County Council and the Greater London Council architects 1888-1975*, London: GLC/Academy Editions.

Glendinning, M. and Muthesius, S. (1994) *Tower block: Modern public housing in England, Scotland, Wales and Northern Ireland*, New Haven and London: Yale University Press.

Grant, C. (1988) 'Old HAT', *Roof*, July/August, p 22.

Gropius, W. (1931) Two essays on housing republished in W. Gropius (1956) *The scope of total architecture*, London: George Allen & Unwin Ltd, pp 117-38.

Hackney, R. (1990) *The good, the bad and the ugly: cities in crisis*, London: Frederick Muller.

Hakim, C. (1990) *Research design: Strategies and choices in the design of social research*, London: Allen & Unwin.

Hall, P. (1988) *cities of tomorrow: An intellectual history of urban panning and design in the twentieth century*, Oxford: Basil Blackwell.

Hamid, F.A. (1990) 'The effect of design and management on selected social problems in public sector housing', PhD thesis, Oxford Polytechnic.

Hampton, W. and Chapman, J. (1971) 'Towards neighbourhood councils', *The Political Quarterly*, vol 42, no 3, p 249 and vol 42, no 4, p 414.

Hansen, K.E. and Andersen, H.S. (1999) 'Strategies for public regulation of urban renewal and housing rehabilitation in Denmark', in H.S. Andersen and P. Leather (eds) *Housing renewal in Europe*, Bristol: The Policy Press.

Hatch, R. (ed) (1984) *The scope of social architecture*, New York and London: Van Norstrand Reinhold.

Heaven, B. (1986) 'Comeback on Coleman', *The Architects' Journal*, 3 September, p 32.

Heck, S. (1987) 'Oscar Newman revisited', *The Architects' Journal*, 8 April, p 30.

Hill, M. (1995) 'Regenerating the five estates in Peckham', *Housing Review*, March/April, p 35.

Hill, S. (1997) 'A roll of the DICE', *Roof*, July/August, p 12.

Hillier, B. (1986) 'City of Alice's dreams', *The Architects' Journal*, 9 July, p 39.

Hirst, C. (1996) 'Waiting in the shadows', *Planning Week*, 26 September.

Hoggett, P. and Hambleton, R. (eds) (1987) *Decentralisation and democracy: Localising public services*, Occasional Paper 28, Bristol: SAUS Publications.

Hook, M. (1973) 'Project ASSIST', *The Architects' Journal*, 10 January, p 61.

Hook, M. (1975) 'Macclesfield: the self help GIA', *The Architects' Journal*, 12 November, p 995.

Horsey, M. (1990) *Tenements and towers: Glasgow working class housing 1890-1990*, Edinburgh: Royal Commission on the Ancient and Historical Monuments of Scotland.

Housing (1981) 'Four day modernisation', August, p 20.

Housing (1983a) 'Special feature: roofs, doors and windows', July, p 26.

Housing (1983b) 'Hillingdon's high-cost high-rise refurb', June, p 7.

Housing (1983c) 'Special feature: insulation', December, p 20.

Housing (1983d) 'Take care with launderettes', September, p 27.

Housing (1984a) 'Report on Middlesborough scheme', October, p 25.

Housing (1984b) 'Report on Salford scheme', February, p 6.

Housing (1985) 'Wimpey Homes Urban Renewal', May, p 10.

Housing (1987) 'Trying a different image', July, p 18.

Housing (1988) Advertisements, May, pp 10, 22 and 36.

Howard, E. (1898) *To-morrow: A peaceful path to social reform*, London: Swan Sonnenschein.

Hugill, B. (1996) 'Miracles do happen', *The Observer*, 9 June.

Inside Housing (1997) 'HAT proves you get what you pay for', 31 January, p 2.

Islington Council (1979) Report to the Housing Committee, 15 March.

Islington Housing Department (1989) *Housing Islington in the '90s*, Islington Council, September.

Islington Housing Department (1996) *Annual Report to tenants 1995-96*, Islington Council.

Jeffries, J. (1982) 'Is the new Housing Project Control System better or worse?', *Housing*, November, p 17.

Jencks, C. (1973) *Modern movements in architecture*, Harmondsworth: Penguin.

Jencks, C. (1975) *Le Corbusier and the tragic view of architecture*, London: Penguin Books Ltd.

Jenks, P. and Fairclough, B. (1997) 'Raising the stakes', *The Guardian*, 18 June.

Jephcott, P. (1971) *Homes in high flats: Some of the human problems involved in multi-storey housing*, Edinburgh: Oliver & Boyd.

JRF (Joseph Rowntree Foundation) (1994) *Lessons from Hulme*, Housing Summary 5, York: JRF, September.

JRF (1995) *Housing demand and need in England 1991-2011*, Housing Research Findings No 157, York: JRF.

JRF (1996) *Housing demand and need in Wales 1991-2011*, Housing Research Findings No 182, York: JRF.

JRF (1997) *Achieving regeneration through combining employment training and physical improvement*, Housing Research Findings No 204, York: JRF, March.

JRF (1999a) *The problem of low housing demand in inner city areas*, Housing Research Findings No 519, York: JRF, May.

JRF (1999b) *Insights into low demand for housing*, Housing Research Findings No 739, York: JRF, July.

Kelly, H. (Director) (1992) Film *An English estate* (Critical Eye) broadcast on Channel 4 on 22 October.

Kutarba, I. (1999) 'Inhabitants of housing estates: territorial aggregates or local communities?', Paper to meeting of CIB W69 Housing Sociology Working Group, Vilnius, Lithuania, September.

LCC (London County Council) (1936) *Working class housing on the Continent and the application of Continental ideas to the housing problem in the County of London*, Report by Lewis Silkin MP, Chairman of the Housing and Public Health Committee, London: LCC.

LCC (1937) *London housing*, London: LCC, May.

LCC (1949) *Housing: A survey of the post war housing work of the London County Council 1945-1949*, London: LCC.

Le Corbusier (1923) *Towards a new architecture*, Paris: Editions Crés/London: The Architectural Press, 1946.

LGB (Local Government Board for England, Wales and Scotland) (1918) *Report of the Committee appointed by the President of the Local Government Board and the Secretary of State for Scotland to consider questions of building construction in connection with the provision of dwellings for the working classes in England, Wales and Scotland and report upon securing methods of economy and despatch in the provision of such dwellings*, Cd 9191, London: HMSO (The Tudor Walters Report).

Liverpool City Housing Department (1937) *City of Liverpool Housing 1937*.

Liverpool City Housing Department (1951) *Housing progress 1864-1951*.

LRC (London Research Centre) (1994) *London housing survey 1992: Social renters, council and housing association tenants in London*, London: LRC.

LRC (1997) *London housing statistics 1996*, London: LRC.

McDonald, A. (1986) *The Weller way*, London: Faber & Faber.

Mars, T. (1987) 'Mersey Tunnel vision', *Roof*, November–December, p 25.

Meehan, C. (1988) *Trying it on: Housing Action Trusts: The struggle begins*, London: Shelter/London Housing Unit, October.

Meikle, J. (1995) 'The house that John built', *The Guardian*, 27 April.

Merrett, S. (1979) *State housing in Britain*, London, Boston and Henley: Routledge & Kegan Paul.

Milner Holland, E. (1965) *Report of the Committee on housing in Greater London*, Chairman Sir E. Milner Holland, Cmnd 2605, London: HMSO.

Mitchell, P. (1990) *Memento Mori: The flats at Quarry Hill, Leeds*, Otley, West Yorkshire: Smith Settle.

MoH (Ministry of Health) (1944a) *Design of dwellings*, London: HMSO (The Dudley Report).

MoH/Ministry of Works (1944b) *1944 Housing Manual*, London: HMSO.

MoH (1949) *1949 Housing Manual*, London: HMSO.

MoHLG (Ministry of Housing and Local Government) (1951) *Housing for special purposes: Supplement to the 1949 Manual*, London: HMSO.

MoHLG (1952) *Houses 1952: Second supplement to the 1949 Housing Manual*, London: HMSO.

MoHLG (1958) *Flats and houses 1958: Design and economy*, London: HMSO.

MoHLG (1961) *Homes for today and tomorrow*, London: HMSO (The Parker Morris Report).

MoHLG (1966) *The Deeplish Study: Improvement possibilities in a district of Rochdale*, London: HMSO.

MoHLG (1970a) *Families living at high density: A study of estates in Leeds, Liverpool and London*, Design Bulletin 21, London: HMSO.

MoHLG (1970b) *Living in a slum: A study of St Mary's, Oldham*, Design Bulletin 19, London: HMSO.

MoHLG (1970c) *Moving out of a slum: A study of people moving from St Mary's, Oldham*, Design Bulletin 20, London: HMSO.

Mowat, C.L. (1955) *Britain between the wars 1918-1940*, London: Methuen & Co Ltd.

Murray, C. (1990) *The emerging British underclass*, London: IEA Health and Welfare Unit.

Nevin, B. (1990) 'Low income, high rise', *Housing*, March, p 7.

Newman, O. (1972) *Defensible space – People and design in the violent city* (first published New York 1972), London: Architectural Press (1973 edn).

Newman, P. and Kenworthy, J. (1989) *cities and automobile dependence: A sourcebook*, Aldershot and Brookfield, Vermont: Gower Publishing Company Ltd.

NHTPC (National Housing and Town Planning Council) (1997) *Still rising high*, London, February.

Olivegren, J. (1984) 'How a little community is born: Klostermuren, Göteborg, Sweden', in R. Hatch (ed) *The scope of social architecture*, New York, NY: Van Norstrand Reinhold.

Orwell, G. (1937) *The road to Wigan Pier* (first published 1937), London: Penguin (1989 edn).

Orwell, G. (1949) *Nineteen eighty-four*, London: Martin Secker & Warburg.

Owens, G.R. (1987) 'Mixed development in local authority housing in England and Wales 1945-1970', PhD thesis, University College, London.

Page, D. (1993) *Building for communities: A study of new housing association estates*, York: JRF.

Parkes, D. (1993) Lecture by David Parkes (RIBA Housing Group) and Lynn Moseley (Circle 33 Housing Association), London, 3 June.

Peacock, M. (1995) Report on Welland Estate, Peterborough, *The World this Weekend*, BBC Radio 4 (1.00pm 26 March).

Perry, J. (1998a) 'Good start, now what?', *The Guardian*, 29 April.

Perry, J. (1998b) 'Power switch?', *The Guardian*, 30 September.

Power, A. (1973) *David and Goliath: Barnsbury 1973*, London: Holloway Neighbourhood Law Centre, November.

Power, A. (1985) 'The development of unpopular council housing estates and attempted remedies 1895-1984', PhD thesis, London School of Economics, University of London.

Power, A. (1987) *Property before people: The management of 20th century council housing*, London: Allen & Unwin.

Power, A. (1993) *Hovels to high rise: State housing in Europe since 1850*, London: Routledge.

Power, A. (1997) *Estates on the edge: The social consequences of mass housing in northern Europe*, Basingstoke: Macmillan Press Ltd.

Power, A. and Tunstall, R. (1995) *Swimming against the tide: Polarisation and progress on 20 unpopular council estates, 1980-1995*, York: JRF.

Power, A. and Tunstall, R. (1997) *Dangerous disorder: Riots and violent disturbances in thirteen areas of Britain, 1991-92*, York: JRF.

Rattenbury, K. (1997) 'Textbook housing for the new term', *Building Design*, 3 October.

Ravetz, A. (1974a) *Model estate*, London: Croom Helm.

Ravetz, A. (1974b) 'From working class tenement to modern flat: local authorities and multi-storey housing between the wars', in A. Sutcliffe (ed) *Multi-storey living: The British working class experience*, London: Croom Helm.

Ravetz, A. (1976) 'Housing at Byker, Newcastle-upon Tyne', *The Architects' Journal*, 14 April, p 735.

Redcliffe-Maud (1969) *Report of the Royal Commission on Local Government in England and Wales*, Chairman Lord Redcliffe-Maud, London: HMSO.

Rex, J. and Moore, R. (1967) *Race, community and conflict: A study of Sparkbrook*, London: Oxford University Press for the Institute of Race Relations.

Roberts, H. FSA (1850) *The dwellings of the labouring classes: Their arrangement and construction* (first published 1850), London: Society for Improving the Condition of the Labouring Classes (3rd edn 1867).

Rowland, J. (1983) 'Housing's hidden assets: private initiative revives thirties housing estate', and 'Estate improvement by community participation', *The Architects' Journal*, 29 July, p 56.

Rowlat, J. (1997) 'Rise of the sell-off solution', *The Guardian*, 2 April.

Seabrook, J. (1984) *The idea of neighbourhood: What local politics should be about*, London: Pluto Press.

Scottish Homes (1999) *Evaluation of CCTV security system at Hutchesontown multi-storey blocks*, Precis no 87, Edinburgh: Scottish Homes, March.

SEU (Social Exclusion Unit) (1998) *Bringing Britain together: A national strategy for neighbourhood renewal*, London: The Stationery Office.

Sharp, T. (1940) *Town planning*, London: Penguin.

Shaw, W. (1995) 'High anxiety', *Observer Life*, 29 October.

Shelter (1972) *Another chance for cities: SNAP 69/72*, London: Shelter.

Sherlock (1991) *cities are good for us: The case for close-knit communities, local shops and public transport*, London: Paladin.

Sim, D. (1993) *British housing design*, Coventry and Harlow: Institute of Housing (Services) Ltd and Longman Group UK Ltd.

Smith, M.E.H. (1982) 'TV Linked entry-phone system offers a life-line to high rise estates', *Housing*, March, p 13.

Smith, M.E.H, Whitelegg, J. and Williams, N. (1998) *Greening the built environment*, London: Earthscan Publications Ltd.

Spencer, S. (1998) 'Downturn in demand', *Housing Today*, 2 July.

Spitties, D. (1995) 'Labour keeps the home fires burning', *The Guardian*, 7 May.

Spray, W. (1992) *Taking the reins*, London: PEP Ltd.

Stoker, J. (1987) 'Pulling in the private sector', *Housing*, September, p 33.

Sutcliffe, A. (ed) (1974) *Multi-storey living: The British working class experience*, London: Croom Helm.

Swenarton, M. (1981*) Homes fit for heroes: The politics and architecture of early state housing in Britain*, London: Hutchinson.

Tarn, J.N. (1973) *Five per cent philanthropy: An account of housing in urban areas between 1840 and 1914*, London: Cambridge University Press.

Taylor, I.C. (1974) 'The insanitary housing question and tenement dwellings in nineteenth-century Liverpool', in A. Sutcliffe (ed) *Multi-storey living*, London: Croom Helm.

Taylor, M. (1995) *Unleashing the potential: Bringing residents to the centre of regeneration*, York: JRF.

The Architects' Journal (1964a) 'Housing at Park Hill Sheffield', 15 January, pp 147-9.

The Architects' Journal (1964b) 'Housing in the Gorbals, Glasgow', 15 April, p 857.

The Architects' Journal (1965) 'Housing', 21 July, p 157.

The Architects' Journal (1967) 'Minister promises flexible housing subsidies', 4 January, p 11.

The Architects' Journal (1969) 'At last – the yardstick revised', 9 April, pp 958-60.

The Architects' Journal (1977) 'Public alternatives', 19 October.

The Architects' Journal (1992) 'Overcladding Northwood Tower', 5 February, p 26.

The Architects' Journal (1993) 'Building study: reinventing the Victorian terrace', 4 August, p 27.

The Observer (1996) 'Britain 1996: an A–Z of wealth and welfare', *The Observer Review*, 15 September.

The Prince of Wales, HRH (1989) *A vision of Britain: A personal view of architecture*, London: Doubleday.

Thompson, L. (1995) 'Room at the top', *Housing*, November.

Torrington, J. (1992) *Swing hammer swing*, London: Secker and Warburg.

Towers, G. (1975a) 'West Cross Route', *Built Environment*, December, p 223.

Towers, G. (1975b) 'Swinbrook: testbed for participation', *The Architects' Journal*, 12 March, p 547.

Towers, G. (1995) *Building democracy: Community architecture in the inner cities*, London: UCL Press Ltd.

Turkington, R. (1994) 'Is there a future for high rise housing?', *Town and Country Planning*, May, p 150.

Turkington, R. (1997) 'Taming the towers', *Housing*, May, p 26.

Ulleri, G. (1987) 'A good reception for a tall story', *Housing*, November-December, p 25.

Wainwright, M. (1996) 'Boy tells how stone slab killed pensioner', *The Guardian*, 22 May.

Ward, C. (1997) *Havens and springboards: The foyer movement in context*, London: The Calouste Gulbenkian Foundation.

Wates, N. (1976) *The battle for Tolmers Square*, London: Routledge and Kegan Paul.

Wates, N. (1982) 'The Liverpool breakthrough: or public sector housing Phase 2', *The Architects' Journal*, 8 September, p 51.

WFHAT (Waltham Forest HAT) (1996) *HAT trick: Homes, jobs, communities* (film), Waltham Forest HAT.

Wilson, S. (1978) 'Vandalism and "defensible space" on London housing estates', in Home Office Research Study No 47, R.V.G. Clarke (ed) *Tackling vandalism*, London: HMSO.

Wintour, P. (1997) 'Ghetto busters to tackle poverty in can-do mood', *The Observer*, 7 December.

Worsdall, F. (1991) *The Glasgow tenement, a way of life: A social, historical and architectural study* (first published 1979), Edinburgh: W & R Chambers.

Yelling, J.A. (1992) *Slums and redevelopment: Policy and practice in England 1918-1945*, London: UCL Press Ltd.

Yin, R.K. (1994) *Case study research: Design and methods*, Thousand Oaks, CA: Sage Publications (2nd edn).

Young, M. and Wilmot, P. (1957) *Family and kinship in East London* (first published 1957), London: Penguin (1962 edn).

Zhukov, K. and Fyodorov, V. (1974) *Housing construction in the Soviet Union*, Moscow: Progress Publishers.

Appendix: Case study research

Rationale and methodology

Five case studies were carried out with the primary purpose of testing the value of the model framework developed from practice and described in Chapter Seven. It is generally accepted that there is no right or wrong way to carry out case studies. The aims of studies, their nature, the numbers involved and their size can vary considerably. For any particular piece of research a rationale and methodology needs to be developed to suit the specific purposes of the project. In order to provide an appropriate test for the model of regeneration, three areas needed to be defined: the criteria for the selection of the studies; the method of collecting the information; and a strategy for analysing the results.

In selecting the estates for study it was essential that they should have experienced serious social problems and, to a degree, technical problems as well. It was a priority to make the selected estates comparable. Criteria were established to ensure that many features were common to all the estates so that differences in the effectiveness of improvements were as clearly marked as possible. Within these criteria it might have been appropriate to select studies which illustrated the full range of types of multi-storey housing – a 'representative sample'. However, it had become clear from practice and research that certain types of housing block readily lend themselves to remodelling. It therefore seemed appropriate that a 'focused sampling' approach should be applied – that is, the selective study of examples which were expected to prove especially illuminating (Hakim, 1990, p 141). It was decided that the focus should be on the types of estate that provide the greatest area of uncertainty in regeneration.

In collecting information it was decided that evaluation of the case studies would not be served by the analysis of statistical data or surveys of residents' opinions. Both these approaches are established in social science and are appropriate for certain types of research. To test the model of regeneration, what was needed was as accurate a picture as possible of the improvement process on each estate and its effects. This picture should reveal the problems of the estate; the way in which the improvement project was developed; the influence of the various participants; the details of the scheme; its impact on the problems; and an assessment of its durability and effect over time. To build this picture the principle known as 'triangulation' was adopted (Yin, 1994, p 144). In this method evidence is taken from several sources, each offering a different perspective. The key sources were the three groups of participants identified in the model: the residents, the designers and the managers. Information was also obtained from documentary sources and site inspections. By cross-referencing these sources a multi-dimensional representation was expected to emerge which was likely to be reasonably accurate.

In analysing the material collected there is no set recipe or formula which can be applied. It is suggested that it is important to establish an 'analytic strategy' in advance (Yin, 1994, p 102). The essence of the strategy adopted was to use the information collected to establish the degree to which each project matched the components of the model. At the same time criteria were defined to assess the success of each improvement scheme. If the model were to prove accurate and valuable a close corelation would be expected between the degree to which each project conformed to the model and the level of success achieved.

Selection of the case studies

In making sure that the case studies selected were comparable, several criteria were applied.

- *First*, it would have been pointless to examine projects which involved complete or predominant demolition. Such schemes must be assessed as any other new build scheme would be. The case study schemes were to consist predominantly of refurbishment or building reuse, although partial demolition could be included.
- *Second*, the schemes selected were to be relatively recent so that contemporary practice could be assessed. All the same it was important that enough time was allowed for problems in use to be revealed. Improvements should have been completed long enough to have stood the test of time, preferably at least two years. Where schemes were phased, at least one phase should have been completed for this period.
- *Third*, all the studies were to be taken from a similar geographical and institutional environment. Inner London contains a very large number of multi-storey estates and offers a wide choice of improvement schemes. Studies selected in London would be drawn from an environment where the social structures and the pressures of housing demand were similar. Selecting schemes carried out by local authorities would ensure that similar procedures were involved. In any case, almost all multi-storey estates were originally built by local authorities and, until very recently, all refurbishment was carried out by councils.
- *Fourth*, all the schemes were to be carried out under a similar financial regime. The time constraints focused the start date for improvement schemes

in the late 1980s and early 1990s. This ruled out both the older and more recent funding systems. Both Estate Action and Housing Action Trusts fit into these periods. However, HATs have almost entirely evolved into vehicles for the demolition of multi-storey estates and, in any case, are relatively small in number. All the case studies were, therefore, to be funded under the Department of the Environment (DoE) Estate Action programme which, during this time period, was by far the largest funding source for estate regeneration.

In selecting the focus of the studies, the first step was to identify those types of estate where the success of regeneration can be predicted with some confidence. It was evident that 'tenement'-type estates can be successfully modernised. For this reason the selection concentrated on more recent estates. Within this sphere – the legacy of estates built in the post-war period – it was also clear that successful schemes could also be developed for tower blocks. As discussed in Chapter Eight, the greatest area of uncertainty is the regeneration of slab blocks, linked slabs and deck access estates. This is the area on which it was decided to focus the sample of estates.

Collecting the information

The information collected was of three types: interviews, documentary material and direct observations. Interviews were carried out with the three categories of participants: housing officers, tenant representatives and designers. In each category there was at least one key interview – with a housing officer who had overseen the development and implementation of the scheme; with a tenant who had been active during the scheme or held a representative position; with the architect or project manager who took charge of the design and specification process. In most case studies more than three interviews were carried out, usually because the housing officer or designer had moved on part way through the process. In collecting information from the tenants, formal interviews were usually supplemented by more causal conversations with other residents.

The main documentary source, in each case, was a report prepared as part of the funding application usually containing considerable detail. In some cases information was available from tenant monitoring following completion of the scheme. Sometimes supporting material was available from professional journals. Observations were obtained from visits to the schemes. The author had been familiar with two of the estates from the mid-1980s. The other three estates were first visited in 1995. All the estates were visited one or more times during fieldwork in the summer of 1997.

From the information collected a general picture was built up. The primary purpose of the case studies was to use this overview to test the model. The data collection process was designed to make possible two assessments. First, an assessment of the degree to which the regeneration process on each estate conformed to the components set out in the model, namely:

1 Effective participation
2 Open options
3 Open design process
4 Technical adequacy
5 Social appropriateness
6 Local management and maintenance
7 Social and economic programmes

Second, to test the model, a comparative assessment was needed of the success of the scheme. Seven 'measures of success' were defined:

1 Graffiti and vandal damage
2 Cleanliness and maintenance of common parts
3 Changes in overall housing quality and 'manageability'
4 Changes in transfer requests, voids and refusals
5 Improvement in comfort of flats
6 Improvement in security of common areas
7 Changes in quality of life on the estate

These 'measures' were selected as indicative of key problems which arise on multi-storey estates which any improvement scheme should address. The first is indicative of the level of abuse of the common areas. The second was taken to indicate the effectiveness of the cleaning and repair service. The third was an indication of the extent to which the estate remained 'hard-to-let'. The fourth was a more specific measure of tenant confidence. The fifth assessed the success of work inside the flats or the need for further work. The sixth was taken as an indicator of crime levels or the fear of crime. The final measure was an assessment based on all the information gathered. It included changes in communal facilities and in environmental quality.

The information on these 'measures' was derived from all the sources. Two – *graffiti and vandal damage* and *cleanliness and maintenance* – were drawn from observations made in extensive inspections of the common areas. Two – *housing standard and manageability* and *transfer request, voids, refusals* – were drawn mainly from the observations of housing officers. Two factors came from the views of tenants or their representatives. These formed the basis of the evaluation of *comfort of flats* and *security of common parts*. The final factor –

quality of life on the estate – was drawn from the author's evaluation of all the other factors. This included the views of the designers.

Strategy for analysis

The presumption behind the definition of the model is that if correctly applied it would lead to successful regeneration which could be sustained over a long period. Ultimately this can only be demonstrated by applying the model to new projects. The hypothesis underlying the case studies is that the model can be tested by applying it to projects already completed. The closer the regeneration process in each case conforms to the model, the more likely it is that the improvement scheme would prove successful. The essence of the analysis was to draw on the material collected to provide an assessment of the degree to which each scheme conformed to the components of the model and the level of success achieved in the seven 'measures'. It would then be possible to apply a score to each of the criteria.

Each of the seven components of the model was scored:

0 – no correlation – *no requirements of the component were met*
1 – some correlation – *the scheme matched the component in a few respects*
2 – good correlation – *most aspects of the component were matched*
3 – complete correlation – *all requirements of the component were met*

Each of the seven measures of success was scored:

0 – no improvement – *no change as a result of the scheme*
1 – some improvement – *some change but well short of complete success*
2 – substantial improvement – *major change but short of complete success*
3 – comprehensive improvement – *as good as could be expected*

The scores were then totalled for comparison. The scores alone, however, cannot be treated as a uniform comparative measure. Several caveats must be entered. For one thing equal scoring does not take account of the relative importance of the various criteria. For example the 'social appropriateness' of the scheme may be much more important than the 'openness of the design process'. Another problem is that some factors may vary in their importance. For example 'comfort of flats' may be a key issue in some projects. In others no improvement to the flats may be necessary, the principle problems being security or communal facilities. It would be possible to weight the scores to take account of this but applying the correct weight would mean making difficult and uncertain judgements. To take into account these possible pitfalls evaluation of the scores was supported by reasoned consideration of the evidence collected.

Care was taken to try to ensure the case study research did not give a distorted picture. The research was done in a systematic way. Multiple sources provided the information and this reduced the bias which might have arisen from a small number of sources. The same factors were examined in each of the five studies. This makes comparative analysis possible and the possibility of distortion was reduced by being able to compare the characteristics of one project against the others. Overall the scores give a good guide both to the conformity of the case studies with the model and the level of success achieved. Comparison of the scores, supplemented by careful analysis, gives an indication of the applicability of the model to each estate improvement studied. It also provides a measure of the effectiveness the model might have if applied as a framework for developing and implementing new regeneration schemes on multi-storey estates.

The case studies

Initial studies were carried out on more than a dozen estates. From these, five estates in inner London were selected as case studies. All were improved by local authorities using DoE Estate Action funding. They are:

A *Market Estate, Islington*
B *Packington Estate, Islington*
C *Gloucester Grove Estate, Southwark*
D *North Peckham Estate, Southwark*
E *Priory Court Estate, Waltham Forest*

The case studies are presented in the order of the date of the start of the improvement scheme rather than the date they were originally built. This allows a picture to emerge of the development of Estate Action procedure. For each case study a survey was carried out using the methodology described above. From analysis of the survey results conclusions on the extent to which each scheme conforms with the model and the levels of success achieved. For each case study a tabulation follows which gives against each of the components and the measures of success its overall score and a narrative summary. This summary provides a descriptive commentary on the scores and sets out how each scheme compares with the model and the level of success achieved. Finally, at the end of the case study reports a summary table is given of the scores for all five estates.

Evaluation of the case studies shows that the model is a valuable procedure which is likely to produce success. Four of the studies show a very close match between the degree to which the regeneration process matches the components of the model and the levels of achievement shown in the 'measures of success'. The fifth – Packington – shows a less strong correlation. This is probably explained by the distortion produced by the strength of the security scheme. Its design and specification makes it resistant to damage and this is supported by a special maintenance regime. These special factors counteract the shortfall in the procedure adopted. Overall the results show a strong correlation between conformity to the model and the success of the schemes. This suggests the model can be used as a guide to formulating an effective regeneration process.

Table A1: *Summary of evaluation: Market Estate*

Match with model		Score
Effective participation	Limited participation. Some public meetings and some discussion with tenant representatives. No wider communication, exhibitions or block meetings	I
Open options	Some options were raised but seem to have been rejected without serious discussion. Demolition was not discussed	0
Open design process	The scheme appears to have been predetermined as a security project rather than starting from an open discussion of problems and possible solution	0
Technical adequacy	There were no serious technical problems with the building. Some unwise choice of materials in the improvements and an over-reliance on technology	0
Social appropriateness	No tenants were able to move. The scheme did not provide for families inadequately housed or address problem families	0
Local management and maintenance	The local neighbourhood office is on site but it is not dedicated to the estate. Tenants sit on the Neighbourhood Forum but have little influence on the management of the estate	I
Social and economic programmes	Community centre opposite and workshops on site but of limited benefit to the estate. Youth scheme belatedly started in 1995	I
Total		3/21

Measures of success		Score
Graffiti and vandal damage	Extensive vandalism and graffiti to three entrances. Almost all security broken down. Internal corridors badly abused	0
Cleanliness and maintenance	Extremely poor. Cleaning system wholly inadequate. Maintenance system cannot cope with volume or nature of repairs	0
Housing quality + manageability	Some initial improvement but over the longer term no improvement discernible. Problems just as bad as before	0
Transfer requests, voids, refusals	The undesirability of the estate eased slightly following the work but has since deteriorated to previous state	0
Comfort of flats	Provision of individual central heating improves comfort but need for more major upgrading	I
Security of common areas	No improvement in the blocks containing family dwellings. There has been improved security on two of the smaller blocks	I
Quality of life on estate	No significant change in quality of external areas of estate. Improving quality of internal access system was critical and this has not happened	0
Total		2/21

Table A2: *Summary of evaluation: Packington Estate*

Match with model		Score
Effective participation	Participation fairly extensive – representative working party, exhibitions and phase meetings. Participation agenda somewhat constrained	2
Open options	Initial tenant consultation on problems. Focus on security without considering wide-ranging options. Demolition not discussed but durability assessed	1
Open design process	The scheme was predetermined as a security project although there was some flexibility in developing the details through discussion	1
Technical adequacy	Some technical problems with the building were addressed. Technical details of the scheme well thought out. There may be some long-term problems with roofs and flat interiors	2
Social appropriateness	No tenants were able to move. The scheme did not provide for families inadequately housed or address problem families	0
Local management and maintenance	On-site office adequate on security but weak on CCTV monitoring and on maintenance. Inadequate tenant participation in management	2
Social and economic programmes	Community centre and workshops on estate. Play areas and adventure playground. Youth scheme running since 1987 although recently reduced	2
Total		10/21

Measures of success		Score
Graffiti and vandal damage	Very limited graffiti. Some vandal damage but generally public areas in good condition	2
Cleanliness and maintenance	Maintenance of security is good. But poor response on other repairs. Cleaning is adequate but not flexible enough to keep fully clean	1
Housing quality + manageability	Substantial improvement. Flats have always been attractive. Scheme has transformed common parts and environment	3
Transfer requests voids, refusals	Turnaround in 'hard-to-let' status with applicants now keen to move in. Partly because scheme now fully effective	3
Comfort of flats	No internal works. Some improvement due to remedying leaks and other defects	1
Security of common areas	Very significant improvement although tenants still complain of frequent breakdowns to lifts and security and inadequate monitoring of CCTV	2
Quality of life on estate	Better security, significant environmental improvement, better community and play facilities. Significant overall improvement	3
Total		15/21

Table A3: **Summary of evaluation: Gloucester Grove Estate**

Match with model		Score
Effective participation	'Project team' with tenant representatives elected at public meeting. Basic discussions not going into detail. Limited involvement of wider population	2
Open options	Superficially a range of options was tabled including demolition but consideration was effectively restricted to security scheme	I
Open design process	Tenants approval sought for scheme but there seems to have been little discussion of design options. No discussion of detailed issues	I
Technical adequacy	Technical details of the scheme well thought out although fire escape doors are a built-in weakness. Improvements to dwellings – heating, windows, kitchens – but problems not entirely solved	2
Social appropriateness	The scheme did not provide for families inadequately housed or address problem families. A few tenants were able to move because of changes in the access system	0
Local management and maintenance	On-site office already in situ but monitoring weak. Tenant representatives sit in Neighbourhood Forum but no estate committee. Control of delegated budgets	2
Social and economic programmes	New multi-purpose community centre includes youth club. Limited employment generation in contract requirements	2
Total		10/21

Measures of success		Score
Graffiti and vandal damage	Very limited graffiti. Some vandal damage but generally public areas in good condition	2
Cleanliness and maintenance	Security system has broken down in too many places. System seems not capable of ensuring rapid maintenance. Cleaning very good indeed	I
Housing quality + manageability	Substantial improvement – scheme has transformed common parts and improved external environment. But high-tech equipment places complex demands on management	2
Transfer requests voids, refusals	The scheme produced high levels of tenant satisfaction. This has been undermined by uncertainty over the blocks to be demolished	2
Comfort of flats	New central heating, windows and kitchens. But there still seem to be some condensation problems	2
Security of common areas	Clear improvement though the system remains vulnerable until/unless maintenance improves	I
Quality of life on estate	Significant improvement in common areas. Some improvement in exterior. Future redevelopment of western blocks presents uncertainty	2
Total		12/21

Table A4: *Summary of evaluation: North Peckham Estate*

Match with model		Score
Effective participation	A wide range of structures – Neighbourhood Forum, elected 'project team', small group meetings and individual customising	3
Open options	A range of options for improvement were discussed. Demolition was discussed in the HAT background and partial demolition carried out	3
Open design process	Tenants and professionals seem to have engaged in wide-ranging discussion and this is reflected in the development and diversity of the scheme	3
Technical adequacy	From Phase 2 onwards full refurbishment was carried out to the buildings. Materials and design solution seem suitable for purpose	3
Social appropriateness	Ground floor tenants were able to move but not those on the upper floors. This may mean that some tenants aren't appropriately housed	2
Local management and maintenance	New management office built on site. Management and maintenance delegated to tenant-led committee. Good standards achieved	3
Social and economic programmes	No new community facilities provided. Limited employment generation in contract requirements	1
Total		18/21

Measures of success		Score
Graffiti and vandal damage	Very limited vandal damage. Public areas in good condition although some entryphone doors unsecured	2
Cleanliness and maintenance	Some entryphones need repair although this is not critical to success of scheme. Cleaning and ground maintenance very good indeed	2
Housing quality + manageability	Comprehensive improvement – scheme has transformed access system and resolved shortcoming of original design	3
Transfer requests voids, refusals	Changes in the improved blocks has turned round tenant confidence. This is partly undermined by uncertainty over the blocks to be demolished	2
Comfort of flats	From Phase 2 onwards, flats have been comprehensively modernised	3
Security of common areas	Insecure access deck eliminated. Common entrances now secure and defensible	3
Quality of life on estate	Comprehensive improvement security and environment. Some lack of social facilities which are to be provided nearby	3
Total		18/21

Table A5: *Summary of evaluation: Priory Court Estate*

Match with model		Score
Effective participation	A wide range of techniques was used including large and small group meetings, block meetings and individual choices and customising	3
Open options	Six options included refurbishment, complete demolition and partial demolition. Tenant decision on redevelopment constrained by loss of status as council tenants	2
Open design process	A 'Design for Real' exercise started the process from which the options were developed for discussion and put to a tenants ballot	3
Technical adequacy	Scheme solves technical problems by addressing leaking roofs, lack of heating and insulation and inadequate lifts	3
Social appropriateness	Almost all tenants were moved during scheme. Most are appropriately housed but the scheme retains family flats on upper floors	2
Local management and maintenance	There is a management office on site but it is not dedicated to the estate. Tenants sit on panel which monitors management contract	2
Social and economic programmes	Local labour clause in contract. Funding obtained under EU Objective 2 for training estate residents. Multi-purpose community centre to be provided. Workshops included in development plan	3
Total		18/21

Measures of success		Score
Graffiti and vandal damage	No significant vandalism. One car fired, one break-in, since repaired. All entrances secure on inspection	2
Cleanliness and maintenance	Excellent. No evidence of shortcoming in cleanliness, ground maintenance or repairs	3
Housing quality + manageability	Comprehensive improvement achieved through improvements to flats, new lifts and secure stairs and better external environment	3
Transfer requests voids, refusals	Comprehensive improvement because almost all tenants decanted and now appropriately housed	3
Comfort of flats	Provision of heating, insulation, new windows, new kitchens and bathrooms. Tenants very satisfied	3
Security of common areas	Stairs not a major problem before although new entrance security helps. Communal gardens private to each block although access not restricted	2
Quality of life on estate	Environmental quality of refurbished and new housing comprehensively improved. Judgement reserved because of limited area complete	2
Total		18/21

Table A6: *Collation of evaluation scores for all estates*

	Market Estate	Packington Estate	Gloucester Grove Estate	North Peckham Estate	Priory Court Estate
Match with model					
Effective participation	1	2	2	3	3
Open options	0	1	1	3	2
Open design process	0	1	1	3	3
Technical adequacy	0	2	2	3	3
Social appropriateness	0	0	0	2	2
Local management and maintenance	1	2	2	3	2
Social and economic programmes	1	2	2	1	3
Total	**3**	**10**	**10**	**18**	**18**
Measures of success					
Graffiti and vandal damage	0	2	2	2	2
Cleanliness and maintenance	0	1	1	2	3
Housing quality + manageability	0	3	2	3	3
Transfer requests voids, refusals	0	3	2	2	3
Comfort of flats	1	1	2	3	3
Security of common areas	1	2	1	3	2
Quality of life on estate	0	3	2	3	2
Total	**2**	**15**	**12**	**18**	**18**

Index

Page numbers in *italics* refer to figures and tables.

Y

Young, Sir Hilton 29–30
Young, Michael 71–2, 74
Young, Raymond 79
young single people/students 129,
    172–3, 197, 202

Z

Zeilenbau 37–9, *38*
zones à urbanisations prioritaires (ZUPs) 210